STALKING FALLOW

Dedication

To my friend, Steven Beale, who first introduced me to stalking the elusive Herefordshire fallow, and his sister, Jenny, who has had to live with me and endure my obsession to write this book.

STALKING FALLOW

John Thornley

Quiller

First published in the UK in 2016
by Quiller, an imprint of Quiller Publishing Ltd

British Library Cataloguing-in-Publication Data
A catalogue record for this book is available from the British Library

ISBN 978 1 84689 224 0

Edited by Paul Middleton
Designed by Arabella Ainslie

Printed in the Czech Republic

Quiller
An imprint of Quiller Publishing Ltd
Wykey House, Wykey, Shrewsbury, SY4 1JA
Tel: 01939 261616 Fax: 01939 261606
E-mail: info@quillerbooks.com
Website: www.quillerpublishing.com

Contents

Illustration credits

Ian MacGillivray	Front cover painting Paintings on pages 10, 34, 60, 76, 96, 116, 136, 156, 168, 186, 206, and 224
British Deer Society	Map on page 15, reproduced by permission
The Deer Initiative	Map on page 16, reproduced by permission
Forestry Commission	Calendar on page 26, reproduced by permission
Dominic Griffiths	Fallow deer measurement sketch on page 53 , reproduced by permission (with amendments)
John Thornley OBE	Photographs except for the following:
Robert Aiken	page 162 (fig 1-5)
Peter Allman	half title verso, title page and pages 68, 115, 124 (right), 143, 150 (bottom), 191 (top), 248 and back cover
Drew Bain	pages 12, 37, 44 (right), 50 and 58
David Barrington-Barnes	backflap
Simon K. Barr	pages 8, 18, 28, 36, 75, 92, 112, 124 (left), 125, 127,135, 159 (top), 189 (bottom right), 190, 209, 223 and 227
Helen Carson	pages 21 (bottom left)
Danny Carter	pages 82, 89 (top) and 90 (top middle)
Graham Downing	pages 78, 153 (below right), 165 and 172
Patrick Faulkner	pages 30 (top left), 46 (top left), 110, 155, 166 (top), 181, 189 (bottom left), 193, 196 and 205
Andrea Green	pages 66 and 69 (right)
Peter Green	pages 142 and 167
Charlie Halls	page 45
Bernard Hluszik	page 229
Alan McCormick	page 40
Des Purdy	page 195
John Robinson	pages 146 (top left) and 154 (left)
Colin Shedden	pages 64 and 119 (left)
Norman Simpson	pages 20, 22, 38, 44 (bottom left), 146 (bottom), 147 and 149
Charles Smith Jones	pages 21 (top and below right), 24, 31, 140 (bottom), 160, 164 and 218
David Stretton	pages 19, 23 (left), 33, 46 (top right and bottom), 47 (top left and right), 148, 159 (bottom) and 166 (bottom)
Lewis Thornley	pages 23 (bottom), 43, 123, 129, 153 (left and middle), 173, 176 (far left), 178 and 219
Sam Walker	pages 57, 63 and 69 (left)
Jack Ward	page 98
Keith Watson	pages 30 (bottom), 94, 108, 109 and 189 (top)

Foreword

John will be well known to many stalkers and landowners for his established expertise in countryside law and legal issues relating to deer and their management.

In this book John turns his attention to the management and techniques of stalking fallow deer. An enormous amount of experience has gone into this book. It provides a comprehensive introduction for those new to the joys and difficulties of stalking and managing fallow deer and the information it contains will make even seasoned deer managers think again.

John's words are enhanced by the evocative paintings by Ian MacGillivray, famous for his highland scenes depicting red deer. Ian has turned his brush to the painting of lowland fallow deer with equal impact. The chapter by Peter Green, an acknowledged veterinary expert on wild deer, provides not only practical advice for the stalker on how to inspect a carcass but a useful resumé on the diseases affecting our generally healthy deer population.

Much has been written about stalking and managing our native red and roe deer and recently even muntjac have been the subject of interest. While there is a significant amount written about the history and ecology of fallow deer, little attention has been paid until now to the growing impact of high densities of fallow deer and the management required to reduce this in parts of the UK.

In his usual precise way John has studied his subject in depth and has drawn not only on his own experience, but on his many contacts in the 'deer world' to ensure the book includes the latest scientific knowledge on the subject. Full account is taken of the current best practice guidance, which in itself reflects the most modern thinking on managing our deer. Indeed, John has played a pivotal role in developing that best practice through his involvement with ACPO, BASC and The Deer Initiative.

This book brings together all the information that stalkers, landowners and managers need to manage our growing fallow deer population effectively and humanely and does so in a way that is a pleasure to read.

Peter Watson
Executive Director
The Deer Initiative

Acknowledgement

There are many friends, associates and stalkers who have helped and influenced what I have written, some without knowing it. I owe them all a great debt of gratitude.

Dominic Griffith, Patrick Faulkner, Norma Chapman, Peter Watson, Norman Healy, Nick Lane, David Barrington-Barnes, Naomi Sykes, and David Brown have been of immense assistance, particularly in their peer review roles.

I am also grateful for the help and assistance given by Charles Smith-Jones, Norman Simpson, David Stretton, Mike Thornley, John Speed, Alistair Boston, Graham Rimington, Blair Smith, Keith Watson, Ian Danby, Jim Stewart, Drew Bain, Alasdair Troup, John Hargreaves, Gareth Hare, Nick Jones, Jochen Algermissen, Bernard Hluszik, Sam Walker, Rob Aiken, Graham Downing, Joal Davies, Richard Harding and Peter Allman.

I consider it a privilege that Peter Green agreed to assist in writing Chapter 8 Identifying Disease. I am thankful for his much valued contribution.

In the late Sixties I had admired the paintings of the son of a colleague; his name was Ian MacGillivray. I was not to know then that all these years later he would illustrate this book for me with such evocative paintings, including that of a lone stalker for the cover. Not only is Ian one of our foremost deer artists, he is a stalker himself, and so the relationship between what is written and what is on canvas catches the very essence of stalking fallow. I am grateful to him for his enthusiasm and help.

My thanks also go to the famous cartoonist, Bill Tidy MBE, who fortunately lives in our parish, for his very apt cartoon that ends the book.

My old friend, previous co-author and colleague, Charlie Parkes, has had a constant role throughout my writings; proof reading everything I have done. I owe him my deepest thanks and appreciation for his patience with me in addition to his technical skills in producing diagrams and photographs.

Finally, I am proud to be in a position to thank and acknowledge the assistance of my son, Lewis, who has become an accomplished stalker since the days when he followed me around the woods as a small boy – sometimes prodding me in the back to point out a deer I had not seen!

John Thornley OBE

Chapter 1

Dama Dama

The enigmatic fallow deer is arguably the most attractive of our six species of deer in the UK and, where they are truly wild, one of the most difficult to stalk. Whether you stalk fallow to shoot, photograph or simply observe them, one has to admire their sheer elegance and ability to survive and spread across our relatively small island. Historically they have clearly been valued not only as a sporting quarry but as a source of food; their venison being regarded by many as the best of all the species. It is no wonder they were once much sought after by royalty and the aristocracy to grace their stately homes.

This is not a book devoted to their natural history, far from it. This has been well documented elsewhere thanks to the efforts of deer experts and scientists including Donald and Norma Chapman, and the late Arthur Cadman.

From the stalker's perspective, however, before venturing out into the woods to stalk fallow, it is important to have an insight into their natural history not only to help recognise their various forms, but to appreciate the broader aspects of their management and welfare. In the UK the voluntary deer management qualifications (DMQ) embrace a requirement for such knowledge as do many mandatory hunter qualifications abroad.

Origin of Species

The fallow deer became extinct in the British Isles during the last glacial period, when populations appear to have been restricted to the eastern Mediterranean. It was speculated that the Romans were responsible for introducing fallow back into Britain. However, the only reliable evidence available until recently suggested that it was probably the Normans, in the early Middle Ages, (Chapman, 1997). The Domesday Book in 1086 records deer that *may* have been fallow kept in a number of parks in nine different counties in England.

Confirmation that the Romans did introduce them back to Britain has now been made through recent archaeological discoveries and subsequent analysis of fallow bones from Fishbourne Roman Palace, Sussex, and several other Romano-British sites. However, it would seem this population did not endure after the collapse of the Roman Empire. Modern British fallow deer herds owe their origins to a second introduction that occurred in the medieval period, around the time of the Norman Conquest.

These recent discoveries are the result of a three-year project*[1] by scientists of Nottingham University into the origins of fallow deer. They have been examining how, when and why the European fallow deer spread around the world from its native homeland in the Mediterranean region of southern Europe. The findings have enhanced our understanding of the natural and cultural history of the species, revealing how fallow deer transformed landscapes and human lives everywhere they were taken.

Classification and Status

Fallow deer form the genus *Dama* and are separated into two subspecies – the European *Dama dama dama* and the Persian *Dama dama mesopotamica*. There are only relatively minor differences between the two, the most obvious being their size; the Persian fallow are larger and the antlers of the bucks tend to have palms nearer the base compared to the European.

Persian fallow antlers from the Drew Bain collection in Scotland

The European fallow deer is not classed as native to Britain and is one of four species*[2] of deer deemed to have been introduced to the UK by human activities. The cut-off date in determining whether a species is deemed native or introduced (non-native) is when the land bridge over Doggerland*[3] was flooded by meltwater at the end of the last glacial period around 7,500 to 8,000 years ago. Animals present in Britain before this occurred are classed as native. Although there is evidence of the fallow deer being present in fossil records there is no evidence of it living in

1 Dama International: Fallow Deer and European Society 4000BC–AD1600
The project, funded by the Arts & Humanities Research Council (AH/102645/1), has been supported by The British Deer Society (BDS). A 30-minute documentary *Dama: The Deer that Walked the World* can be viewed via the BDS website www.bds.org.uk

2 Fallow, sika, muntjac and Chinese water deer

3 Doggerland was an area of land, now lying beneath the southern North Sea that connected Britain to mainland Europe during and after the last ice age

Britain immediately prior to the land bridge being lost, therefore it is considered an introduced species.

Although classed as a non-native species and one that has impacts that require us to actively manage its population, it is not deemed to be an invasive species that is likely to threaten our current environment, human health or economy. This is most likely due to the time it has been here and that any fundamental change to our environment as a result of its presence has long since taken place.

In practical terms the fallow deer's status is now effectively that of a native species with its place in our cultural heritage now being recognised by government*[4]. By contrast, the relatively recent introductions of sika, muntjac and, to a lesser extent, Chinese water deer are deemed invasive and so additional focus is placed on these species in deer strategies for control and even local eradication in some situations.

The legal status of fallow remains one that is applicable to all wild animals, albeit they were introduced and captive at some point to facilitate their transportation. Once released into the wild and free to roam they are considered to be *ferae naturae* and thus owned by no one (*res nullius*). The right to shoot them is vested in the owner of the land where they occur; this right extending to third parties with permission, e.g. a stalker. Hence, neither the objectives of management nor the implementation of that management are currently under the control of national or regional authorities. The right to manage (or not to manage) rests simply with the landowner.

Protection

Separate legislation protecting fallow deer exists for England and Wales, Scotland and Northern Ireland. Each imposes a close season; prohibits certain methods of taking or killing; and stipulates the types of firearms and ammunition permitted (see Chapter 4 for details of permitted calibres and ammunition).

The Fallow Deer Close Season

	England, Wales and Northern Ireland	*Scotland*
Bucks	1 May to 31 July	1 May to 31 July
Does	1 April to 31 October	16 February to 20 October

The legislation provides a number of exemptions to killing during the close season, including killing to prevent the suffering of any injured or diseased deer and dependent fawns. Exemptions also exist in respect of crop damage and these are dealt with in

4 DEFRA Wild Deer Action Plan in 2005

detail in Chapter 10. Stalkers should familiarise themselves with the vagaries of these exemptions before assuming they have carte blanche legally to take action.

Distribution and Density

The distribution of fallow deer is now widespread across the globe and they are one of the most widespread ungulates in Europe. They have been introduced to many countries where they were not native or had become extinct, e.g. the British Isles.

Their reintroduction to the British Isles in medieval times saw the emergence of numerous parks and chases, where they were kept and protected for hunting purposes and as a source of food. In later years they became a popular adornment of many stately homes throughout the country and this continues to this day. Escapes, which were inevitable, particularly through the war years, were to reinforce a wild population that is now distributed widely throughout the UK. Their unprecedented increase in numbers and spread over recent years has outpaced their management in many areas.

The increase in their range on the UK mainland is confirmed by the results of surveys conducted by the BDS*[5] with its members and other relevant organisations in 2007 and 2011. These provide evidence for the expansion in the range of all six species of deer with the overall rate of change for fallow being 9.4 per cent compared to 10.3 per cent for muntjac and 5.9 per cent for roe.

Density

Fallow deer in some areas of the country extend over considerable areas, many of these being privately owned estates. At the present time there appears no reliable figure of the current population in the UK and unless counting is done by a reliable method over a landscape scale any estimation may be inaccurate. Fallow deer have relatively high rates of recruitment, which seem comparatively insensitive to density dependence (Putman *et al.*, 1996).

The Deer Initiative for England and Wales has recently reviewed all relevant information to determine density thresholds of the major species, including fallow, above which significant damage or risk of damage may occur with respect to:

- Agriculture
- Commercial and amenity forestry
- Regeneration of unfenced broadleaved woodland and other conservation sites
- Deer vehicle collisions
- Disease transmission to livestock and humans

5 The British Deer Society – www.bds.org.uk

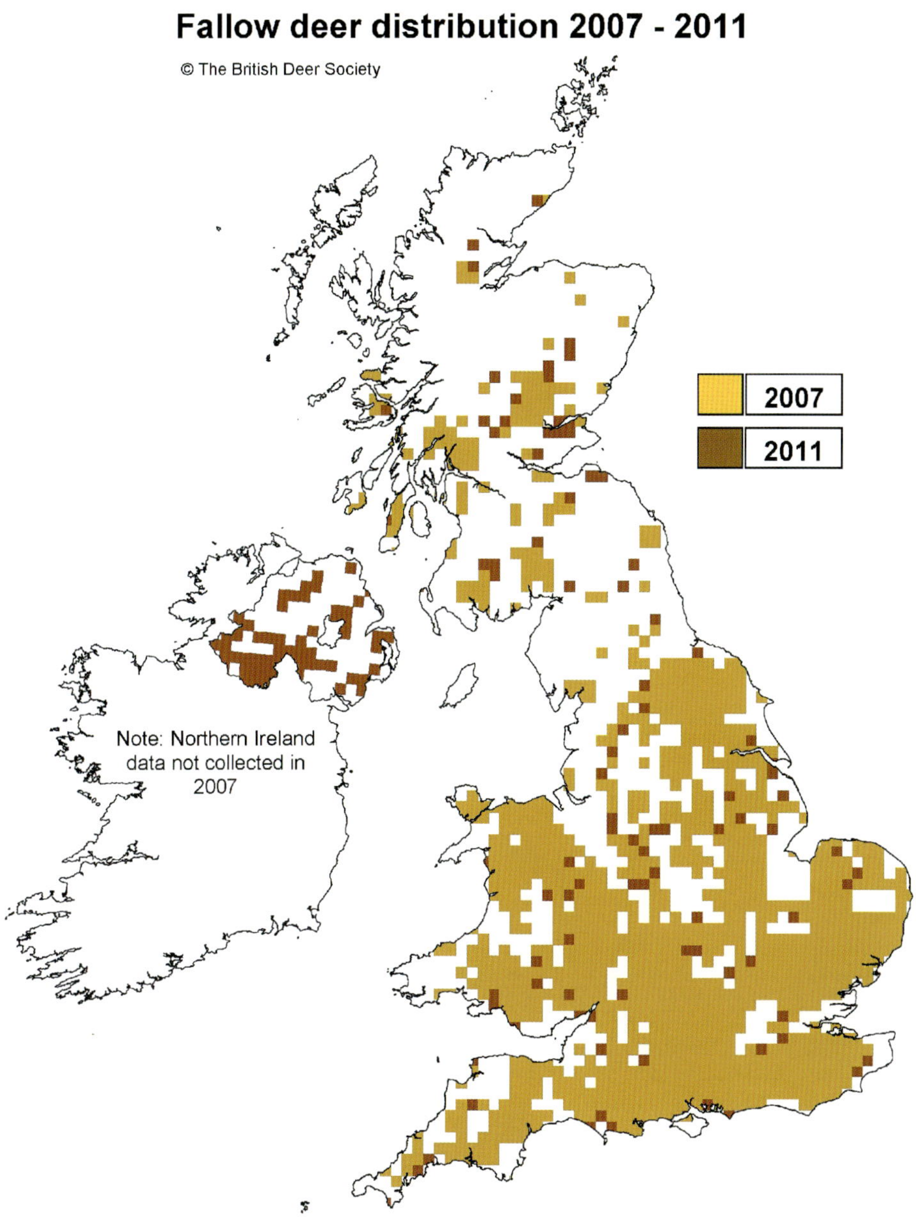

Records are based on at least one reported sighting within the 10km grid square. The survey is repeated at five-yearly intervals with results of the latest survey being available in 2017. Park deer are included. Future distribution information can be found on the BDS website

Fallow density in England and Wales

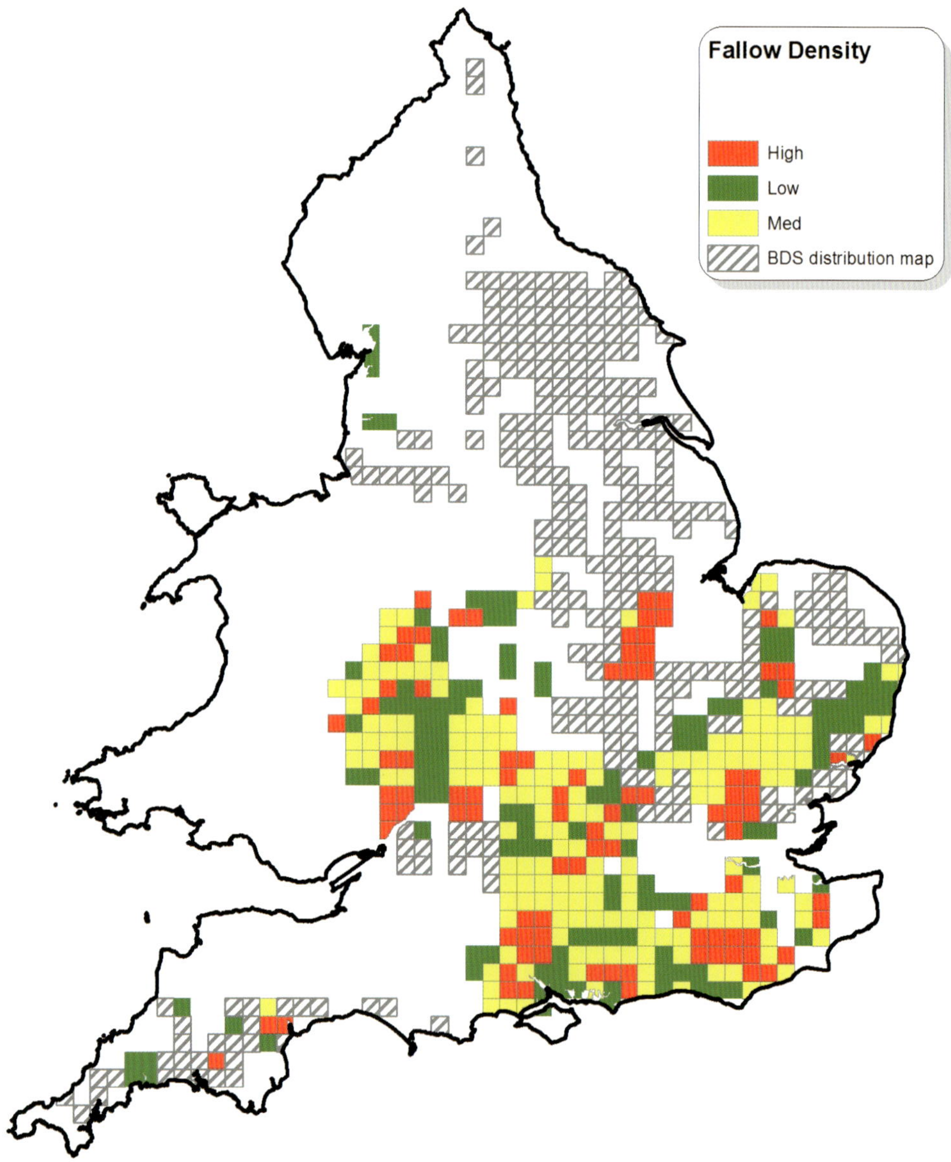

Deer impact maps have been created by using both quantitative and qualitative data gained from verifiable sources. The scale is at 10sq km level, giving a general impression of how deer impacts are likely to vary across England and Wales, both by species and in general. The methodology for collating and integrating the various data sources is still evolving. The data is being updated constantly with some areas incomplete at the time of writing (2016). The map shown on the left gives an indication across England of fallow deer densities per 10sq km. The coloured squares indicate data received from the various sources and the relevant density level.

The hashed 10km squares mirror the BDS distribution map shown previously in respect of England only. Density is yet to be determined in some squares together with Wales, in addition to new areas of the country where fallow have spread.

Characteristics and Description

Characteristics of fallow deer are their long tails, spotted coats on many varieties and palmated antlers of the mature bucks. Chapter 2 is devoted to their antler growth and development. Stalkers should note the ears of the buck protrude at a more horizontal angle to that of the doe. This together with an obvious tassel of hair protruding from the penis sheath provides the selective stalker with confirmation of the sex when antlers are not present or cannot be seen.

Size

Average height at the shoulder:
Bucks: 35 to 39in (90 and 100cm)
Does: 31 to 33in (80 and 85cm)

Weight

Average weights will vary considerably depending on many factors including age, food availability, time of year and quality of life. The greatest variation in weight is that of the mature bucks that lose considerable weight during the rut.

The following typical range of weights refer to what I would call 'carcass weight', which is used commonly and recorded in cull returns, and upon which weights are recorded for the purposes of payment by game dealers, i.e. in the skin with head, distal (lower) limbs*[6], internal organs and gralloch, etc, removed.

Bucks: Pricket:	80 to 90lb (36 to 41kg)
Mature buck:	110 to 150lb (50 to 68kg)
Does:	55 to 75lb (25 to 34kg)
Fawns: mid-season around	45lb (20kg)

6 The cut being at the knee on the front legs and lower hock joint of the back legs

Age

Average life span is twelve to fourteen years. Being able to estimate the age of deer is an important aspect of their management and Chapter 7 gives the stalker an insight into what to look for before the decision to shoot is made. It is difficult to age deer accurately in the wild, particularly females, unless their birth date is known and they have been marked conspicuously to enable subsequent identification. Bucks in the wild can be aged from the development of their antlers up to around four years, after which it becomes more difficult, as can be seen from the photographs shown in Chapter 2. Consequently, they are identified commonly within the categories of 'fawns', 'yearlings', 'middle aged' and 'old' for the purposes of management planning and cull records. Analysis through examination of the teeth provides the most accurate judgement to be made in determining the age of the young and suggests an age class in adults through teeth wear. The Deer Best Practice Guides*[7] provide information and diagrams to assist in this process.

Reproduction

Fallow have an annual breeding season that becomes intense during what is known as the 'rut' when the majority of the does are served by the most dominant bucks.

Bucks will hold a number of does together and usually remain with them throughout the period of mid-October through to early November. It is the bucks that establish and protect what is known as a 'stand', albeit it will be the principal territory of the does. The area of the stand may be quite small with activity taking place within the confines of perhaps a quarter of an acre. Typically, bucks of varying

A master buck defends his territory during the rut

7 www.thedeerinitiative.co.uk

ages will frequent the periphery of the protected territory and some may present a challenge to the master buck. Younger bucks will seek to take advantage of any stray does, often chasing them away into a safer area.

Bucks will defend their stands to the death if necessary, albeit this is rare; their antlers being less of a lethal design than those of the roe buck. They will actively seek out any imposter, whom they will challenge and fight. I recall sitting quietly in a high seat some years ago looking down to a stand below a steep wooded ridge some 100 metres away, when the master buck left his does suddenly for no apparent reason. He trotted up the ridge past me and beyond to challenge and fight with another buck 50 metres further on that I had not seen! Quite how he had detected the other buck remains a mystery.

Leading up to the rut the bucks will thrash and mark trees around a much larger area of the stand in addition to pawing the ground in several places, leaving what are known as 'scrapes'. These areas on the perimeter, often on the outside of the wood or field margin, will be patrolled regularly and the scrapes revisited frequently and pawed upon. This is reinforced by the leaving of scent on trees and scrapes, which communicate to other bucks the extent of the territory and the dangers of encroachment.

Does give birth to one fawn in early summer. Twins are born occasionally but this is generally rare. The does that are not covered during the rutting period will more than likely be served later, resulting in a later birth the following summer.

Above: A typical scrape of a buck during the rut

Left: Fallow fawn

See Chapter 5 in respect of the implications of reproduction on population management.

Terminology

Males are referred to as bucks, females as does and the young as fawns. The following terms are used to describe the ages:

	Buck	Doe
1st year	Buck fawn	Doe fawn
2nd year	Pricket	Yearling doe
3rd year	Sorel	Doe (and subsequent years)
4th year	Sore	
5th year	Bare buck	
6th year	Buck	
7th year	Great buck	

Colour of Coat

A wide range of colours are found within the European fallow with different names and variations around four main colours found typically, i.e. common, menil, white and black. This variation of coat, with a further change in colour during the winter months each year, means the fallow stalker cannot rely on looking through the woodland canopy for one particular colour. While some areas of the country may have one colour that predominates, the stalker has to expect and recognise any variation quickly.

Common fallow

Common Variety

The 'common' variety is distinguished in summer by a rich chestnut brown colour covering all but the lower regions. The brown coat is covered with white or yellowish spots over the back and upper flanks with none on the head and legs. Midway along the flanks the spots often form a distinctive continuous line. The underside of the body is coloured by various shades of white. The coat has a broad black stripe down the entire length of the back running through and over the tail, with a black line also around the white rump area in the shape of an inverted horseshoe. This area is referred to as the 'speculum'.

In winter the coat turns to a darker brown/grey colour with the spots hardly noticeable and the white under parts sometimes turning somewhat duller.

Menil Variety

The menil variety is quite similar to the common but tends to have a paler brown coat with more prominent white spots. The line running down the back, tail and around the buttocks is a less distinctive brown colour compared to the black colour of the common variety.

In winter the brown coat changes to a duller brown/grey colour with the spots remaining visible.

Above: Menil fallow

Below left: Black fallow buck, with a stare like a buffalo, in summer coat

Below right: Black fallow can be surprisingly well camouflaged – the snow helping detection on this occasion

Black or 'Melanistic' Variety

The black variety can vary between shades of a sooty black through to greyish brown. In summer the coat is usually a glossy black on the back, buttocks and tail, turning to a grey/brown colour on the lower body. The coat lacks the distinctive white spots of the common and menil variety. However, when viewed close up brown/grey spots can usually be seen. The lower parts are a light grey to mushroom colour.

The winter coat remains dark but is duller and less glossy than in the summer and often turns into a grey/brown colour. The novice stalker may be misled into thinking black fallow will be seen easily within the woodland canopy but this is not the case. In

the poor light of a winter's day they can be surprisingly well camouflaged among the dark trunks and stumps of trees.

The 'White' Variety

The coat of the white fallow becomes increasingly more distinctive as it matures. They are not albinos (these occur but are rare) and their eyes are a normal colour. In summer the coat is often a light cream colour turning to creamy-white in winter.

There are no spots or dark colours in the coat. From being a sandy/cream colour with occasionally very slight paler spotting at birth, they become progressively paler at each moult (Chapman, 1997). The time taken to reach a completely white coat clearly varies and can take a number of years.

From a stalker's point of view the white variety tends to be noticed easily, with all other variations achieving very effective camouflage in their natural habitat. For this reason it is the white variety that is often culled, not necessarily because they tend to be spotted easily, but more likely for the purposes of poaching prevention as the herd's location is unwittingly revealed by their presence.

Above: White fallow with common above

Right: The group's location is unwittingly revealed by the presence of a white fallow

Left: Long coated fallow

Below: A long coated fawn shot in south Shropshire – note the tufts of hair protruding from the ears, which are more prominent in the adults

Long Coated Fallow

Fallow with an unusual coat known as 'long coated' exist to this day within the area of the Mortimer Forest in Shropshire. Having access to stalking in this locality I have had the opportunity to observe them. Their coats have hairs that are up to three times longer than the average fallow with distinct long tufts protruding from the ears and making their tails look extremely long. The doe also has tufts of hair on the forehead and when stalking within the woodland cover they can give the initial impression of a buck. At first glimpse a dark fawn can look like a large shaggy dog.

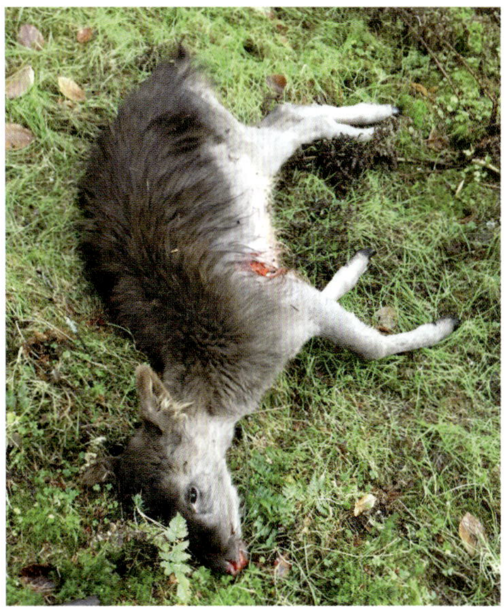

Long haired fallow were first recognised more than fifty years ago by Gerald Springthorpe, then wildlife co-ordinator for the Forestry Commission. Until recently a number were kept in captivity in an enclosure behind the forestry ranger's cottages at Ludlow. These have now been released into the wild and will no doubt interbreed with those of the normal variety as others have done previously, resulting in some intermediate forms. The variety has been subject to past research indicating the long hair is the expression of a dominant autosomal gene (Whitehead, 1993), this appearing to be insufficient to consider them as a sub-species, once suggested as *Dama dama springthorpei.*

Fallow or Sika?

The closest species to fallow deer in size and appearance is the sika and the novice stalker is at risk of misidentification. While their appearance is similar in many ways there are distinct differences that should be noted.

The sika is the slightly smaller of the two with a recognisable difference in size when compared together. However, when viewed in isolation among the woodland canopy, it is not easy to distinguish between the species on size alone.

The confusion between the two species is more likely to be between the females and young males, particularly in the summer when the coat colourings of the sika, being a rich chestnut brown with white spots, are similar to that of the common fallow. The winter coat is not unlike that of the black fallow.

The summer coat of fallow usually shows a distinct lateral line. On the common and menil this is formed by the white spots joining together, whereas the sika is not so defined. The rump markings are also similar but the heart-shaped white caudal patch of the sika has a black border that does not impinge into the white area as it does in fallow. Sika also have a shorter tail than fallow. The metatarsal glands on the outside of the back legs of sika are more prominent than those of the fallow.

Above and right: Sika hinds in summer coat can look similar to fallow does

Antlers of the two species are quite different and make identification of the males less confusing. The antlers of the sika stag are not palmated like those of the mature fallow buck. However, this alone should not be a deciding factor as you will occasionally see fallow bucks with little or no palmation. The formation of the antlers of the sika stag are distinctly different, with the main beams leaving the pedicles in more of a vee shape and giving a more upward appearance than that of the fallow buck. The single spikes of the first head of both species can look similar.

I tend to look at the head and face of deer in the first instance, this being part of the anatomy that catches the eye and often all that can be seen due to the ground cover. The facial appearance of sika can appear sharper, the eyes appear more pronounced and the ears lack the copious inner hair of the fallow. The head of the sika hind has a domed appearance compared to that of fallow. Both the sika stag and hind have a light-coloured horseshoe shape line on the forehead, giving the former a fearsome look. It is often said that the face of a sika stag is like that of the devil – with a look as if you owe him money!

The study of photographs backed up by the experience of observing both species in the field should alleviate any misidentification. The deer stalking certificate qualification (DSC1) requires this competency to be met. (See Chapter 3, Stalking Opportunities.)

Senses and Behaviour

Fallow are a herding species but do not be surprised while stalking to find solitary animals or small groups seemingly in isolation to bigger herds. Their habits and behaviour change throughout the year, as shown on the Deer Calendar (overleaf).

For much of the year the does, fawns and followers (previous year fawns) will be split into small groups of perhaps six to twelve. These small groups are led usually by a matriarchal type doe that will make key decisions to protect the group from any perceived danger. Limited feeding will concentrate these groups together, forming large herds in the locality of the food source. This is often on agricultural crops, much to the embarrassment of the stalker. Groups will lie-up (couch) for varying lengths of time chewing cud and resting. They are crepuscular, feeding mainly at dawn and dusk when they are most active. Under the pressure of culling activities where their safe feeding is restricted during the daytime they will become nocturnal and feed during the hours of darkness. Where they are safe they may be seen to feed at regular intervals throughout the day with less feeding at night.

Bucks will form bachelor-only groups both in the summer months, when they are often to be found lying in the corn, and in the winter following the rut when relationships become more congenial. They will join the does for a brief time in the

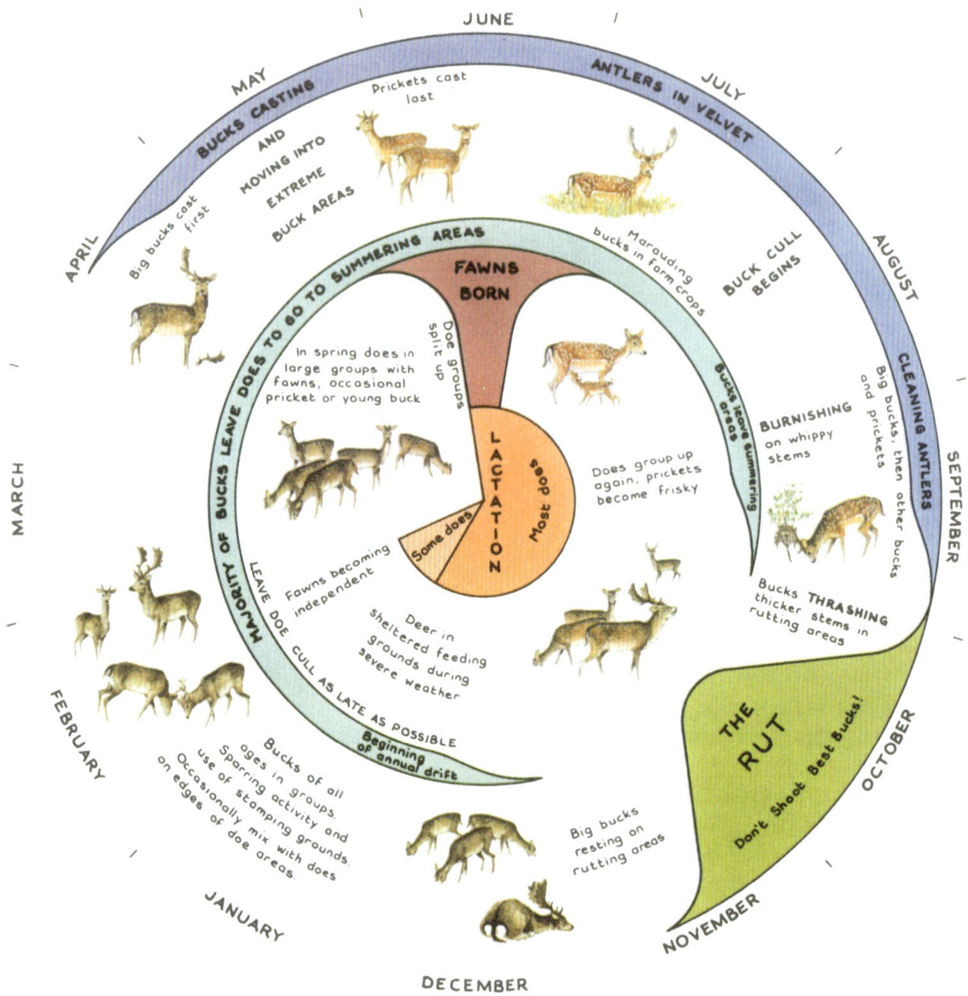

The Fallow Deer Calendar (Reproduced by kind permission of the Forestry Commission)

early spring when all may be seen feeding together.

Where their numbers are high and grazing limited they will feed close to domestic livestock, albeit given the choice they will avoid sheep. While they do not tend to be seen or associate with other species of deer they clearly coexist in many areas. However, the greater their number the less tolerant they may be if competing for food or sanctuary. Roe and muntjac share their general habitat commonly but not necessarily their range of food, which may explain the common ground exploited.

Senses

The stalker should appreciate that when comparisons are made between the key senses of man and deer our own are quite pathetic. We no longer hunt to survive as our ancestors did. Some of our senses, once used to detect danger or quarry in the natural world, have long since become redundant; fallow deer's have not and their sense of smell – their scenting ability – is superb and far superior to ours. This, together with their acute hearing, keeps them out of danger the majority of the time.

Their ears have very active muscles and you will note they are able to be turned through a wide radius to the front and rear while the head is stationary. While their eyesight is less effective and different to that of humans, it is still extremely good at times and capable of picking up the slightest movement or different shade of colour. This is why wearing suitable clothing and remaining absolutely still at times is so important to the stalker.

Their individual senses support each other in warning and confirmation of potential danger together with an uncanny ability to pinpoint your exact location. This is backed up by their cognitive sense in recognising the warning signs of other creatures, which are inevitably acted upon by a swift departure from the area without ever being seen by the stalker.

Fallow are quick to learn stalker behaviour patterns, including times, locations used and routes taken. They have an uncanny ability to discover areas they will not be targeted in through the habits of the stalker not shooting for safety reasons. And they determine the safe havens where they have vantage points to detect predatory danger easily. This is why fallow at times are so difficult to stalk.

The frustrations of stalking fallow are compounded by what appears to be their sixth sense – one of a psychological awareness of danger. I have related this to our own in Chapter 6. On occasions I have been confident of being unseen, unheard and not scented by them or any other wildlife and yet, for no obvious reason, they have become suspicious and taken flight during a stalk. Most frustrating!

Fallow are also extremely patient and persistent in their quest to stay alive. They are also inquisitive. They will stand for long periods of time with all senses finely tuned towards areas of potential danger. This constant risk assessment is a way of life – as it should be for the stalker. They are quick to learn the habits of humans and have an innate sense to recognise those that pose a danger and those that do not. This is why many stalkers are faced with the embarrassment of being told by those walking their dogs or driving the tractor how many deer have been seen! All this should prompt you to change your stalking tactics from time to time, as discussed in Chapter 6.

Communication

Fallow communicate with each other in many ways including by voice, scent and behaviour. The tail, of some 9in (23cm) in length on mature animals, is often lifted when the deer are suspicious or alarmed. It is also swished regularly from side to side, this sometimes being the first movement seen by the stalker when the deer are in cover. When suspicious, fallow will also sometimes take a few steps towards the perceived threat, raising and lowering their head as they do. This behaviour is particularly prevalent in does with young fawns to protect. Bucks will also do this in an adversary fashion during the rut.

A potential danger has been detected among the trees and their tails are up!

Pronking

The lifting of the tail when suspicious is occasionally accompanied by the unusual gait of fallow, known as 'pronking', where they bounce away on stiff legs with all four feet leaving the ground simultaneously. One can only speculate on the reasons for this behaviour and it is assumed it is done to alert other deer of potential danger. However, it should also be noted that when fallow pronk in this way their head is held high providing for a more visual reconnaissance and assessment of the potential danger as they move. The behaviour is not confined to responses to danger as occasionally you will see fallow, particularly the young, practising the art playfully. May be they are just practising for what is to come?

Having witnessed pronking behaviour in many different circumstances while stalking, it often results in their downfall, literally, as the pronking is usually followed by a stand and stare, providing the stalker with an opportunity for a shot. In my experience this rarely occurs when fallow have actually winded you (scented) – this usually resulting in a determined gallop away without hesitation. If following a shot a beast is seen to pronk at any point, rather than run, this usually confirms a clean miss. (See Chapter 7 for details of shot reaction.)

Vocal

Fallow may appear relatively quiet animals for the majority of the time. However, they can be discreetly vocal between themselves at times, uttering soft peeps and indescribable little noises to communicate to one another. These noises go unheard unless you are very close by.

As a stalker, the first occasion you may realise fallow can be vocal is when you are barked at; your presence having been detected. And more often than not, it will be a doe with a fawn at foot. The doe will give out a short, sharp, deep bark, perhaps repeated as she retreats from the perceived danger. When compared to that of the roe buck it tends to be shorter and less guttural, and it lacks the echo effect of the muntjac. It is rare to be barked at by a buck. The bark of a doe is often backed up by the stamping of a front foot and the raising of the tail, creating not only a threatening posture but communicating the danger to her fawn and any others nearby.

During the rut the mature bucks will repeatedly make a loud and deep belching noise commonly described as 'groaning'. This can be heard over a considerable distance, sometimes up to half a mile or so dependent on wind and weather. It is often prompted by the soft whickering noise of the does around the rutting stands, which generally go unheard.

Vocal communication between does and their fawns is an important welfare strategy. Fawns will bleat or scream if in danger or distressed, as will adults sometimes if handled when injured. Both doe and fawn will make a peeping noise to communicate. The doe will also make a deeper bleat sometimes to make contact and locate her fawn.

Scent

Fallow have several scent glands, the most obvious being the metatarsal on the outer side of the hind legs just below the hock and the sub-orbital glands below the inner corner of the eyes, all of which are thought to play an important role in communication between individuals.

Signs, Habitat and Food

Signs

Where fallow are abundant it is not difficult to detect their presence from the signs they leave. Familiarising yourself with the footprints, tracks and droppings they leave is an important aspect of deer management, enabling you to estimate numbers and assess their range and impact.

Heavily worn tracks known as 'racks' are a sure indication of the frequent use and routes taken of fallow, some having been used over many years.

The footprints, commonly referred to as 'slots', left by fallow will only be obvious on damp or wet ground where an impression of the cloven hoof will be left. If the ground you stalk supports roe deer too then care needs to be taken in disseminating the small slots of young fallow from those of mature roe, which tend to be more closed and rounded at the front. Close examination of slots will also reveal the pace of the animal; the cloven hooves widening like a pair of scissors when running. In the latter case, an impression of the two dew claws may also be left to the rear of the main slot. The doe's slots tend to point directly forward, whereas the bucks splay out to their respective side slightly.

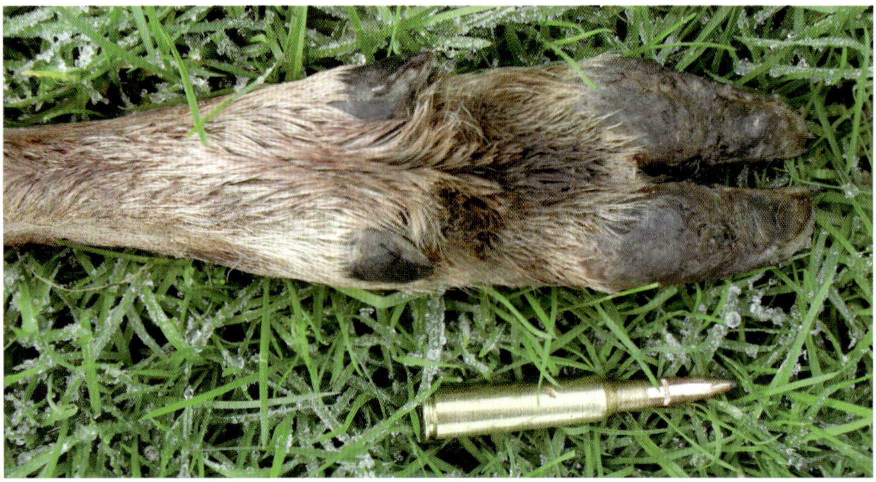

Above: A well-worn rack in constant use

Above right: Posterior view of the back foot of a fallow pricket showing position of the dew claws. The comparison rifle cartridge is 7.8cm in length

Right: Muntjac slot

Middle: Roe slot

Far right: Fallow slot – note the marks left by the dew claws. Cartridge is 7.4cm in length

The droppings (fewmets) from fallow are black solid pellets that on dropping to the ground normally disperse over a small area. The droppings of the buck are larger than those of the doe and are slightly concave at one end, the latter being more rounded. The size of the pellets will vary proportionate to the size of the animal.

More information in respect of signs is given in Chapter 10 relating to crop damage and protection.

Fallow droppings (fewmets)

Habitat

Fallow have become increasingly adaptable to a wide range of habitat but they have a preference for deciduous woodland. If that woodland also contains a thick, warm belt of conifers in which to couch up and hide then even better. Add to this some nearby agricultural land with grassland interspersed with arable ground on which crops are rotated then as far as the fallow are concerned they have Utopia. Where a network of woodland exists their range may extend over a large area, sometimes of several thousand acres, using hedgerows and wooded belts to travel along. Fallow in this situation can become nomadic and travel long distances for the best food and shelter. However, where they are left undisturbed provided there is an adequate food supply their range will be less extensive and they will heft to that area.

Their ability to extend their range once disturbed creates a management problem if their numbers exceed the carrying capacity*[8] for the area. This is further exacerbated if they are able to find sanctuary in an area where no management is practised. This is discussed in more detail in Chapter 5 Population Management.

Food

Fallow are predominantly grazing animals and will eat a wide range of plants, especially grasses which form a major part of their diet. They are big animals and consume a considerable quantity of food. In a park environment this may be up to 6kg a day. They will browse broadleaved trees and shrubs. In winter, with less grass available, acorns, beech mast and chestnuts will be eaten and most varieties of bramble will be browsed along with ivy and holly.

Being grazers they will readily seek out and feed on agricultural crops, including cereals, beans, beet and rape, sometimes causing considerable damage by both eating and trampling. (See Chapter 10, Crop Damage and Protection.)

8 Carrying capacity is the number of deer that the area can potentially support taking into account the wider impacts to the environmental, habitat and social perspective

Fawn, Pricket, Sorel, Sore, Bare Buck and Buck

Today I stood behind a tiny fawn:
Beauty and innocence so newly born.

Dappled shadow, sleeping beneath the fern,
Born yesterday.
The world is yours: and you've all to learn.
Go, run and play
Before you find that life is harsh and stern.

Seek out the woodland paths and winding burn:
Go where you may.
Hold still and watch – experience you'll earn.
And then, one day,
Antlers held high, a Great Buck, you'll return.

The late Arthur Cadman

Chapter 2

Antlers

Development, Recognition and Measurement

An outstanding feature of fallow deer is undoubtedly their uniquely shaped palmated antlers, which, on a mature buck, take on the splendour of the king of the forest. Beauty is, of course, in the eye of the beholder. Many stalkers consider the antlers of the mature fallow buck to be the most attractive of our six species of deer in the UK. Indeed, they have an aesthetic appeal to the general public and are sought as ornaments or adapted into items of furniture and light fittings.

Table and light fittings

Antlers fascinate stalkers and become talking points, whether they are on the wall or still on the head of a living buck. It will often be the sight of an antler or its movement that first catches the eye and alerts the stalker of a buck's presence. At certain times of the year, particularly in the late summer, that may be all that is seen of a beast couched up or moving within a deep crop of rape. It may also be the sound of clashing antlers that first alerts the stalker to the presence of bucks fighting during the rut in October and November.

It may be the sound of clashing antlers that first alerts the stalker

Knowledge of their development and appearance provides the stalker with valuable information on which to base cull decisions in the field. Such decisions may have to be taken quickly so experience of observing fallow bucks of different ages will be invaluable to your decision making and management plans. Such knowledge becomes invaluable when converting the half chance of a cull animal quickly and efficiently, as elaborated upon in Chapter 6 on stalking techniques. So taking time to observe bucks of different ages can pay dividends in your overall management plans.

While we tend to use the size and shape of antlers as a barometer of the quality of deer by no means does a poorly antlered fallow head necessarily mean the animal is not otherwise of sound body and good weight. In fact, many of the top weights of fallow bucks I have shot have actually had poor quality antlers. For many stalkers, very average and poor heads are the norm, particularly in areas where the fallow are not descendants of those that in former times were bred selectively by the aristocracy in estate parks for their large antler size compared to their otherwise small physique.

Good quality antlers depend on a variety of factors, not least inherited shape and formation. There is no doubt that a quality of life arising from a stress-free environment with good nutritious food all year round has an important bearing on antler growth potential. But genetics are a key ingredient in the first instance to quality antlers and so selective culling of deer with poor antler development should form part of your management plans whether you stalk simply to control deer or as part of a commercial enterprise where the quality of antlers matters.

However, in some areas of the country the population of fallow is so high that any idea of selective culling is not feasible and bucks are shot on sight irrespective of antler quality.

Fallow antlers can vary tremendously, even within the same territory, so assessment of what qualifies as a good quality head for your ground is essential in your management objectives. If you have the opportunity to cull bucks selectively as part of your wider management plan then identifying those with poor quality antlers requires patience and good observation. Bucks lacking consistent wide palms and giving a 'fish tail' appearance due to forked or split palms (bifurcated) should rank high in your cull plans, together with old bucks that are often referred to as 'going back'. This is a term used to describe bucks that are deteriorating through old age. I know many stalkers that, given the opportunity, will always take the younger bucks, often the prickets, first. While this may appear to be good practice and provide the best venison it can be a mistake unless you have been able to assess the buck's quality carefully on the basis of its overall appearance rather than a judgement on the strength of its antlers alone. Consequently, too few good prickets are left to mature. Assessment of a buck's overall appearance is dealt with in more detail in Chapter 7 on the decision to shoot.

Examples of bifurcated (split) palms in mature fallow bucks from the Drew Bain Collection

Careful judgement should be made prior to shooting prickets

Antlers are not grown without purpose. They fulfil a number of functions that are not restricted to matters associated with the mating period, during which they can be seen in use, both in attack and defence. Communication, visual recognition in the social order and sometimes their use to facilitate feeding are all justifications for their evolution. As a weapon of defence against predators they can be most effective, as will be observed when a dog holds an injured buck at bay.

While competitive bucks and potential predators are at risk of injury from antlers so too are stalkers, and this is not restricted to the trophy falling off the wall on to your head! The stalker needs to be aware of the potential danger from antlers when in close proximity to a buck that may be injured or trapped. Post-shot checks for confirmation of death should be done with caution. Even in circumstances where death is confirmed some movement of a buck can occur during the gralloch and, if your head is down, you may be vulnerable to a strike in the face. Recognition of this risk should be noted in risk assessments, as outlined in Chapter 12. However, pure accidents can and do happen in which antlers can cause serious damage or injury. A beater on a game shoot was injured recently when a fallow buck in a cover crop of maize was panicked into a headlong dash for safety and collided with him; presumably both were unsighted in the thick cover.

Growth and Development

Antler growth is restricted to the male of the species. A number of factors appear to dictate growth, which appears to be initiated through exposure to light, with darkness inhibiting it. Research has also shown that electrical activity is an important feature in antler development (Lake, F. T., Davis, R. W. and Solomon, G. C., 1982). Unlike horns, which are permanent, antlers are grown and subsequently cast each year. Their growth is rapid and in fallow this can exceed more than a centimetre a day. In a healthy buck both antlers grow independently and at the same rate, each matching the other generally in size and shape. Antler growth is slowest at the beginning and end of the process (Chapman, 1997). The annual cycle of growth and later casting (shedding) is adapted to the length of daylight, hence casting and growth commencing in the spring as the days lengthen. The whole process appears pointless, although there are some advantages suggested later for this natural phenomenon. Rarely in the natural world are things done without purpose and the growing and casting of antlers is no exception.

The first antlers develop on a buck fawn from two permanent stumps of bone situated on the skull between the ears known as the pedicles. These are covered in hair similar to that covering the head and lower legs. Fallow bucks are born without pedicles and the skulls of newly born male and female fawns are indistinguishable in shape.

The pedicles appear to be formed from the membrane (periosteum) covering the frontal bones (Chapman, 1997). They develop following an initial surge of testosterone in the foetus, which leads to antlerogenic tissue development on the frontal bones of the skull. Buck fawns are distinguishable by pedicles from about eight months of age and the small bumps are evident if you look carefully from about December. Pedicles become thicker and shorter in old age.

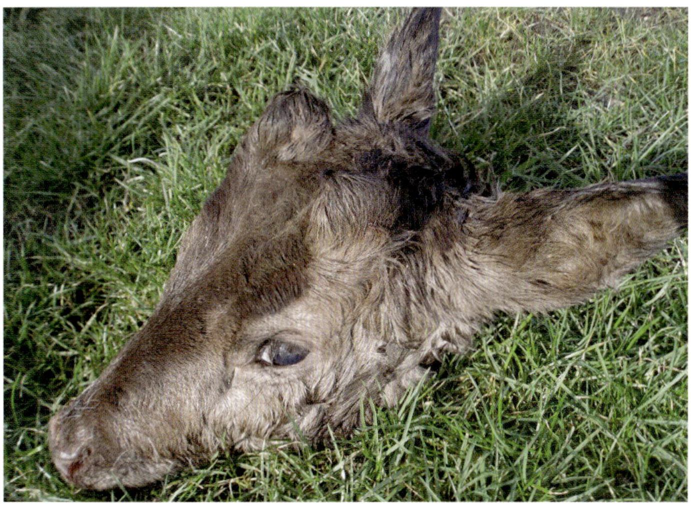

Eight or nine-month-old buck fawn showing bumps

As the pedicles grow, the skin over them becomes sparse and a type of velvet develops from which the first antlers appear. As the antler grows, a ring of bone forms around its base just above the pedicle and this is known as the coronet. Antlers grow firstly from the tips and secondly in the body of the antler. Antlers are bone and on a mature fallow buck have been found to consist of 10 per cent water, 50 per cent ash and 40 per cent organic matter (Kerckerinck zur Borg, 1987). The percentage ratio of these components will vary dependent on age. As the antlers grow (irrespective of the age of the animal) they are covered entirely in small hairs, creating a sensitive and furry surface. This is known as 'velvet' due to the texture of dense hair that grows at right angles to the surface of the antler. Its colour in fallow deer tends to match the coat (pelage) of the particular animal. The velvet feels greasy to the touch. This is due to a substance secreted by the sebaceous glands known as sebum, which produces an oily, waxy substance that lubricates and waterproofs the skin and hair.

Contained under the velvet, as well as inside the antler, are numerous blood vessels and sensory nerves that explain why, even after velvet loss, the buck has an awareness of exactly where the tips of his antlers are. When the antlers are fully grown the blood supply ceases and the antlers themselves become dead bone and cannot grow again, even if damaged. The velvet, now redundant, dies and starts to drop off. This is aided by the buck rubbing aggressively against trees and vegetation. This process combines territorial marking with cleaning the antler of velvet, often resulting in damage to vulnerable young trees. The whole process is achieved within a few days, although you will find some bucks may carry the remains around for longer. Eventually the antlers reach a stage that is referred to as 'clean' with little or no remnants of the old velvet left. Fallow bucks are usually clean by late August or early September. The initial colour of cleaned antlers is pale and often blood stained. This soon darkens as the antlers complete the drying process and the colour of varying shades of brown becomes enriched from constant rubbing against vegetation and soil deposits.

Mature bucks with antlers in velvet matching pelage of coat

A buck's first antlers will usually consist of nothing more than single spikes or small growths of knobbly bone; the latter being referred to commonly as a 'flat-topped' pricket. The spikes can vary considerably in size and shape and, as mentioned earlier, are not necessarily indications of the overall quality of the buck.

Casting of Antlers

The annual casting of antlers begins when the young buck (pricket) casts his first antlers at around two years of age. The older bucks cast their antlers from around April to May and this will usually be two to three weeks earlier than the younger ones, which often cast later into June. The open season for bucks, covering a period both before and beyond that of the doe, means there is never a time of year when only the does are in season and the bucks are not. Stalkers are free, therefore, of any dilemma over mistaking a cast buck for a doe as can occur with roe. There are, of course, other important indicators apart from antlers with which the stalker should be familiar in terms of differentiating between the sexes and these are elaborated upon in Chapter 1.

Antlers become detached from immediately below the coronets; they literally drop to the ground. The detachment is the result of a decrease in testosterone levels instigating the activation of the osteoclast layer of cells. These begin to absorb calcium from the antlers, causing the bone to weaken and eventually fall off either entirely of their own accord through gravity or as a result of the slightest tap or contact. The experience of this biological change is thought to be painless and can be somewhat of a surprise to the buck when it occurs. Bucks have been observed to suddenly spook at the experience of the falling antler but then return to the cast antler in an inquisitive mood.

The base of the cast antler at the point where it has become detached from the pedicle is referred to as the 'seal' and its surface is rough and porous. A corresponding shape is left at the top of the pedicle that bleeds a little and scabs over quickly, following which the annual antler cycle of growth and development is repeated. The seals are normally convex on deer that still have potential to improve in later years; conversely they tend to become flatter and sometimes concave in deer that are starting to 'go back' through old age (N. Simpson, 2015).

Both antlers may be cast within the same day but often a buck will be seen with just one remaining antler that drops off some days later. It is rare to find these cast antlers in the wild and it is thought some are actually eaten by the deer themselves in addition to other mammals as a source of minerals. If not eaten, they soon become buried or concealed in the undergrowth, which, at the time of casting, is increasing in density.

Cast pricket antler with convex and rough surface

One of the reasons suggested as to why deer cast and replace their antlers each year is not only to replace breakages but to enable their size to keep pace with bodily growth (Whitehead, 1993). It is apparent that the timing of casting and growth during the summer months ensures that fully developed hard antlers are in place for the period leading up to the rut when they may be needed for territorial dominance and defence.

Ownership of Antlers

I was once asked by the great deer enthusiast and authority, G. Kenneth Whitehead, who owned cast antlers. Kenneth was accustomed to seeking legal advice on deer-related matters and usually behind such queries there was a story to be told. At the time I imagined Kenneth, having picked up some cast antlers for his collection, had been challenged by some irate landowner. Of course, prior to being cast, the antlers of wild deer are ownerless (*ferae naturae*), as is the animal itself, and they remain such until the deer is in some way 'reduced into possession', e.g. shot by a stalker. A cast antler is a different matter. Once cast the first claim of ownership falls (pardon the pun) to the landowner of the ground where they are found and although there are exemptions for the picking of mushrooms and wild fruit by the public no such exemption within the law applies to antlers. In defence of the casual taking of cast antlers from open land one may consider if challenged that the taking of the antlers was done with a belief that the owner of the land had abandoned all rights to them. However, if a case was pursued against the finder the individual circumstances would be a matter for the prosecutor to consider and ultimately the courts to adjudicate upon should a case be seen to be in the public interest to pursue.

A number of hypothetical situations come to mind where ownership may be in dispute but, providing the taking was legitimate, ownership of cast antlers will be apparent. Anyone subsequently acquiring legitimately owned antlers without permission may therefore be guilty of theft as they become property capable of being stolen. The issue of ownership becomes more relevant when you consider the potential value of antlers that achieve trophy status and have been prepared as such. In this latter situation strict liability for theft would apply where they are taken without permission.

Antler Deformity

The Effects of Disease or Injury to the Body

The nature and shape of antlers, while dictated mainly by genetics and diet, can be affected severely by outside influences. The causes of some antler deformities are unknown and self-fulfilling prophesies arise where disease or parasites are found within the body and thought to be the cause. Anything that causes ill thrift over the summer when antlers are growing will have an effect on antler quality and conformation – liver fluke, bowel worms, lungworm, TB, Johne's Disease, mineral deficiencies – all may result in weak and deformed antlers.

Antler deformity in fallow bucks will occur as a direct result of injuries to the body during the period of antler growth. When the injury is sustained prior to full growth of the antler, deformity will usually affect the remaining growth and may manifest itself in a different form annually if the injury is permanent. If sustained following full antler growth then it will be the next head grown that may be affected. Fallow bucks are inquisitive and their size and tendency at times to live in close proximity to farming practices and highways mean they are injured frequently through entanglements with fences, debris and collisions with vehicles. Hence, antler deformity is quite common.

A classic leg trap for deer causing death or the loss of a lower limb leading to antler deformity. It is caused through the leg entering between two closely strung horizontal wires that then become entwined as the deer jumps

Road accidents in which deer are injured are estimated to exceed 10,000 across the whole of Britain, with 40 per cent involving fallow. In both England and Scotland fallow are the most common of our species of deer associated with localised hot-spots of accident risk. Many of these accidents result in injuries to deer at a time of year when their antlers are still growing, resulting in subsequent antler deformity in that and later years.

It is often the case that injury to one side of the body will result in deformity of the opposite side antler, e.g. injury to the left leg resulting in deformity of the right antler. There has been considerable speculation and disagreement over this contralateral effect. In my own experience I have found injury on one side of the body has, in the majority of cases, resulted in deformity of the opposite side antler but not in all cases.

I asked Peter Green, veterinary, who has written Chapter 8 on identifying disease, for his opinion. His enlightened view on the subject is as follows:

> *There is received wisdom and anecdotal evidence that a severe lameness, perhaps including the loss of a limb, gives rise to an abnormal antler on the opposite side. There is certainly no doubt that deer with injured or absent limbs develop antlers frequently that are not symmetrical and one antler may be severely malformed, but it is not a consistent finding that the effect is upon the opposite side. Sometimes it occurs on the same side as the injured leg. There has been limited research on this subject, mainly because deliberate injury of an animal experimentally needs a strict licence in most countries, but the scientific evidence seems to suggest the reason for the antler malformation is not anything to do with the internal nerves or metabolic signals within the deer but is caused by the limp. When a deer walks or trots (the two most common gaits)*

it has a diagonal weight-bearing action: the left foreleg and the right hind leg bear weight together and so do the right foreleg and left hind leg. In the normal walk or trot of a healthy deer this gait gives rise to a gentle side-to-side motion of the head.

As the antlers are growing they are covered in velvet and are very heavily perfused with circulating blood. The side-to-side rocking of the head in a healthy deer during normal motion places equal kinetic, inertial and gravitational forces on both antlers. The sideways rock-and-return motion will have an effect on blood flow (in just the same way as bleeding from a cut finger is increased if you gently shake your hand downwards), but if the deer is rolling its head equally both left and right the effect is symmetrical.

But, a deer with an injured or absent leg does not rock its head equally from side to side in both directions. It develops a limp. And a limp usually includes an eccentric head motion. A limping deer nods or rocks its head far more one way than the other, depending upon which leg is disabled. It is this uneven nodding or rocking of the head when the antler is in velvet that appears to give rise to the deformed antler. The repeated unnatural downward nodding of the head to one side disrupts the fine-tuning that shapes the development of the antler and a deformed one is formed. This is different from the hormonal effect upon antlers caused by damage to the testes. In such cases the bizarre effects are almost always symmetrical.

Below left: A perruque fallow head

Below right: Perruque fallow from the New Forest ex John Willet collection (from the Drew Bain collection)

On rare occasions fallow bucks have been known to develop a 'perruque' head, which is more common in roe deer. This is often the direct result of injury or disease to the testicles, effectively castrating the buck and cutting off the supply of testosterone while the antlers are still growing. The result is that the antlers continue to grow, producing excessive rough bone. The velvet is not shed and the malformed antlers fail to turn to hard bone. The buck often dies through infection in the unusually large growth. In roe bucks this can be quite grotesque, often covering the eyes. Such large growths are not so common in fallow.

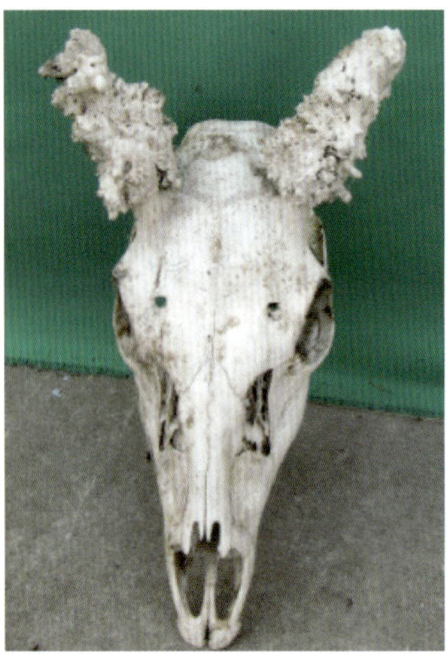

Hummels

Where the growth of antlers does not take place at all is itself an abnormality and is more common in red deer than most other species. These stags are known as 'hummels' and although they are also known to occur in roe bucks as well as red deer they are not as evident among fallow. The condition appears to be the result of a lack of pedicle growth or some abnormality in their development. Quite why this occurs is not certain. One suggestion is the condition may be the result of delayed puberty caused by malnutrition in early life (Suttie and Kay, 1981). The animal's appearance and biological development remains normal and they are capable of breeding and producing healthy offspring with no such abnormality. Over the years hummels have been reported to exist in fallow but I have yet to see any evidence of this. If they do exist they are rare. I know of many stalkers who think they have seen fallow hummels. I suspect on the majority of these occasions they were not true hummels and what they have observed or shot have been flat-topped prickets or more mature beasts that through some injury or disease have failed to grow a normal head in that particular year. However, I would not be so brave as to suggest they do not exist at all. The late Arthur Cadman, respected for his knowledge of fallow deer, used to say hummels were rare in fallow. A record was found of a fallow hummel having been shot at Bramfield in Hampshire in October 1968. The buck was estimated to be six or seven years and had flat-topped pedicles (Chapman, 1997).

The Effects of Injury or Damage to Antlers

Any damage to the antlers that are still growing and in velvet will normally result in bleeding and often some deformity to the antler itself. The latter results in the growth of unusual antlers, attracting much interest from stalkers, particularly visitors from abroad who see them as valuable trophies due to their bizarre appearance. Such heads, while relatively common in roe deer, do occasionally occur in fallow as a result of injury caused through road accidents, entanglements with fences, thorns, agricultural equipment and rubbish while the antlers are growing.

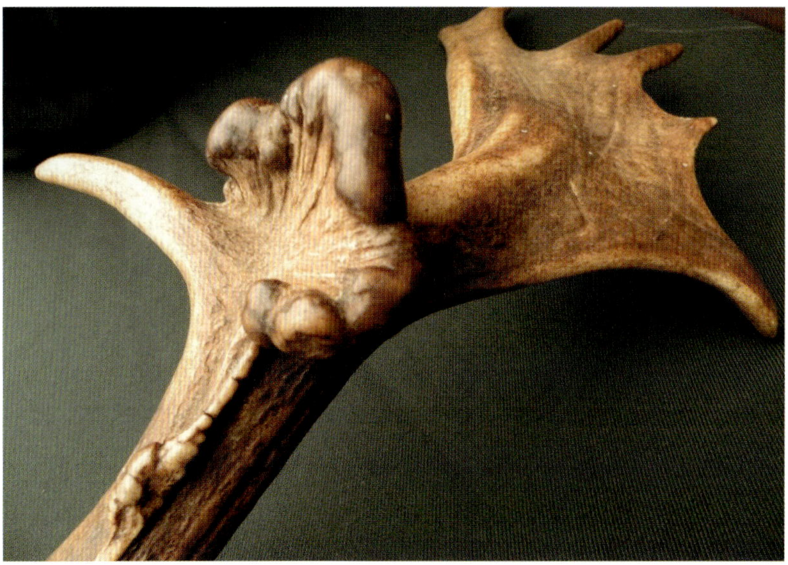

Mushroom type growth on main beam due to injury caused during antler growth

Fallow bucks are particularly prone to becoming entangled in a wide variety of agriculture-related equipment and rubbish, some of which they will carry aloft in their antlers for weeks. When such adornments are acquired when the antler is clean no resulting deformity will occur and often the debris rots away or is lost by the buck's activity and frustration. Many bucks do not escape their dilemma, resulting in fatal consequences. On many occasions antlers are broken off through the pressure of sheer leverage, leaving the buck devoid of the antler and giving an unusual appearance.

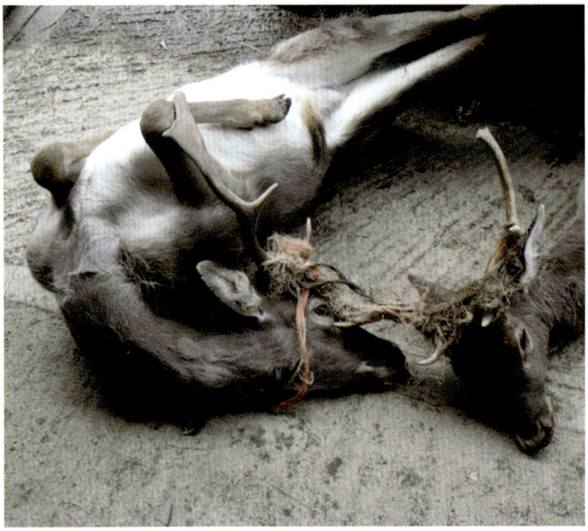

Entanglements can have fatal consequences

Above left and right: It is rare for injury to the pedical and/or skull to occur

Left: A sorel with both main beams broken giving the stalker the impression of a pricket at first sight

During the later months of the year, as the undergrowth diminishes, broken antlers are more likely to be found than the ones cast naturally in the spring. If you do find broken antlers they are always of interest. You may actually recognise them and know the buck that lost them.

I recall being in the company of a Scottish stalking friend, Maitland Rankin, who during a stalk for a fallow buck came across the obvious signs of a buck's scrape adjacent to a high forestry fence that had been damaged. The immediate area had been disturbed on both sides of the fence. A few feet away he noticed a broken antler, which he picked up and kept. Producing this from his pocket later, Maitland was as pleased with the found antler as he would have been had he shot the buck that had lost

Maitland's matching antler

it. The assumption was the buck, a sorel, had lost the right beam of his antler during the rut in battle with a buck on the opposite side of the fence.

Maitland did not get a shot that day but took the antler home to Scotland. Some months later I was back stalking in the same area and saw a very peculiarly antlered buck, giving the appearance at distance of a pricket. The buck was lame and fortunately I managed to shoot it. On finding the buck I could see both antlers were broken at similar distances up the beams above the brow tines. My mind went back to the antler found by Maitland and I decided to keep the head to see whether it matched the right beam of the remaining antler. In due course we compared the two and there was an obvious match, as you will see from the photograph above. No doubt the left antler would have been broken at a similar time. The head with reunited right antler remains a talking point on Maitland's wall and is now referred to as 'the buck he never shot'.

Assessing Age from Antlers

While the antlers of young fallow bucks are a clear indicator of age, assessing a mature buck's age from the appearance of its antlers is by no means an exact science, particularly if they have access to supplementary feeding or are captive. To illustrate the difficulty, the photograph below shows the consecutive cast antlers of a captive fallow buck kept by stalking friend, Jochen Algermissen, in Germany. These can be compared to cast antlers of wild bucks as shown in the photograph opposite.

Consecutive cast antlers of a captive fallow buck

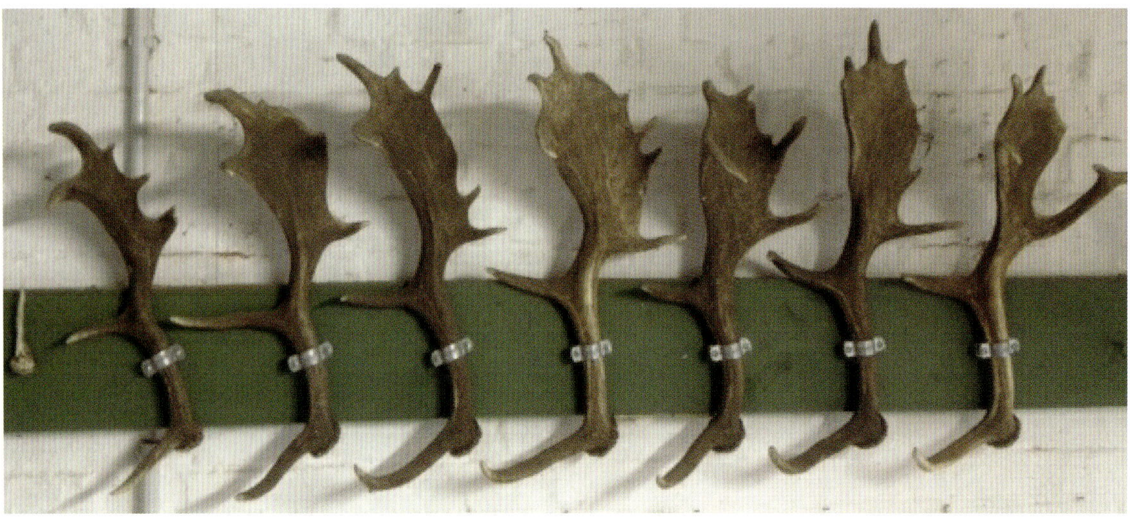

As can be seen, with the exception of the first head of the pricket at two years of age, if any of the antlers are viewed in isolation, ageing the buck from this perspective alone is difficult. At the age of nine years the antlers can be seen to be at the start of the 'going back' process.

In the wild a more accurate judgement of the age of a buck from its antler development can be made, as depicted in the photograph below of typical cast antlers from two years to seven years. It will be seen that once 'buck' status is achieved at six years (fifth head) it becomes more difficult to determine age from then on until the buck is clearly quite old and 'going back', as indicated in the cast antlers of the captive buck aged nine years. Many third and fourth heads of bucks will be at least equal to bucks a year older respectively in other areas where antler quality is known to be better, often for no apparent reason.

A buck's antlers are usually at their best around six to seven years and starting to decline (going back) after nine years.

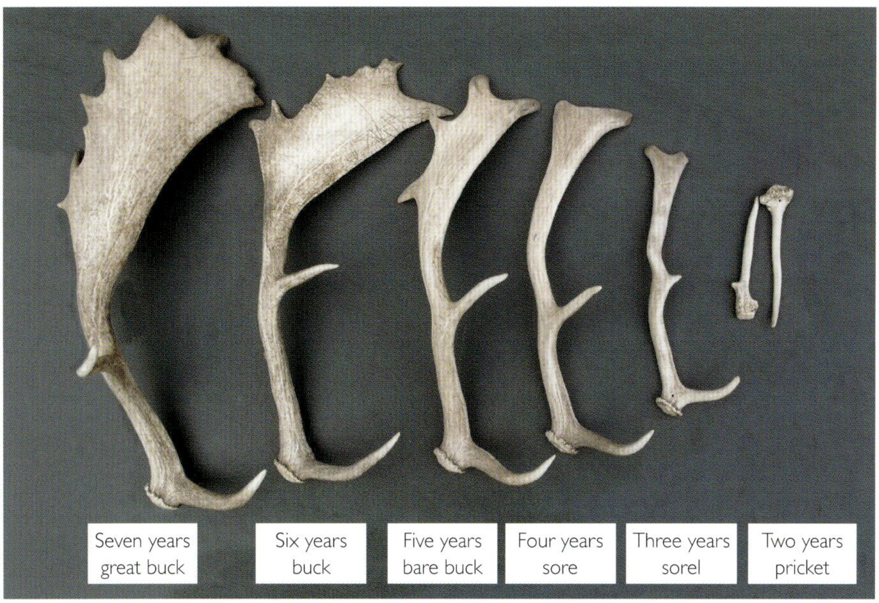

Ageing bucks in the wild can usually be achieved up to their fourth year (third head – sore), after which it becomes more difficult

While ageing bucks in the wild, as opposed to those in captive conditions where supplementary feeding takes place, may be easier it emphasises the fact there are more reliable methods of ageing deer, particularly from examination of their teeth as related to in Chapter 1. Of course, ageing bucks by their teeth alone is not possible while stalking in the wild when faced with decisions over which bucks to cull. Once a buck is shot subsequent examination of the teeth can prove your decision right or wrong and so expand your knowledge and experience in the process of ageing bucks from their overall appearance and conformation. A loss of condition due to disease or injury can also make assessment of age difficult.

Heads of Interest

Above left: This historical head was originally from the collection of J. G. Millais and is the head embossed on the front cover of the classic work *Deer and their Horns* by J.G. Millais. It now forms part of the Drew Bain collection

Above far right: A fine example of a very large fallow head from the New Forest in Hampshire with a score of 186.61 CIC points, from the Drew Bain collection

Right: This abnormal English fallow head where the antlers bend back is from the collection of Drew Bain (Ex G.K. Whitehead and ex J.G. Millais collections)

Trophies and their Measurement

It has been a long established tradition for hunters to treat the skins, tusks or horns of particularly large animals, usually males of the species, as 'trophies' in recognition of their achievement in stalking and culling the animal. Deer are no exception and their antlers in particular have become prized possessions. As a means of recognising the biggest as 'best', assessment criteria have been established over many years. A number of institutions have been involved worldwide and assessment criteria have varied. Generally, the criteria have centred on physical measurement of, for example, antler length, tine length, girth and weight. Awards in the form of certificates and medals are given dependent on the 'score' achieved through the assessment process.

I have mixed views over the subject of 'trophies' as much harm can be done in terms of the welfare of the species if the shooting of bucks is done for the sole reason of hanging a trophy on the wall. The challenge for me has always been in the actual stalking, be it for a buck or doe. If shooting a buck is justified through your own management plans or those of your host's then the fact it may fall to be a medal class trophy should be viewed as a bonus. However, we should recognise that in many areas, particularly abroad, it is the revenue generated through hunting in pursuit of trophies that has been ploughed back into conservation and done so much to benefit not only the quarry species but the wider natural environment in which other species survive.

Taxidermy has become popular in recent years and it is now seen as fashionable to have a set of deer antlers on the wall, or indeed a full mounted deer head. And what better than a fine pair of fallow antlers with their majestic wide palms? Whether or not the actual head is of a medal quality status matters not to the wider public. But, of course, it does matter to many stalkers who go to great lengths, and sometimes expense, to shoot a medal class trophy-antlered buck. Many stalkers have collected heads over the years that are not medal class but nevertheless are attractive or unusual in some way. Such heads make valuable trophies in their own right. The bizarre heads are particularly sought after by many of our foreign guests. Whatever the quality of antlers it matters not as they are often memories of individual stalks taking one back to a time and place long past. They also serve as talking points, perhaps over a glass of whisky with friends.

If you think you have shot a buck that may be medal class then you should consider having the head measured by a trained and experienced measurer from one of the two awarding bodies:

1. The International Council for Game and Wildlife Conservation (CIC)
2. The British Association for Shooting and Conservation (BASC) in partnership with Sporting Rifle and the British Deer Society (BDS)

There is no universal system for the measurement of fallow antlers and in Europe the criteria initially adopted by the CIC has been the benchmark. Prior to November 2014 both evaluation services measured to these basic criteria. However, the CIC now measures to a revised formula and this revised system applies across all member states in Europe and further afield. Stalkers seeking measurement by the CIC are now requested to present full skull trophies. However, if this is not possible the head can still be measured. The revised system is to benefit the classification of a number of species by enabling additional key measurements to be taken that do not affect the final score.

The BASC/Sporting Rifle/BDS Service, which has become increasingly popular among UK stalkers, has continued to be benchmarked to the old CIC methods enabling measurements to be compared to the data collated over the past forty years in the UK.

If you are not sure if a head may qualify for medal status you may decide in the first instance to take some key measurements yourself, which given a good eye and an insight into the technique, is not too difficult. Done correctly, it will give you a good

Expert trophy measurer Dominic Griffith measures a typical head with the author's assistance. Dominic heads up the BASC, Sporting Rifle and BDS trophy measuring service

indication of a possible score and potential for a medal. By way of example, to achieve a bronze medal antler length should be in the region of 60cm; brow tine length about 16cm; palmation size 30cm × 14cm; circumference of coronets about 20cm; upper and lower beam about 12cm; dry net weight around 3kg. This is only a guide and you should be aware that a low score in one area may be compensated by a high score in another, bringing the trophy into a medal category. The full criteria and method to do this, based on the BASC/Sporting Rifle/BDS service, are described below.

Ideally the head should be measured after it has been clean-boiled and is dry, although this is no bar to measurement under the BASC/SR/BDS system. The drying process may take up to several months depending on the type of skull cut and the relative humidity of the environment. If you submit a head for measurement prior to drying an estimated weight within the formula may be determined. Whether you decide to prepare the head as a standard cut, long nose cut or full skull mount is a matter for you as the type of cut will be taken into consideration during the measurement process. You will need a good flexible tape that does not distort under tension, ideally a thin metal one, together with a set of scales from which you can suspend the head to take the weight measurement and a notepad and pencil. Be mindful that if during the process you decide to mark the antler to aid measurement you do so sparingly as you may find it difficult to remove, particularly if you use chalk. You will also find the task is aided by having an assistant, not only to hold the antlers, but to double-check your measurements.

Fallow deer measurement

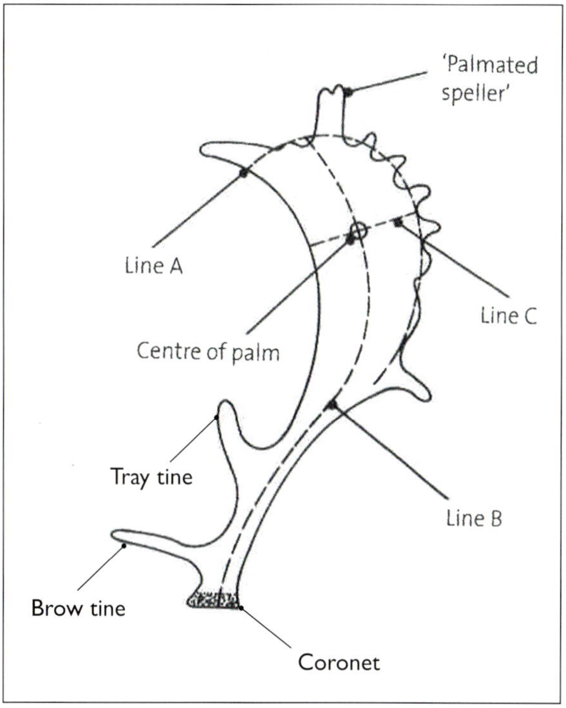

The sketch on the right of a typical fallow antler provides a visual reference to the measurement process described below.

1. Length of antler

First you should view the palms individually to determine the basic shape of each one (imaginary line A). You will note the sketch shows what is referred to as a 'palmated speller'. These are not common but an understanding of how they are defined is essential in trophy measurement because when they do appear on the antler they should be discounted with regard to length measurement. A palmated speller is defined as a mass of antler lying outside the basic shape of the palm and where the width of that mass, measured at its widest point, is less than 50 per cent of the width of the palm itself. If the width is greater than 50 per cent then it is considered as a normal extension of the palm and may then be included for the purposes of length measurement.

The length measurement should be taken to the nearest 0.1cm along the outside surface of the beam and parallel to its leading edge, from a point level with the underside of the coronet to the highest point of indentation of the palm (not to the highest point of the antler itself). Allow the tape to fall naturally over the coronet on to the beam, pressing it to the beam at a point 2cm above the coronet. Follow an imaginary line up the central line with the tape as indicated (line B) to the highest indentation of the palm. Both antlers are measured in this way and the average of these measurements multiplied by a factor of 0.5 to establish the points scored for this element of the process.

2. Length of brow tine

This measurement is taken along the underside of the tine from the upper edge of the coronet to the extremity of the tine and is made easier if you turn the trophy upside down. Determine the average length of both tines and multiply by a factor of 0.25 to establish the points scored.

3. Length of palmation

This measurement is taken from a point 1cm above the narrowest point of the circumference of the upper beams where the palms begin to broaden, again laying the tape along the imaginary line B up the centre of the outside surface of the antler and parallel to its leading edge terminating at the highest indentation. Determine the average of both palmation measurements to establish the points scored.

4. Width of palmation

This measurement is determined by taking the circumference measurement of the palm at its broadest point where an indentation appears on the back edge. Loop the tape around the palm to find the widest point, pressing the tape into the palm as necessary. The tape should follow the imaginary line (C) through a point at 90 degrees to line (B). Remember, just as with the antler and palm length measurements, it is taken from the indentation and not the tip of a speller. Divide the circumference measurement by two to determine the palm width. The average of both palms is then multiplied by a factor of 1.5 to establish the points scored.

5. Circumference of coronets

Measure the circumference of each coronet, taking care to ensure the tape does not slip off on the blind side. This measurement can be a little tricky if the coronets are uneven. If possible, get assistance to support the tape on the back edge of the coronet while you take the measurement. The average of the two is determined for the points scored.

6. Circumference of lower beams

This measurement is taken at the narrowest point between the brow and tray tines of each beam. Loop the tape around the beam until the lowest measurement is found. The measurements for each antler are both included in the points scored.

7. Circumference of upper beams

This measurement is taken at the narrowest point between the tray tine and commencement of palm of each beam, the latter point having been determined earlier in the process of palm measurement. Loop the tape around to find the lowest measurement. If this measurement scores more than 130 per cent of the lower beam measurement the excess over this must be discounted. This allows for a measurement to be taken and included where no tray tine is present. Both measurements for each beam are included in the points scored.

8. Dry weight of antlers

This is best done by suspending the scales/spring balance on a secure anchorage, ensuring the scales are zeroed to take account of the weight of any hooks and so on used to suspend the head. The weight is taken to the nearest 10g. A deduction of 250g (0.25kg) is made for full skull trophies and 100g (0.1kg) for a long nose cut trophy. In the case of non-typical cuts a fair estimated deduction should be made bearing in mind weight should not be added where severe cuts have been made. The dry net weight is multiplied by two to determine the points scored. In the event the trophy has already been full shoulder mounted by a taxidermist, the BASC/SR/BDS service will apply an estimation of weight and annotate the measurement form appropriately.

9. Beauty

Points can be awarded as shown for colour, tine ends, mass, form and regularity.

a. *Colour*

Pale yellow or artificially coloured	0 points
Grey or medium brown	1 point
Brown to black	2 points

b. *Tine ends*

Short, few thin spellers on both sides	0 points
Spellers along a third of palm	1 point for each side

Spellers along two thirds of palm	2 points for each side
Spellers along entire length of palm with back tine	3 points for each side
Maximum being six points for tine ends.	

c. *Mass, form, regularity*

Mass between 2.75 and 3kg	1 point
Mass between 3.01 and 3.25kg	2 points
Mass over 3.25kg	3 points

Up to two points can be awarded for good shape and regularity, making a maximum score in this section of five points. Where differences are evident between antlers sensible judgement over points awarded should be made.

10. Penalties

Points should be deducted from the overall score for insufficient span, faulty palmation and irregularities.

a. *Insufficient span*

Measure the span at the widest point between the middle of the palms. This is usually best done from the back holding the tape between the palms to determine the widest point. The tape needs to be held horizontally before the measurement is taken.

Calculate the measurement as a percentage of the average length of the beams i.e. (*show as fraction*) span over average length × 100.

Deduct points as follows:

Span less than 85 per cent of average beam length	1 point
Span less than 80 per cent	2 points
Span less than 75 per cent	3 points
Span less than 70 per cent	4 points
Span less than 65 per cent	5 points
Span less than 60 per cent	6 points

b. *Faulty palmation*

The following points up to a maximum of ten can be deducted for palm faults as described:

Swollen, diamond or triangular-shaped palm	1–3 points each side

Bifurcated (split) palm	2–4 points each side
Jagged palm	3–5 points each side
Spike or dagger-shaped palm	4–5 points each side

c. *Unnatural edges of palmation*

Up to two points can be deducted for smooth, worn or porous palm edges.

d. *Irregularities*

Up to six points can be deducted for antlers that are irregularly placed on the pedicles, or show obvious differences between the two beam lengths, brow or tray tines.

Establishing the Overall Score

Having recorded the points scored under each section of measurement these should now be added together with those points for beauty. Subtract any penalty points to give the final score.

Scores achieved within the following ranges will determine the level of medal awarded as shown:

Bronze	Silver	Gold
160–169.9	170–179.9	180+

Medals

World and UK Top Heads

The top three world record heads all come from Hungary (all free range). Their scores are follows:

1. 237.63 CIC points, 2002, Guth (Hungary)
2. 233.11 CIC points, 1991, Guth (Hungary)*[9]
3. 227.57 CIC points, 2013, Pincehely (Hungary)

A world record head for length of antler at 95cm was pictured in the *The Field* magazine in 1955. This animal was from near Karaboga, Turkey. However, the head shown below measured under the Rowland Ward system exceeds this length.

This massive head, now in the Drew Bain collection, is the world No.1 fallow in the records of big game in the Rowland Ward record. It was shot by Jurgen Josch in Karpathia, Slovakia, in 1999. Details of measurement: length 39⅛in, circumference 4in, tines 17in, width of palm 6in, outside spread 31⅛in, tip to tip 22⅛in

9 A photograph of the head shown at 2, shot in 1991 at 233.11 CIC points (Nagygyorgy Sandor), is shown in Kenneth Whitehead's *Encyclopaedia of Deer*

Top Ten Record Heads in the UK with details of Measurements

	Name	Country	Date	Weight	Beam Length		Lower Beam Circumference		Palm Length		Palm Width		CIC
					Left	Right	Left	Right	Left	Right	Left	Right	Score
				Kg	Cm	Cm	Cm	Cm	Cm	Cm	Cm	Cm	Cm
1	John Plant	Hampshire	Nov 04	3.30	68.4	69.7	13.1	12.5	45.8	47.4	29.2	35.8	215.10
2	G. Knight	Hampshire	Feb 06	4.20	76.2	76.5					17.7	16.4	205.78
3	P.S. Yates	Hampshire	1985	3.95	68.8	72.3	25.0	24.4	44.7	48.8	19.3	21.2	204.34
4	D. Quarrell	Wiltshire	Aug 07	7.20	82.9	76.6	23.3	23.4	48.0	48.6	14.2	14.3	197.21
5	John Powell	Hampshire	Oct 05	4.10	71.7	74.8	11.4	11.0	46.4	47.0	18.0	16.0	196.66
6	J. Powell	Hampshire	Oct 05	4.10	71.7	74.8					18.0	16.0	196.66
7	M. Brackstone	Hampshire	Feb 08	3.30	64.1	70.2	36.8	18.4	40.0	46.2	10.4	10.7	196.63
8	G. Gundersen	Sussex	Oct 08	3.30	73.0	71.0	49.0	48.0	24.5	16.5	11.5	11.3	194.46
9	A. Prince	Kent	Oct 12	3.91	64.2	65.8	10.9	10.9	42.2	42.8	20.7	16.5	194.00
10	A. Prince	Sussex	Nov 12	3.93	68.0	68.8	11.3	10.8	43.8	46.2	18.4	16.9	193.40

Chapter 3

Stalking Opportunities

Wild fallow are a real challenge to stalk and the opportunity to do so should not be missed, whether by way of invitation as a guest, paying for the day or securing your own ground through lease, licence or agreement.

There are a number of ways in which you can enhance your chances of securing stalking successfully when given the opportunity. Becoming fit and competent by acquiring the necessary skills, knowledge and qualifications is one of the most important.

Becoming Fit and Competent

The days when one could stalk deer without qualification or evidence of experience are coming to an end and, like it or loathe it, becoming fit and competent by way of formal qualifications is becoming a necessity if you wish to take many of the opportunities to stalk that are available. In most European countries hunters must undertake training and be tested before they are allowed to hunt large game animals such as deer.

Currently in England and Wales, chief constables are obliged to grant a firearm certificate if you are able to show you have good reason to possess a rifle for deer stalking and do not present a danger to the peace. In practice this means providing evidence of your opportunity to stalk, which may amount to a specific invitation, booking with an agent or providing evidence of land on which there are deer and your authorisation to shoot there.

There is no legal requirement for you to actually provide evidence of qualifications, although you will on occasions be asked to show this by the police. There are many stalkers that do not consider this satisfactory since public safety and deer welfare may be at risk from the unqualified and incompetent individual shooting a high powered rifle without some form of basic training. Fortunately, the stalking fraternity can be proud of its self-regulation, with the uptake of voluntary qualifications sufficient at the

present time to resist the need for a mandatory requirement for formal qualifications. Qualifications do add weight to your good reason and suitability to be entrusted with a rifle for deer stalking and it is sensible to pursue some basic competence training before embarking on shooting deer. This need for competence has been recognised at government level.

In Scotland during the development of the Wildlife and Natural Environment Act, 2011, (WANE Act) the Deer Commission advised the government that the right to shoot deer in Scotland should also be subject to a competence requirement and the policy is now that all people who wish to do this should either hold a deer management qualification or be accompanied by a qualified hunter. Rather than enforce this requirement through regulations the government decided to take a voluntary approach and allow training and certification to be delivered through shooting organisations and rural colleges, effectively encouraging self-regulation. This voluntary approach is currently under review by Scottish Natural Heritage (SNH). There is provision to introduce a competence requirement through legislation if necessary in the future.

Qualifications and Training

Deer Management Qualifications (DMQ) is the awarding body for the Deer Stalking Certificates 1 & 2

If you have recently taken an interest in deer stalking and need further advice and guidance, gaining some form of sector-recognised qualification will give you a wider understanding of stalking techniques and deer management. It should be recognised there is much to learn and experience. In gaining some basic qualifications you will be laying the foundations for further learning, most of which can only be achieved through gaining actual stalking experience.

There are a number of training courses and qualifications available from the various bodies within the deer sector, all of which are voluntary. However, as mentioned earlier, you will find some qualifications are essential if you wish to take up many stalking opportunities. The two basic qualifications that are normally required and have been recognised nationally are those awarded by the Deer Management Qualifications body (DMQ)*[10], known as the Deer Stalking Certificate (DSC) 1 & 2. The Scottish government has recognised that these qualifications may in some situations meet the standard for being fit and competent (see Chapter 10).

10 admin@dmq.org.uk, DMQ, Administrative Centre, Marford Mill, Rossett, Wrexham, LL12 OHL

Qualifications are essential for many stalking opportunities

The aim of the standard and related assessments is to enable candidates to demonstrate their understanding of basic deer management principles and to show competence in legally, safely and humanely culling deer, and dealing with carcasses hygienically.

DMQ is a 'not for profit' company, is limited by guarantee and is supported by a large number of organisations including DEFRA, Scottish National Heritage and The Deer Initiative. It maintains the Deer Stalking Certificate standards, quality assures the assessment process and administers the awards. Acting as the awarding body for the qualifications, it does not carry out assessments or training. These may only be offered by approved assessment centres*[11].

DMQ's role is to develop and maintain a progressive approach to deer management standards and assessment, linked to the recognised Occupational Standard.

The DSC1

The DSC1 is a basic qualification for deer stalkers. It is a largely knowledge-based qualification that enables candidates to demonstrate their understanding of basic deer management principles and meat hygiene, and to show competence in shooting at simulated targets. There are a number of assessment centres offering DSC1, the main ones being the BASC and the BDS.

The assessment tests knowledge and skills in the following five areas:

1. Deer biology and ecology
2. Deer identification
3. Safety
4. Shooting
5. Large game meat hygiene

There are five assessments to pass within the above areas; written, visual, safety, shooting and game meat hygiene, and should you fail any of these they can be retaken within three years of your registration date.

11 www.dmq.org.uk/assessmentcentres.htm

The DSC1 shooting test

In taking the DSC1 qualification you do not need to have actual stalking experience or have your own rifle or firearms certificate; rifles and ammunition will be provided for candidates that need them. Clearly, in presenting yourself for assessment you need to have sufficient knowledge of the deer management areas to be examined. You must also be a competent rifle shot, as no rifle instruction will be provided prior to the assessment. A number of organisations, including BASC, currently offer pre-DSC1 training to assist you if you have little experience of using centre fire rifles. It is advisable therefore, even if you are experienced, to consider first taking one of these training courses, many of which lead to a consequent assessment for the award.

Once registered, candidates have three years to complete the assessments, but they can be completed in one day. The DSC1 qualification incorporates the large game element of the Wild Game Meat Hygiene requirements to meet the Food Hygiene regulations 2004, and is a prerequisite for DSC2.

The DSC2

This is a practical-based qualification that enables you to demonstrate your knowledge and competence in culling deer legally, safely and humanely and dealing with carcasses hygienically. It is assessed on the basis of evidence that you collect in a portfolio, which you are provided with on registration. This evidence is based mainly on your ability to demonstrate the whole process of culling deer on a least three separate occasions, these being in the presence of an approved witness. It is therefore strongly recommended that you obtain some experience under the guidance of a competent person before embarking on this qualification. A list of approved witnesses is obtainable from DMQ.

Once registered, you have three years to submit the portfolio; any evidence that is more than three years old will not be considered. The portfolio is then subject to assessment to ensure the evidence gathered meets the required criteria and is recorded correctly. This qualification should be seen as recognising a stalker's knowledge and skill over a considerable period of time. It is not the type of qualification to be taken lightly, attempted quickly or by dubious means.

It is unlikely that you will be able to satisfy the requirements of this qualification without having stalked and culled deer on a number of occasions previously. Many approved witnesses charge for their services, the cost of which may vary dependent on what is on offer. While the experience of stalking is always valuable, if you are paying for a witnessed stalk and are not up to the standard required, it may be a costly experience with no evidence gained. So my advice would be not to arrange to have a stalk witnessed until you are confident in all areas in which you will be assessed. Remember, the approved witness is there to observe and ask you relevant questions; not guide or assist you in what you do.

Best Practice

DMQ strongly recommends that you obtain practical experience under the guidance of a competent person before registering. Depending on where you live or stalk, you are also advised to consult the best practice guides issued in England and Wales or the best practice guidance for Scotland*[12].

Best practice guide

The birthplace of best practice could be said to be within the minds and skills of the practitioners involved over many years. They were the stalkers we have held in high regard because of how they did things, their consideration for deer welfare and public safety. In the olden days the best way of doing things was communicated by word of mouth and demonstrated in the field, whether that was in the techniques of actually stalking or in how to deal with the carcass once the trigger had been pulled. Over time this has been supplemented by articles and books written by those with the ability to write about what they practised. The best practice guidance focuses upon that body of knowledge and practice among our deer stalking fraternity.

12 www.thedeerinitiative.co.uk and for Scotland www.bestpracticeguides.org.uk

David Stretton demonstrating best practice in carcass preparation at a game fair

Best practice guidance was first introduced in Scotland and later to England and Wales with a remit to make best practice common practice in a user-friendly format. For the most part, they illustrate general principles and are not necessarily a rigid prescription. They are intended to give practitioners, landowners and managers confidence that when following the guidance they are acting humanely, responsibly and effectively, and carrying out their duties in a rational and considered way based on the best current information.

It is useful to consider where best practice guidance fits into the bigger legal picture associated with the risks and liabilities of deer management. While none of the guides are mandatory, the Scottish guides are seen as a supportive document to the Code of Practice on Deer Management contained within the Wildlife and Natural Environment (Scotland) Act, 2011. Best practices are used to maintain quality as an alternative to mandatory legislated standards. The growing trend to use them to support codes of practice within legislation is worthy of note and should be seen as an opportunity to further enhance self-regulation.

The guides now provide sufficient information to be considered a major contributor to the national standards and the required training material, together with ancillary qualifications such as the Deer Stalking Certificate (DSC). Approved witnesses for the DSC2 qualifications should be using best practice as a benchmark and asking relevant questions based on the guides.

Continuous Professional Development

There are a number of training courses that both support and complement the DSC qualifications and many effectively lead to a programme of continuous professional development (CPD). This has been recognised over many years by various organisations and training providers within the sector who have run specialist courses designed to develop skills and enhance the basic deerstalking qualifications. Best practice events run jointly between The Deer Initiative, BASC and the BDS have been particularly successful in skills development.

A recent initiative by the British Deer Society, in response to the need for CPD, has been the introduction of a training initiative entitled the BDS Skills Award. The award is aimed not only at deerstalkers and deer managers but anyone with an interest in increasing their knowledge of deer. This is a timely initiative as concerns over 'skill slippage' have been voiced by individual stalkers and landowning bodies keen to ensure standards are maintained, particularly where high risk sensitive areas are stalked over.

The award is available to both BDS members and non-members and takes the form of a progressive learning programme based on the continuous acquisition of skills, with awards being made at bronze, silver and gold levels.

Each level of award comprises a number of different course components, some delivered by the BDS and some provided by a range of other organisations. Certain course elements are mandatory while others can be chosen according to the student's preference. Each course component is awarded a points value and when enough points have been awarded the relevant level of award may be claimed. All courses can also be taken as part of personal skills development programme without the need to pursue the award.

Mandatory elements of the training include achieving Deer Stalking Certificate 1 (DSC1) for the bronze level, DCS2 for the silver level, and attendance at a BDS Deer Management Course, or equivalent, for the gold level. Other areas of BDS training include advanced shooting skills, habitat assessment, butchery and high seat use. Points will also be awarded for training delivered by providers, such as all-terrain vehicle and off-road driving, NRA range conducting officer courses and attendance at best practice events run by The Deer Initiative.

Finding Stalking

Stalking is unique in many ways in that within the sport there is a considerable range of opportunities from which to choose covering different species and terrain. Many opportunities will require stalking qualifications as a prerequisite, but there are chances for the complete novice to gain experience. While many stalking opportunities are sought from those that are advertised, actually instigating your own enquiries or requirements should not be ruled out as a means of securing these. However, unless you are well qualified it is doubtful that this direct approach will be productive.

You should not necessarily restrict yourself to looking specifically for fallow stalking as the experience of stalking a variety of species can be beneficial to your all round ability as a stalker. Differing species and terrain demand different skills and techniques. For example, stalking the hill for red deer in Scotland will give you a great appreciation of the need for stealth, the use of dead ground and the power of scent and its effects over long distances, all of which are relevant to fallow stalking. Skill in recognising deer other than fallow can also be very useful if your ground holds a number of different species.

Skill in recognising deer other than fallow can be useful

The Internet

Finding stalking is not difficult in this technological world. A search using the appropriate words on the internet will provide you instantly with a number of options. These will be mainly commercial stalking offers at a price and in circumstances where you will be accompanied, which is desirable if you are a novice. If you do not have access to the internet the shooting press carries advertisements regularly for a variety of stalking opportunities and details of sporting agents. The powers of social media are such that you should be able to check out the credentials of individual providers to ensure they are honest, reliable and provide value for money. You may find The Stalking Directory*[13], a source of information both in terms of feedback and stalking opportunities.

13 www.thestalkingdirectory.co.uk

Stalking Syndicates

Occasionally you may see advertised the opportunity to apply to join a stalking syndicate. These opportunities are most suitable for the more experienced stalkers as they will usually involve stalking alone; demanding experience of taking the shot, carcass handling and preparation. Some of these can offer good value for money dependent on the number of stalkers involved and size of the stalking area. You should be mindful of the distance to be travelled to the ground and your ability to make sufficient visits to enable you to make a useful contribution to the cull.

Shooting Associations and Clubs

The British Association for Shooting and Conservation (BASC)*[14]

BASC has a dedicated deer department to assist stalking members. It offers a number of courses designed to develop stalking skills. It is an approved assessment centre for the DSC1 qualification. Specialist advice is also available to members from the team within the firearms department should you have issues or concerns over aspects of your firearms certificate or its conditions.

The association has a number of different stalking schemes across the UK available to its members, catering for the complete novice with no qualifications to the more experienced stalker. The schemes cover a wide range of opportunities, from stalking sika deer in Northern Ireland on the famous Baronscourt Estate and red deer on the Isle of Arran in Scotland, to stalking fallow, roe and muntjac in southern England. The schemes offer excellent value for money and, of course, becoming a member brings the benefit of insurance cover for stalking activities.

The BASC has a dedicated team to assist its stalking members and provides stalking opportunities through a number of schemes catering for all levels of experience

14 www.basc.org.uk

British Deer Society

The society*[15] was formed in 1963 from a deer group within the Mammal Society. It is a registered national charity with a charter to promote the welfare of deer. The society provides technical advice to government, organisations and the public on deer management, legislation and conservation, and is involved in education of all age groups about the importance of deer in our environment. It has a major training function both for the novice and more experienced stalker and, as described earlier, is involved in encouraging continuous professional development through its skills development programme. The society is based at Fordingbridge, Hampshire, and publishes the magazine *Deer* for its members. Membership also provides insurance cover for stalking activities.

The St Hubert Club

The St Hubert Club of Great Britain*[16] was founded in 1953 and is concerned primarily with the training of its stalker members. It was the first organisation to run a formal programme of training for stalkers. Over the years the club's training scheme has been extensively revised and its Qualified Stalker Certificate is now linked to Occupational Standards and is approved by LANTRA. To gain the certificate the trainee has to undergo a considerable programme of training over a minimum of four years, including being supervised and assessed on all club stalks for at least two years. Finally, a portfolio of evidence has to be produced and verified.

The club provides stalking opportunities for members both on privately owned land and Forestry Commission woodland in the Thetford and Kielder areas.

Securing your own Stalking Ground

Being in a position to manage your own stalking ground is the ultimate opportunity in the stalking world. Looking at the evening sky and deciding at the last minute to venture out upon your own stalking ground, rifle in hand, is an exciting prospect and a real privilege.

There are now more stalkers in the UK than ever before and finding your own fallow stalking in some areas of the country can be a difficult task, despite deer numbers being at an all-time high. The perception by many is that the majority of stalking opportunities fall to a privileged minority of stalkers; less fortunate stalkers becoming frustrated through what they perceive to be a lack of opportunity. The reality of some stalkers having more ground than they can manage effectively adds to the frustration. But then, no one should expect to get into a sport and immediately

15 www.bds.org.uk

16 www.sainthubertclub.co.uk

compete with those who have spent years building up their experience and expertise. However, if you are prepared to gain the experience and qualifications suggested then when the opportunity does present itself you will be in a strong position to take it.

Securing your own fallow stalking should not be taken on lightly. It involves a responsibility far greater than just culling deer. It is also physically demanding. If a substantial cull is required you will need to show you have the experience, the necessary equipment and facilities to achieve it. Establishing this position will often be the deciding factor in whether you are successful in being given the opportunity to manage the ground.

Living in an area close to good populations of deer will increase your opportunities not only to stalk but also to obtain your own ground. It is a distinct advantage as you will need to be in a position to make sufficient visits, not only to achieve the cull but to attend to the ancillary tasks associated with deer management.

The opportunity of securing some stalking has been much to do with being in the right place, at the right time or just knowing the right person. The old saying, 'It's not what you know but who you know' is still a fact of life. That said, acquisition of stalking by these means does not always get the right person for the job and can often result in disaster for the landowner, deer and habitat concerned. Qualifications, proven experience and insurance will in the future play an increasingly important role in who gets to stalk what and where.

Authorities to Stalk

The exclusive right to stalk over a piece of ground is normally vested in the landowner unless the rights have been separated from the land or let. Simple verbal permission is the minimum requirement for you to be authorised but it is advisable for this to be in writing. If it is the only stalking to which you have access it will need to be in writing for the purposes of your firearm certificate conditions. However, it is likely that the owner will seek a more formal arrangement by permit, licence or lease.

The trend in recent years has been to move towards the governance of stalking through licence rather than lease. There are valid reasons for this as there are distinct legal differences between a lease and licence. Stalking licences are more appropriate as they provide greater freedom and flexibility for the licensor to end their arrangement with the licensee. They can also be administered locally for relatively short periods, e.g. twelve months, and, as they are concerned with personal rights and privileges rather than legal interests in the land, they tend to be most appropriate for most stalking activities.

Application to Tender for a Licence

Landowners and forestry companies that provide the opportunity for stalkers to tender for ground, usually under the provisions of a licence, are not necessarily looking for the highest monetary bid and your experience and ability to show you are a safe pair of hands will be the deciding factor. However, you should be realistic in your bid offer. Where there are a number of candidates equally suitable and qualified then whether or not the offer is a fair one may be a deciding factor.

On receipt of the application forms you need to read them carefully and abide by the requests for information and deadline dates. Not to do so will risk your disqualification from the process. If you have built your own portfolio of evidence, as described later, you will give yourself the best chance of success, particularly if there is considerable interest from other stalkers.

Recent years have seen the raising of standards required of stalkers with owners mindful of increased access to the public and accountability to reduce the risks to their safety. It is likely you will have to provide evidence across a broad spectrum of deer management, take a shooting test and be successful at interview. Gaining qualifications in the relevant areas and building a portfolio of evidence is, therefore, essential preparation.

Your Portfolio

A typical portfolio may include the following information and documents:

- Brief résumé of experience and ability to achieve a cull
- References
- Firearms certificate with appropriate open condition for deer
- Public liability insurance to a minimum value of £10 million
- DSC1 and 2 certificates
- Attendance at best practice events
- Additional course certificates, e.g. carcass handling, deer dog
- ATV qualifications, chainsaw, etc
- Participation in collaborative team culls
- Management of stalkers and assistants
- Generic and site specific risk assessments
- Cull records, carcass handling and disease recognition
- Larder/chiller facilities
- First aid qualifications
- Deer dog ownership details, including experience and training

Site Visit

Following the registering of interest in the tender process you may have the opportunity to visit the stalking ground in question and you may subsequently be asked for a résumé of the area with the application. This is an important part of the process since it provides you the opportunity to assess whether the ground has potential and what value you may put on it.

Interview and Skills Test

If you are successful and called for interview you should be prepared to respond to a wide range of questions including, firearm security and safety, food hygiene, and public relations. You may be required to undergo a form of skills assessment, which may include a shooting test. If this is the case you will be advised in advance and you should go well prepared with adequate ammunition and a zeroed rifle. This may sound common sense but you would be surprised at how many stalkers fail to prepare adequately and consequently fail the test.

Licence Particulars

If you are provided with an example of the licence during the application process you should not be deterred by the exhaustive nature of the document or legal terminology. Read it thoroughly and check it meets your needs as well as those of the licensor. Check it does not compromise you. We all make mistakes and solicitors are no exception. I have read and reviewed a number of licences that have been in the standard format for years, sometimes becoming outdated in legal content and not sufficiently detailed in respect of risk assessment.

Prior to entering into the agreement you should read the small print to ensure you are aware of your obligations and agree with them. In particular, you should look to see that the following points are covered to your satisfaction:

- Boundaries – check they are maintained and indicated clearly on an appropriate map.
- Species to be shot – are all species of deer present or likely to be found included?
- Rifles and ammunition – are your calibre(s) and ammunition type you require to use permitted. Check if sound moderators are obligatory?
- Assistants and guest stalkers – is there appropriate provision to allow for assistants or guest stalkers if this was agreed initially?
- Access – is adequate access permitted for vehicles, particularly ATVs for extraction purposes?
- High seats – is there provision for their installation and use together with the cutting of sight lines?
- Venison – is the financial agreement over the sale or retention of venison clear? This is an important element and can assist in calculating the offer price/bid.
- Use of buildings, estate chillers, etc – this should be specified if relevant.

- Shooting out of season or specific days – check there is clarity with regards to the policy of shooting out of season or on specific days where legal exemptions may apply, particularly in respect of serious crop damage.

Should you have any concerns or queries it is better to take these up with the licensor prior to signing. Once you are satisfied with all aspects of the licence you should sign the document in the presence of a witness if required and return all copies. It is normal practice for the licence to be then signed by the licensor and a copy returned to you for your information and retention. A pre-commencement meeting with the owner or representative is advisable and provides an opportunity to iron out any final issues and walk any difficult areas of the boundary.

Retaining the Opportunity

If you are fortunate enough to secure stalking ground, providing you do a good job, you may retain it into the future, giving you the opportunity to manage the deer in a balanced manner and pursue objectives to improve the quality of the herd. Once established, investment in high seats and influence over the management and husbandry of the woodland may also be possible. However, do not take the matter for granted. You should endeavour to maintain your level of skills, ideally through annual skills testing. Make sure you do your best to manage the deer effectively and with some regard for their welfare. Ensure you submit cull returns promptly and pay the required rent on time. Establish good working relationships with those on the ground and ensure you abide by the licence conditions.

I recall the words of my old stalking friend and roe expert, the late Ken MacArthur, who always reminded me never to take the privilege of having your own stalking ground for granted, 'One never knows what is around the corner or who else may be knocking on the door.'

Chapter 4

Stalking Necessities

Fallow are big heavy animals and no one should set out to stalk them unless they are equipped adequately. Not only is a suitable rifle and ammunition required but also the equipment to manage the whole process, from both taking the shot through to carcass extraction and preparation. Being attired suitably and protected from the elements helps not only personal comfort by keeping warm and dry, but your ability to stalk and shoot effectively.

My views expressed with regards to rifles, clothing and equipment are personal ones, born out of trial and error. Those I favour have worked for me but you will make your own decisions based on personal choice. In the long run, good quality kit performs the best and is a pleasure to own. It also lasts longer and so is cost-effective. So buy the best you can afford.

Rifles and Ammunition

The subject of rifle calibres and bullet types provokes much debate among stalkers. The truth is that any legal calibre with a suitable bullet placed correctly is perfectly adequate for fallow stalking. While stalkers have an ample range of rifles and ammunition from which to choose, their choice is governed to a certain extent by legislation and, of course, cost. Deer welfare is central to the legal requirements, as my experience one early morning in Essex underlines.

I was sat in a high seat in the darkness waiting for the first light to peep through an overcast sky. As the light came my senses tuned in to the sound of a cracking branch behind me. A fallow buck appeared from my left side. As it ran past I had the impression that it was moving with an uneven gait and on high alert. It paused briefly to enable a shot to be taken. At the shot the buck took off at great speed and ran for some 80m before disappearing into the dense canopy of the woodland, from where it was eventually found a further 70m on with the help of a dog.

Examination of the animal revealed my shot had passed through the lungs, but

more obvious was an old surface wound to the right shoulder that appeared to have been caused by an inappropriate calibre and/or ammunition. The bullet had caused a cavity the size of a golf ball and disabled the right foreleg but had not penetrated the shoulder blade or entered the ribcage. The wound was probably less than a week old, but the loss of condition of the animal was already quite evident.

The fallow buck shot in Essex – the surface wound on the right shoulder was probably caused by an inappropriate calibre and/or ammunition

The incident serves to underline why the law is as it is, and the welfare implications that follow when people break the rules. All too often, it seems, some people are unaware of the requirements or think ammunition that falls below the prescribed limit is still acceptable to use against large animals such as fallow. Perhaps, faced with the opportunity for a shot at a deer, they are simply tempted to have a go. Inevitably, the result is an injured animal.

Legal Requirements for Fallow Deer – Rifles and Ammunition

England and Wales

Calibre not less than .240in or muzzle energy of not less than 1,700ft/lb*[17]. Bullet must be soft nosed or hollow nosed.

17 The criteria for England and Wales are based on both calibre of rifle and its muzzle energy (not either/or as the wording of the legislation tends to suggest), whereas in Scotland they are based on the ammunition, muzzle energy and velocity.
In Northern Ireland it is a combination of both rifle calibre, ammunition and muzzle energy. Details of the exemptions relating to the use of shotguns are given in Chapter 10 for crop damage.

Scotland

Bullet of not less than 100 grains AND muzzle velocity of not less than 2,450ft per sec, AND muzzle energy of not less than 1,750ft/lb. Expanding bullets designed to deform in predictable manner.

Northern Ireland

Calibre of not less than .236in (6mm). Muzzle energy of not less than 1,700ft/lb. Expanding bullets designed to deform in predictable manner and not less than 100 grains.

Choice of Calibre and Cartridge

The late Ken MacArthur, roe expert and good friend, used to say, 'Beware of the stalker with only one rifle, he probably knows how to use it!' and how true this is. Those stalkers changing their rifles constantly or building up arsenals of differing calibres are often guilty of blaming their tools for a bad job. That said, there are occasions where there is 'good reason' for the possession of more than one calibre of rifle and chief police officers should be sympathetic to the genuine stalker's need.

Choosing a commercial cartridge has the advantage of a good source of rifles and, more importantly, ammunition. A rifle is purchased infrequently, as opposed to ammunition that needs to be available frequently to purchase or load. Typically, your choice of rifle will be chambered to accept one of the following cartridges, all of which are suitable and legal for shooting fallow: .243 Win, 25 06, 6.5 × 55, .270 Win, 7 08, 7 × 57, .308 and 30 06.

There are differences between them and you should research the ballistic properties of each, bearing in mind the type of stalking you have and the size and weight of fallow deer. If you are able to test fire different calibres and cartridges prior to purchase this will help you determine what suits you best. You may well get seduced by the ballistics of one calibre and cartridge combination over another but you may change your opinion if a rifle is unpleasant to fire. A flinch is most difficult to cure. Your choice of ammunition should be confined to those that are designed for the job and meet the energy levels required to ensure clean and humane kills.

Confidence in the rifle of your choice is paramount, assuming it is well founded. There are some excellent accurate rifles you can buy 'off the shelf' without breaking the bank, e.g. The Tikka T3 lite. Save your money for a top quality scope to put on it. While the .308W cartridge is a great all-rounder, my favoured one for fallow is the 6.5 × 55mm Swedish (6.5mm bullet diameter and 55mm case length). This has a soft recoil, is quite flat shooting out to 200m and, with a 140 grain bullet, is heavy enough to do the job without too much damage to the carcass.

The .243 W cartridge requires special mention since it is much maligned. For many years I shot all my fallow with a .243W and was perfectly happy with its performance using the 100 grain bullet. The problem arises when a lightweight frangible bullet is used and a beast is three-quarters facing you. The bullet may not get through the shoulder to do the damage necessary for a clean kill. Light fast bullets are also prone to severe carcass damage. They may fail to meet the legal requirements in terms of energy and therefore their ballistic performance should be checked prior to use.

A further issue can arise with this round in that it may not exit, leaving very little blood to follow up on, albeit the animal will have been shot humanely. A heavier bullet in a larger calibre will normally give this and make finding the carcass easier.

The simple answer is provided the .243 bullet used is of sufficient weight the cartridge is quite adequate for the job.

Whatever rifle you eventually decide upon it should be cleaned religiously after use with special attention paid to the bore. If you buy a new one take the trouble to shoot the barrel in. There are a number of published procedures for this and the one I have relied upon can be found on the Border Barrels web site*[18].

Sound Moderators

Moderators have changed opinion of late and have transformed the shootability of some rifles, e.g. the 30 06 family of cartridges.

For some years I resisted the idea of fitting a moderator, which I considered spoilt the balance and aesthetics of my rifle. However, once tried it is difficult to ignore their advantages, not just in ear protection. Greater accuracy can be achieved together with low recoil, enhancing your ability to observe the reaction to the shot. A low level report can also be an advantage when culling in sensitive areas by keeping disturbance to a minimum from a community and public relations perspective.

Many professional stalkers do not have the choice and are required to use moderated rifles as part of their employer's health and safety risk assessment. In the UK sound moderators fall within the definition of a firearm and therefore their possession and use is subject to the same controls as your rifle. In some countries abroad their use remains prohibited.

Rifles can now be purchased with the barrel screw cut by the manufacturer ready to receive a moderator, with the crown of the barrel protected by a simple threaded ring for use when one is not fitted. When buying a moderator you should ensure you get the correct size not only for the calibre but also the thread of the barrel. There is a compromise to be reached when selecting a moderator, that being between its efficiency in suppressing sound against its weight and size. Therefore, you should

18 www.border-barrels.com

resist the temptation to go for the lightest on the market. If you value your rifle, the moderator should be detached when you are not stalking to prevent corrosion to the thread and bore.

Rifle Scopes

My advice is to buy the best scope you can afford, even if that means searching the second-hand market for one of quality. Swarovski, Zeiss, Schmidt & Bender and Leica are among the market leaders but there are some good alternatives if you have to economise, e.g. Leupold.

For stalking fallow, where you are mainly shooting at between 100 and 200m (less in many woodland situations), you do not need a top end scope that provides the ballistic technology for long range shooting. It is simply an unnecessary expense, in my opinion. A quality scope with a variable magnification ranging from 2 to 12 × 50, and an illuminated reticule facility is as much as any fallow stalker should need. If the budget does not run to one then go for a fixed power of 6 or 8 × 50 with a reticule of your choice, ideally illuminated.

The illuminated reticule is a really useful facility, helping you to determine the crucial point of aim in poor light when a conventional cross hair can be lost against the dark background of a beast. I tend to only use mine in these conditions. Many models are designed to enable you to adjust the illumination level and to turn off automatically should you forget, which is really useful and extends battery life. When stalking you should adjust the setting as the light changes, providing for a low illumination that is not distracting.

You should invest in quality mounts or a fixed rail system to fix the scope to the rifle and ensure these are fitted professionally if necessary. Accuracy depends on proper scope alignment, eye relief and secure fixings. The scope should be adjusted with the use of a bore sight, which will save you time and ammunition when the finer adjustments are made when zeroing, the latter being done by yourself. A rifle zeroed by someone else will not necessarily be correct for you.

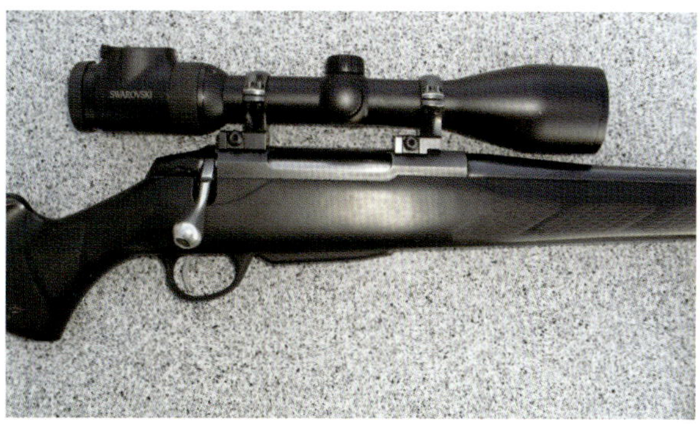

If your budget is tight spend the money on a quality scope rather than the rifle – the author's 6.5 × 55mm Tikka T3 lite rifle and Z6i scope with illuminated reticule

Clothing

The old Scandinavian saying 'There's no such thing as bad weather just bad clothing', while not strictly true, is more relevant nowadays than ever before as modern fabrics, design and technology have combined to provide the stalker with a superb range of clothing with which to combat the elements.

If you are cold and wet you will be uncomfortable and your motivation to stalk on or wait that crucial bit longer in the high seat will diminish. In addition, when the opportunity presents itself you may not shoot well. Being cold and wet dulls the senses and stiffens the body, making the shot more difficult and increasing the risk of a misplaced one. Your choice of clothing will vary dependent on the time of year, the type of stalking you have and the prevailing weather conditions.

Stalking on Foot

If you are to stalk on foot you will not need such warm clothing as required for a long spell in a high seat. If you plan to do both, then a compromise has to be reached to ensure you are both warm enough when sitting for a long period in the seat, yet comfortable enough when stalking actively. When stalking actively you do not want to be overburdened with the excesses of clothing or equipment. You should bear in mind you may have to crawl at times in wet conditions. It should be comfortable and quiet, enabling you to keep warm and dry throughout the day.

I prefer a short jacket when stalking, which is quiet when brushed against foliage and allows you to bend and creep about the woodland easily. A long coat is restrictive when having to crouch or crawl under the canopy. Whether you choose a camouflaged type pattern or a plain coloured jacket is a matter for you. The image that camouflage patterns create in the minds of the onlooker can be a negative one and wearing something plain can appear more professional. What matters is the colour tone, which as far as possible should match the surroundings, so avoid anything too dark. It follows that when stalking in snow you should consider whites, which are now available from some stockists*[19].

The colour tones of your clothing should match your surroundings

Wearing the right footwear is vital. I prefer boots to wellingtons and have to admit I have somewhat of an obsession for them, in which I know I am not alone in the stalking world. Boots tend to provide more control on foot placement (see Chapter 6 on stalking techniques) and greater support than wellingtons on steep ground. I also find them quieter and more comfortable. I have had some with the most infuriating and incurable squeaks and those that have resulting in wet feet; needless to say all have become relegated to non-stalking duties.

Boots 20 to 30cm in height give good ankle support and protection against the wet. Wearing

19 www.bushwear.co.uk

gaiters made from material that is quiet is a good combination. Look for a boot that is waterproof, relatively light and not too stiff in the last (sole), allowing for ease of flexing in situations where your footwork needs to be precise. In this regard, the Danner range of boots is excellent, as are some Austrian boots I purchased recently from WH Shoes*[20]. Much of my woodland stalking over the years has been through thick strong bramble and leather takes some punishment if not protected on the front edge, therefore boots providing a rubber or Kevlar-type protection to the front and sides are ideal.

It is the face and hands that are spotted quickly by deer and masking their appearance helps you to remain undetected among the woodland canopy. So wearing a hat and, if you can put up with it, a face veil helps you remain undetected. Gloves in the form of fingerless mitts are an advantage, not only as protection to the back of the hand from a cold wind but more importantly as camouflage. I wear some old treasured mitts that were made originally for the equestrian market; they have no palm and so provide complete dexterity and are ideal for use all year round.

Preparing for the High Seat

If your stalking activity is confined to long periods of waiting with little or no foot stalking, then you can afford the luxury of more clothing and equipment than would otherwise be necessary. You may find a roe sack or small rucksack useful in this regard.

During the colder months thermal underwear is an option to consider and building up a number of base layers of good quality garments under a substantial coat is a must. I have found some of the ski gear in merino wool to be ideal and a respected stalking friend recommends thin fabrics made from bamboo extracts for their wicking ability and warmth.

Boots with a waterproof Gore-tex lining and a high thermal rating will help keep your feet warm. You should have gloves or hand warmers with you. Keeping your hands warm is important when handling the rifle. There are now all-in-one thermal suits available on the market and while these are too bulky and warm to walk any distance in, they can be taken to the high seat and then slipped on quickly. Alternatively, taking a simple woollen or loden-type blanket with you to wrap around the legs once in the seat has to be tried to be appreciated on a cold day. This is common practice for many hunters in Europe, where waiting for wild boar can be a long drawn out affair.

A considerable amount of heat is lost from the head and so a hat will keep you warm as well as dry if it rains. If it has a peak all the better, since dipping your head to block out the light of the sky will improve visibility into the woodland canopy and open ground around you. If you have a considerable distance to walk to your chosen high seat then it is better to travel light and carry extra clothes with you that you can

20 www.wh-jagd.at

put on later. Arriving at your seat sweating is not a good idea as your clothing will become damp. When this coincides with a drop in your body temperature after an hour or so you become chilled and uncomfortable, and in severe weather the early signs of hypothermia can develop. The use of a thin insulated seat pad will provide extra comfort and warmth.

Equipment

The amount of equipment you carry has to be considered carefully as you should aim to travel as lightly as possible, whatever the type of ground to be stalked. The more kit you carry the more difficult the task of keeping quiet, out of sight and taking a shot quickly becomes. I am amazed constantly at the tendency for novice stalkers to overburden themselves with every imaginable device, stuffed in pockets or lassoed around the neck, making the idea of remaining inconspicuous and quiet almost impossible. The saying 'all the gear, no idea' springs to mind.

Get into the habit of a final physical check before stalking to ensure you have the essentials with you, i.e. rifle with adequate ammunition, knife, bipod or sticks, plastic gloves for carcass work, binoculars and a means of communication. The latter is for health and safety purposes if stalking alone. I am not convinced of the value of carrying a full first aid kit for lowland stalking of fallow. To be of practical use it would need to be quite large and this becomes a disproportionate incumbent given the level of risk involved. You can carry some basic items, e.g. plasters and bandage, and keep a larger kit at base or within your vehicle if this is nearest.

You may wish to carry a small device for assessing wind direction, particularly on the calmer days, as referred to in Chapter 6. Taking a small amount of toilet roll can also be most useful. There should be no need to carry a roe sack or any other form of backpack as extraction of a fallow carcass will have to be by more practical means, as described later. If you are intending to stalk through to last light then a small head torch is useful should you have to search for a shot beast or a dropped round of ammunition.

Binoculars

The value of binoculars when stalking is no better proven than when you have to stalk without them, having left them behind. Their use is elaborated upon in Chapter 6 on stalking techniques. There are some superb glasses now available to suit most pockets. For fallow stalking it is not necessary to buy the most expensive glasses that have the advanced technology to assist long range shooting but those now incorporating a rangefinding facility can be useful, as referred to later.

As with rifle scopes, you should aim to buy the best you can possibly afford. If your budget is tight consider buying a second-hand pair, which will enable you to obtain a higher quality item than you could buy new for the same price. You should be seeking a compromise between what is practical to carry and quick to use and the performance in poor light conditions. This latter point is the reason why you should never buy a pair at a game fair on a sunny day without first knowing how they perform at dawn and dusk.

In terms of which binocular specification to choose from it is the performance in poor light that is crucial for stalking purposes. This is referred to as the light transmission factor. The simple laws of physics mean the larger the objective lens is, the more light will be admitted into the system. When magnification is increased, not only does the light transmission fall but any movement of the binocular in the hands is emphasised, thus forcing yet another compromise to be considered.

Binocular expert Eric Wood*[21], who sources and supplies used, top quality optics, provides here some useful technical definitions used in specification:

- Magnification is expressed as the number of times the apparent image size compares to the real size of the object in view
- The objective lens size is expressed as the number of millimetres that define the diameter of the lens
- The field of view of a binocular is expressed as the apparent number of metres across the visible image view per 1,000m
- Exit pupil size is the diameter of the image circle seen through the eye lens and can be calculated easily by dividing the objective lens diameter by the magnification. This can effectively be seen as a measure of the total relative brightness of a binocular. The 'normal' adult's eye pupils will open in normal daylight to a maximum of 7mm at age twenty and less than 5mm at age seventy. In conditions of early light or evening dusk, this human pupil size will be considerably less. The exit pupil size of the binocular should match or slightly exceed that of the eye pupil to allow the maximum light reaching the pupil to pass through. For stalking, 5mm is about right
- The twilight factor is a measurement of the theoretical measurement of the brightness of the specification, which does not take account of the efficiency of the optical quality and is an out of date figure that cannot be relied upon. Since there is no satisfactory alternative at present, the image brightness of a binocular can only be judged reliably by using or testing the binocular
- The eye relief is the distance from the eye pupil to the surface of the eye lens. In spectacle wearers, this needs to be greater to accommodate the spectacle frame

21 email address: ericwood992@msn.com, eBay User I. D. ericwood992.choiceoptics

between eye and lens. It is generally considered that spectacle wearers need a minimum eye relief of 14mm to achieve the full field of view of the binocular.

Your chosen binocular should be comfortable in the hands with sufficient weight to enable a steady hold, without being too heavy to carry all day. The focus wheel and dioptre adjustment (to balance both eyes) should be within comfortable reach and the eye cups should be capable of being adjusted precisely to your needs and comfort. The carrying strap should be wide to allow for the weight to be spread around the neck. A harness has the advantages of supporting the binoculars from above and below and prevents them swinging in front of you when bending or crawling.

A harness provides additional support and comfort

When testing a binocular before buying, particularly if second-hand, make sure to look at the collimation (alignment of the optics). After looking through the binocular for some minutes, the eyes should feel relaxed as normal. If there is any sign of strain, set the eye lenses at about 15cm from the eyes and view a horizontal line (a nearby roof will do nicely) through both eyepieces simultaneously. The line should continue through both lenses without interruption. If there is any deviation in this line, the optics are not aligned correctly. This can happen after a shock or bump, and usually denotes insecure optics in the binocular body. High quality optics are very resistant to shocks but do go out of alignment from time to time if not treated carefully.

Try the focusing mechanism, which should be smooth and progressive. For stalking, quick focusing is required so the amount of rotation of the focusing wheel to achieve the correct sharp focus should be minimal. This varies considerably between different manufacturer's models.

Do not be tempted to go for the highest magnification available. Binoculars with too high a magnification can limit both your field of view and ability to hold them steady.

Above 8× magnification much of the extra detail available is lost due to slight vibrations. It is much better to have a binocular that is rock steady in the hands and up to 8× magnification will provide for steady viewing. For woodland stalking it is also useful to match the magnification of your binoculars with that of your telescopic sight as far as possible. If your stalking area covers large expanses of open arable ground then choosing binoculars with a higher magnification may be an advantage, particularly for census work. You may consider the use of a telescope, to be kept in your vehicle, for extra-long distance spotting. Your choice may also be influenced by your stalking activity. If you are only operating from a high seat then a binocular with a large objective lens may be accommodated, giving you the advantage in the poor light of dawn and dusk.

One of my favoured pairs of binoculars are some old Swarovski SLC 7 × 30 Bs that I used for many years and readers should note they can still be sought on the second-hand market. They are small, light to carry and quick to use, and while their performance can now be bettered they still provide a quality image. The practicality of these glasses for general woodland stalking makes them somewhat treasured. My view is that the 7 or 8 × 42 (8× magnification × 42mm objective lens diameter) is one of the best specifications for woodland stalking. I now use a pair of Leica 8 × 42 Ultravids, which I find the ideal compromise between size, weight and performance in poor light. If the budget allows, go for the HD model with the latest lens coating. It is important to ensure you keep the lenses clean; there is little point in buying top quality optics if their performance is masked by dirt.

Left to right: Zeiss Victory HT 8 × 42. The author's Leica 8 × 42 HD Ultravids and old Swarovski SLC 7 × 30 Bs

Swarovski's EL range' 8 × 42 and Leica's Geovid 8 × 42 HD-B binoculars incorporating rangefinder facility. The latter model also incorporates the facility to determine ballistic data for adjusting telescopic sights for long range shooting

The relatively new range of binoculars that incorporate a rangefinding facility can be very useful, providing confidence and practice at judging distances for those occasions when you need to be shooting rather than looking. But note they are usually bigger and heavier, and they may not be as practical for woodland stalking as some of the binoculars I have mentioned. Your choice, therefore, will always be a compromise between practicality and performance. If you decide to purchase a pair you should test the same model/specification with and without the rangefinder facility to ensure the image quality is not compromised. The Leica Geovid and Swarovski EL range of binoculars give excellent performance. One advantage of buying the Swarovski products is the company's excellent after sales service.

Thermal Image Cameras/Units

The use of thermal image cameras (infrared) for census work is elaborated upon in Chapter 5. Their use is not confined to this work and a growing number of stalkers now use them for detecting deer in poor light conditions. Some may consider this cheating and detracting from the true sport of stalking. There is also a danger of encouraging some shots to be taken during the hours of darkness when it is unlawful.

However, for some stalkers with a cull figure to achieve it can give them an advantage by giving advance warning of the presence of deer previously unseen without the use of such equipment. They also have a use in locating deer in woodland that have been shot in the last hour of daylight.

Providing shots are taken within the legal time frame, i.e. one hour before sunrise to one hour after sunset, their use can be justified.

Shooting Supports

Carrying some form of support for the rifle for use when taking the shot is a wise precaution as natural supports are not always available. The type of support you decide upon depends on the nature and topography of your stalking ground.

Stalking fallow in a large expanse of arable land, where there is little or no ground cover and a likelihood of shooting over greater distances than in the woodland, will dictate a bipod fixed to the rifle. This will enable you to take stable shots from the prone or, if capable of extension, the kneeling position. My preference is for this latter design, which is particularly useful in situations where you are using field margins or game crops as cover during your approach.

Shooting Sticks

For woodland work, where most shots are within 100m, with little chance of taking shots prone due to ground cover, the use of a separate full length bipod, tripod or set of quad sticks is more practical. The stalking world has come a long way since the single hazel stick was used as support and a wide range of designs are now available, many of which are adjustable for shooting from differing heights, some automatically through the operation of a trigger mechanism. But bear in mind that no matter how sophisticated they may be you are going to have to carry them for long periods of time and their use needs to be quiet and quick to deploy. Manufactured sticks in metal or plastic can be heavy and chill the hands on a cold day, whereas wooden equivalents are lighter, warmer and quieter. All these factors may influence your choice.

Provided you can become proficient in their use, there is no doubt that quad sticks enable the most stable of rests as the butt of the rifle can be stabilised, enabling a longer range shot to be taken with confidence. They also have a further advantage over the tripod sticks in that they only have two points of contact with the ground. The disadvantage is that they are heavier and bulkier to carry around and not as quick to deploy in some woodland situations where the ground cover restricts positioning. In

Above: The extendable fixed bipod is particularly useful for situations where the ground slopes away or where there is ground cover or crops to negotiate

Left: A wide range of sticks are now available, many being adjustable in height. The three bipod sticks on the right are home-made

Above left: The tripod has greater stability over the bipod but has the disadvantage of having to stabilise a third leg where ground cover is dense or uneven

Above middle and right: Quad sticks have the advantage of supporting the stock of the rifle, providing stability for longer range shots

addition, some repositioning is necessary over a certain tolerance if the angle of shot has to change as a result of the beast moving position. For these reasons many stalkers, including myself, opt for using home-made bipod sticks of simple design, which are not only comfortable and easy to carry but quiet and quick to use.

Whatever the type of sticks*[22] you opt for make sure you practise with them – before you stalk. Quad sticks*[23] have the advantage of supporting the stock of the rifle, providing stability for longer range shots. They are also useful for use in standing crops where no alternative support is available.

Knives

Not only do I have an obsession for boots but also knives. But, you only need carry one when stalking for the purpose of the bleeding and the gralloch. A quality knife of good design with impervious handle should be a cherished item of essential equipment. And despite what you may see and hear, it does not need to be a big knife, but it does need to be sharp.

Where I live in Derbyshire I was fortunate indeed to have the late Harry Boden reside. His knife-making skills were once well known within the stalking fraternity and I had the pleasure of giving Harry a stalker's perspective on his designs. Another renowned knife-maker is Alan Wood*[24] in the Borders, much famed for his stalking and bush craft knives. Alan's knives, like the late Harry Boden's, are of high quality and

22 Most UK stalking equipment suppliers stock a range of sticks. Low cost telescopic sticks including those with trigger mechanisms for quick height adjustment can be purchased from www.bushwear.co.uk

23 These are the Viper-Flex quad sticks manufactured by a Danish company and can be supplied by www.hammondsporting.co.uk

24 www.alanwoodknives.com

Left: Knives made by Alan Wood and Harry Boden. The smaller knife made by Alan Wood is called the 'mini hunter' and is ideal for the gralloch. Note the dropped point design and conspicuous tags, enabling them to be seen among the leaves of the forest!

Below: The small mini hunter knife in use at the gralloch, in the upturned position

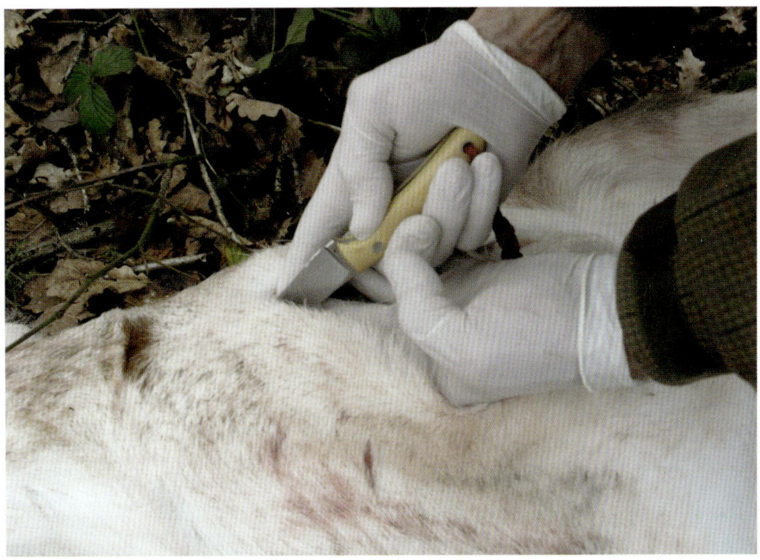

practical design with blades that keep a fine sharp edge, even after considerable use.

Whether you opt for a fixed or folding blade is a matter of choice but I favour a fixed blade, protected by a deep sheath. These have the advantage of safe use and ease of cleaning compared to a folding blade that may default on the lock and is more difficult to keep clean. Look for a blade of between 6.5 and 9cm in length and no more than 2.5cm wide. It should have a dropped point as this will be less likely to pierce the stomach when used in an upturned position to cut through the skin to facilitate the gralloch. Irrespective of blade length, the handle should be big enough to provide for a secure comfortable grip. The beauty of a smaller knife is the control that can be exercised when cradled in the hand for internal work. It is also less obtrusive to wear and more comfortable on the belt when sitting, bending or crawling.

Knives for additional carcass preparation and skinning will be larger and of varying design for butchery work and should be kept for use back at the larder.

Carcass Handling

It is in the process of carcass handling that you need to be equipped adequately. I speak from experience, having undergone keyhole surgery on both knees to repair cartilage damage caused by dragging heavy fallow. That was in my younger days when I knew no better and could not afford the luxury of a quad bike. With the equipment available today it is not difficult to be able to follow best practice and make use of modern technology to reduce the risk of injury and extract carcasses hygienically.

Where possible you should avoid dragging or lifting a carcass without assistance or a mechanical winch. If vehicular access is not possible in woodland or field crops and a drag has to be carried out you should seek help ideally and make use of a drag bag/sled, which will reduce friction and contamination of the carcass. I have tested a sled from the Napier range of products*[25], which is ideal for fallow; it is strong, well made and designed to pull the carcass rather than the bag. However, it is equipment to have available rather than carry with you while stalking.

Try to avoid a long drag and consider using a drag bag/sled if there is no alternative

Owning your own all-terrain vehicle (ATV) or having access to one is essential if you are managing a large area of ground with a large cull to achieve. Their use in areas not accessible by a 4×4 vehicle in winter when the ground becomes wet and boggy makes extraction of carcasses less arduous. You should familiarise yourself with the

25 Napier of London, www.napieruk.com

The modern equivalent to the garron for extracting lowland fallow

appropriate health and safety and best practice guidance on their use*[26], and consider taking the relevant qualifications and training courses that are available.

When carcasses have to be transported in vehicles this should be done in a hygienic manner using a suitably large clean tray and guarded from any possible source of contamination, including access by dogs.

If you have access to a purpose-built larder facility close by then, once a beast has been gralloched, preparation to the point of acceptability for the game dealer or chiller should be carried out there. If this is not possible further carcass work can be achieved in the field by either suspending it with a small pulley*[27] or by using a specialist piece of equipment, e.g. a tilting cradle. This is without doubt an invaluable piece of equipment in the field or larder and with the incorporated winch a carcass can be lifted from ground level without assistance. A titling cradle is also available*[28] that is designed for a quad bike, providing for both transport and carcass preparation.

26 HSE guidance AIS33 – Safe use of all-terrain vehicles in agriculture and forestry. Deer Best Practice Guides – Carcass Extraction and Transport, www.thedeerinitiative.co.uk

27 Napier of London, as referred to earlier, also produces a useful retractable ratchet hoist for suspending a carcass away from the larder

28 Available from Keith Watson at www.keithshighseats.com. Tilting cradles and general larder equipment are also available from a number of other manufacturers, including David Stretton at www.doningtondeermanagement.co.uk

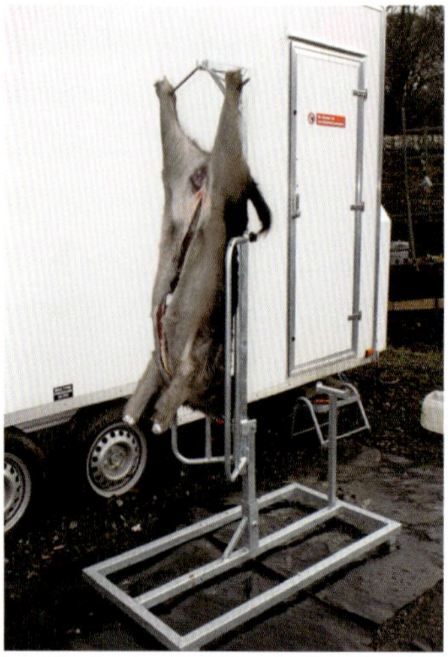

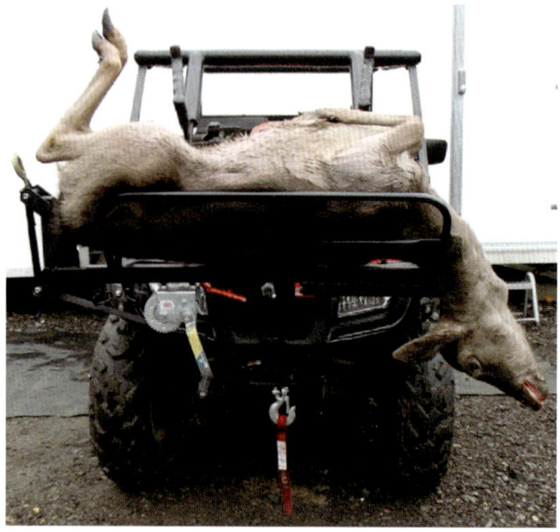

Above left: Tilting cradle incorporating a winch for lifting a carcass from ground level when necessary

Above right and below: Quad bike with tilting cradle providing for both transport and carcass preparation

Dogs

Last but not least is, of course, this essential facility – a dog. You should not stalk deer unless you own a trained dog or have access to one when the need arises. I am not one to advocate their use while actually stalking but when you are faced with recovery of either a beast that is wounded, or one that you cannot find, their use is invaluable. This is why seeking some stalking opportunities as described in Chapter 3 may be limited without proof of ownership or prompt access to a trained dog.

There are several breeds to choose from that will naturally track a blood trail and with some training become a real asset. I am reluctant to recommend a breed as many dogs vary, even within the same litter. The perfect dog for the UK stalker is yet to emerge. I own a Bavarian mountain hound and while she is a friendly sort and trouble-free in the vehicle she is not always sociable with other dogs. However, when it comes to the business of tracking, the breed takes some beating.

'Dogs for deer' training and courses are available from a number of providers should you consider having your own deer dog. These are linked to best practice and provide guidance and training in working your dog on deer.*[29]

The author's Bavarian mountain hound, Heidi, after a long but successful track of a fallow pricket shot low and back twenty-four hours earlier

29 Courses and training are available from the BDS, BASC, The Deer Initiative, UK Deer Trace & Recovery and the Bavarian Mountain Hound Society

Chapter 5

Population Management

Of all the six species of deer in the UK it is fallow that are arguably the most mismanaged. Such has been the speed of population increase and spread of the species that the stalking world has been taken almost by surprise, with management remaining ad hoc in many areas. A planned approach to their management is required, enabling a balance to be struck between their negative and positive impacts on the environment.

With a rising population of fallow, attempting to achieve a sustainable population whether for sport, habitat or crop protection is not simply a matter of culling more or fewer deer. Halving the number of deer on the ground does not necessarily halve the problem. A holistic approach is called for that includes not only culling to maintain or reduce numbers to an acceptable level, but landscape design, habitat management and physical protection. In this sense, culling to minimise the negative impacts may be viewed as only one tool in the bag. However, it is an important and effective tool and one on which this book is centred.

Most stalkers are now taking deer management very seriously, including some with relatively small areas of permission. Population assessments and cull plans are now undertaken regularly as part of their overall management plans. However, for some any notion of a planned approach to fallow management is irrelevant from a practical point of view as they simply will not have access to a wide enough area of the deer's range. They will be culling deer that visit or migrate through their small area of ground, not knowing whether the number, sex and age of the deer they shoot are appropriate in terms of the wider population. This is not ideal. Where large populations of fallow exist the most effective way is to manage them on a landscape scale through the co-operation of landowners and neighbouring stalkers wherever possible. Occasionally even a planned approach can be thwarted through inappropriate interference that obstructs your objective of achieving a balanced cull. Restrictions on where and when you can stalk within the existing boundaries, are not helpful but then you have to accommodate other users of the ground, whether that be for game shooting interests or otherwise.

Those with influence but little practical knowledge of deer management can often frustrate cull planning decisions by inappropriate interference. I speak from some experience of not only being restricted in terms of where and when I could stalk but also what should or should not be shot.

I had been asked to manage the fallow on a small estate open to the public. Following assessment of numbers and the impact within the woodland it was clear there were too many deer and a heavy cull was required that would have to be repeated over a number of seasons. Shooting was to be restricted to only a few days during the season and had to be completed on each occasion within a two-hour time frame, with security manning public access points. In addition to these restrictions I was asked not to shoot any of the mature bucks and this was to include a buck that had been injured previously and had only three legs. I was not too happy over this as I had seen the three-legged buck, which was deteriorating through age and infirmity, i.e. he was going back, and should be culled. But he had to be left.

I assembled a small team of reliable rifles to assist and we made a good start in reducing the population during the first season. However, as time passed I became increasingly obstructed by the estate management, who clearly thought they knew more about managing the deer than I. To make matters worse, and without the courtesy of consulting me, the estate allowed the local pest controller to shoot 'some deer' in certain areas. I remained patient, being determined to reduce the numbers and improve not only the quality of the fallow but also the woodland habitat. However, matters were to get worse. Some of our planned days were cancelled at short notice and, when we did shoot, one had the distinct feeling that someone had been in before us. The deer that were seen were stressed and the whole matter was becoming tiresome. When old 'three leg' was seen in a pitiful state, the estate management finally decided perhaps he should be shot. With that final job done I decided enough was enough and withdrew my services.

Below left: Old Three Leg in his better days

Middle and right: Old Three Leg suffered as a result of interference in cull planning

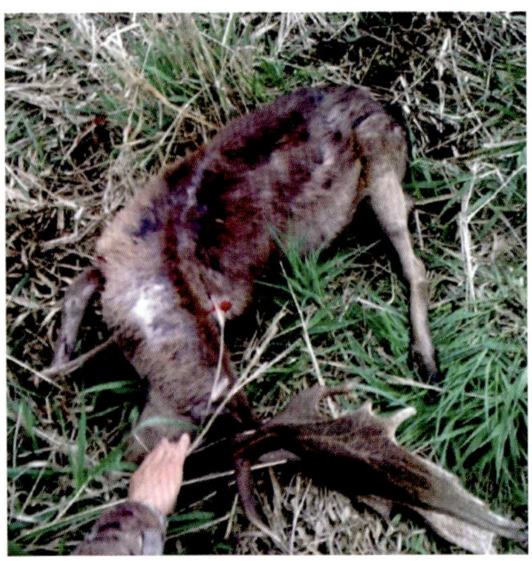

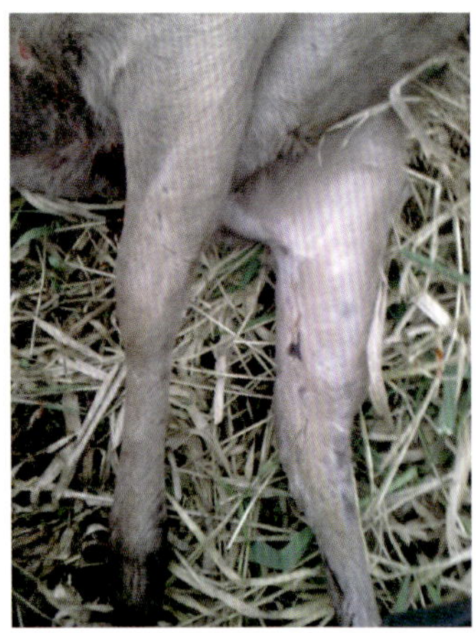

The Right to Manage

While there is a growing expectation nationally for deer to be managed sustainably there is no means of enforcing this ideal. In England and Wales there exists no legal framework or authority at central or local government level to enforce deer management; the right to 'manage' (or not to manage) remains vested in the landowner. Even in Scotland landowners cannot be compelled to manage deer on their land, albeit powers exist for independent intervention.

In the UK and much of Europe wild deer are considered to be *ferae naturae* (wild by nature) and the owner of the land where they are found has sole right to take them or delegate authority to do so. Currently, if an individual landowner wishes to exterminate all the deer on their land, provided they are in season, he can legally do so. The deer could be the last remaining herd of the 'long haired' fallow referred to in Chapter 1; they would be gone forever with nothing that could be done to prevent their extermination.

Conversely, a landowner can abrogate responsibility to manage the deer on his land and allow their numbers to rise to unsustainable levels, causing considerable damage to the environment. While this is unacceptable there are currently few sanctions south of the border to prevent this either.

North of the border the minds of civil servants are being exercised not only on how deer are managed and by whom, but also the distinction between 'management' and 'sport', the former potentially attracting greater concession when compared with sporting rates.

The question remains as to whether mandatory control is necessary or appropriate within an industry that has a very healthy climate of self-regulation. A voluntary approach to deer management with stronger management groups operating on a landscape scale, as described below, enhances this climate and should be welcomed by stalkers; done effectively it negates the need for any mandatory option.

The Need for a Landscape Approach

If you manage a fallow stalking area in isolation to others nearby, your efforts may be thwarted considerably, since fallow know no boundaries and are quick to seek out sanctuary. On the other hand, leaving a master buck one day only to find it shot over the boundary the next is disheartening and your management plans may only be as good as they are allowed to be by your neighbouring stalker. Indiscriminate commercial trophy shooting that fails to take into account the objectives of good deer management can create an imbalance within the population that is detrimental to deer welfare. There is concern in some areas for the distinct lack of mature fallow

Fallow are quick to seek out sanctuary

bucks, leaving their demise to speculation. Trophies, where scope exists for their culling, should be seen as a by-product of purposeful management, with the number and age of bucks shot falling within an overall cull plan.

To achieve management at an appropriate scale in areas where deer density is out of balance with the environment, co-operation and agreement between landowners is essential, otherwise migration into and out of the area may negate your efforts; you can still do your own thing, but in an informed way that should reap benefits for your own stalking area and that of others.

The Deer Initiative recommends that deer management should be carried out at a scale 'appropriate to the natural range of a deer herd'. The mobility of fallow, a herd species, means that in most cases their management will need to encompass a wide geographical area, typically in excess of 5,000 acres. One of the most effective ways to achieve this is through the formation of a Deer Management Group (DMG), although this is not essential if co-ordination can be organised by neighbouring stalkers and landowners.

Writing Management Plans

An increasing number of major landowning bodies now require stalkers to complete a deer management plan (DMP) together with a risk assessment*[30]. A central

30 See example given in Chapter 12

principle of such plans is that good deer management should aim to maintain healthy populations in balance with their environment, incorporating the anticipation of deer populating new areas.

If you only manage the deer on a relatively small area of ground you may question the need for any form of written plan, particularly if the owner has not demanded one as part of the arrangement. However, there are benefits of setting about the task with some documented objectives in mind, even if your area is small. The smaller the area of your stalking is the greater the need to liaise with your neighbours over how each of you can manage the deer in the area in a cohesive manner. Not to do so can nullify your intended plans, as alluded to earlier.

How the deer have been managed previously and how they are viewed in the context of the history of deer in the surrounding countryside should be taken into account. Their aesthetic, economic and recreational value should be recognised and management plans may need to take account of the importance of deer being part of our cultural heritage. The landowner's views should be acknowledged and balanced against the implications for both the welfare of deer and their environment. In the process of planning you should consult with other users of the land and take account of their views. This is essential as managing the deer effectively should be seen as being in everyone's interests. Consulting other land users may also provide an opportunity to promote your own role as a stalker.

A DMP does not need to be a complicated document and the use of a simple format will help you compile the detail required in a logical sequence. It can be written to extend over a period of years provided annual review of the plan is undertaken or whenever circumstances change that may have a bearing on the objectives. In essence the latter is much about adapting plans to suit changes in both the population dynamics and environment and so management must be responsive to enable the plan to be adjusted along the way. A system of monitoring of the objectives against the plan is essential.

The following outline plan is based on a guide that is available from The Deer Initiative*[31]. It is designed to cover a wide range of situations and can be modified to suit your needs. If you manage a small uncomplicated area of stalking you may consider using only parts of the plan relevant to your needs or use the shorter version that is available. Conversely, the plan can also be enhanced by additional material if necessary.

Title of Plan

The title of the plan should form the front sheet with details of the writer and review dates.

31 www.thedeerinitiative.co.uk

1. Background Information

1.1 Ownership and Contacts

It is useful for details of the owners of the land and those responsible for the plan to be named here together with their respective addresses and contact details.

1.2. Location

The location should be shown on a suitable map providing information as to the size of the area (normally in hectares), boundaries, woodland, buildings and all access routes, both public and private. Footpaths and other rights of way should be shown clearly. It may be necessary to append a number of maps to the plan, each indicating different aspects of the ground. An overview can be given of the type and classification of the woodland together with any specific features including its use by the public. You may wish to comment further on safety issues, e.g. close proximity to a busy road or buildings.

1.3. Deer – Current Situation and Trends

Species present and current situation with regard to their numbers, trends and impact on human interests should be shown. Indicate the type of census methods used. Attach a map with the current species distribution, including 10km beyond the boundary if possible.

1.4. What Are the Current Impacts?

Describe here the level (low, medium or high) of impact on the woodland canopy and crops, e.g. damage by browsing, fraying and bark stripping. All other impacts should be shown, including damage to agricultural crops and road vehicle collisions. A simple judgement can be made on whether their impact is acceptable or not. This should be an informed judgement following the census findings. See later for information on impact assessment.

1.5. Describe the Current Deer Management

Future plans will need to take account of the current management and this should include measures in addition to culling that have been taken to maintain a sustainable population of deer, e.g. fencing. The involvement of any local Deer Management Group and its influence should be included. The adequacy of current equipment should be commented upon, including high seats and larder facilities.

1.6. Perceived Obstacles to Achieving Effective Deer Control

There may be numerous obstacles that hinder the process of deer control. Some will be out of your control, such as unpredictable deer movements and agricultural workings. However, there will be a number that you may be in a position to negate and these should be listed together with how the problem can be addressed. Historical information can be included together with any operations planned for the future that have a bearing on deer management, e.g. tree felling and new plantations.

2. Future Management

2.1. Land Management Objectives and Monitoring
A key objective here will be the protection and promotion of biodiversity under any statutory obligations. Areas or features such as Special Sites of Scientific Interest (SSSIs) should be noted, cross referenced and indicated on a map. Monitoring of such sites should be in place, together with other areas subject to woodland improvement grants and the like. Impact assessment of woodland, ground flora and where necessary agricultural crops will dictate the need for objectives and targets to be set.

2.2. Deer Management Objectives
Species and numbers of deer collated by the various methods should be shown together with the intended cull details. Targets should be set together with how they are to be monitored throughout the season. A cull record should accompany the plan. Additional objectives and targets can be set relating to other objectives desired, e.g. venison and trophy production.

This section of the plan should be amended annually with the forthcoming cull objectives for the year ahead. The cull plan will need to be monitored at an appropriate time throughout the season to ensure targets are met. Determining the cull is dealt later in this chapter, on page 104.

2.3. Deer Management Action
Information indicating the number of men and days required to achieve the cull including all culling methods, e.g. collaborative team culls, can be shown here if necessary. Ancillary action should also be included, e.g. Deer Management Group meetings and work conducted to protect habitat.

2.4. General Cull Strategy
State the overall cull strategy of all species present and provide a holistic view of the deer management, e.g. to maintain a healthy population of wild fallow as an historic and distinctive wildlife feature of the estate.

Cull records can act as a useful baseline for determining future culls but will need to reflect any changes required as a result of impact assessment and environmental issues, e.g. road vehicle collisions and complaints of damage. Issues that influence the strategy and not mentioned earlier within the plan can be included here.

3. Health and Safety Issues

Risk assessments should be prepared for all relevant areas of deer management described within the plan. Any further actions necessary with regards to control measures should be noted and subject to monitoring to ensure they are in place. For guidance and advice in respect of the completion of risk assessments see Chapter 12 Safe Stalking.

4. Costs

Capital expenditure, ongoing costs and income sources can all be shown if required.

5. Annual Review/Trend Summary

A template entitled Annually Reviewed Cull/Trend Summary is available from The Deer Initiative.

Appendices

Examples of additional documents to be submitted with the plan:

- Boundary map
- Approximate deer species distribution map
- Past cull data (before start of this plan)
- Current larder records (from start of this plan)
- Past impact assessments
- Risk assessments
- Formal stalking agreement or contract
- List and location of current grant and designations documents
- Other useful contacts and information.

Determining the Cull

This may be a fait accompli in that the cull requirement may be dictated to you by the owner or it may be included within the terms of a stalking licence, in which case you have no control over the matter. You can only hope that the figure has been determined through proper assessment of the ground and falls within clear objectives set within the management plan. If the cull requirement is not dictated in the strict terms of a licence one would hope that you, as the stalker, may have some influence over what is or is not shot.

There are some key factors that affect culling planning, including overall density of the population and what it comprises of in terms of sex ratio and age structure. There are also natural factors such as reproductive, mortality, emigration and immigration rates that must be taken into account.

Carrying Capacity

Historical cull records are often used to form the basis of determining the forthcoming cull figure in the absence of a census of deer numbers or sufficient account of their effects on the environment, habitat and crops. And so a totally unrealistic figure may have evolved with a cull figure that is inadequate or impossible to achieve. By taking into account the wider impacts of deer from an environmental, habitat and social perspective an indication can be gleaned as to the number of deer that the area can potentially support. This is commonly referred to as the 'carrying capacity' for the area and although the concept is far more complex than I describe here, it is sufficient for the purposes of a basic cull plan.

Assessing Population Density

Estimating the population size for the area together with the sex ratio and age class structure is crucial to cull planning. The difficulty that arises with fallow is that, if your counting method is not efficient and not done over a sufficiently wide enough area covering the natural range of the population, then your figure will usually be an underestimate. The problem tends to add weight to other factors of assessment, e.g. impacts on woodland habitat and crops. Some counting methods, such as direct counts in heavily forested areas, may be flawed from the outset unless adequate measures are taken to achieve accurate counts.

On a practical level, simple continuous observation and recording by the stalker who visits his ground regularly can frequently produce results as accurate as any other and this should be seen as an important contribution to the annual census.

Irrespective of the method used you will rarely count every animal and so some estimation needs to figure in setting a cull target. Comparing past cull records to subsequent visual counts can be quite an effective tool to indicate population size. This method was used over a number of years in the Mortimer Forest in Shropshire where an estimate of deer not seen in the count was found to be frequently in the region of 25 per cent, e.g. an annual count of 280 was increased to an estimated population of 320, on which a cull of 25 per cent (80) was based. The following year the annual count proved to be similar, substantiating the estimate of a population 25 per cent over what was actually counted. If the visual count increased or decreased the cull could be adjusted pro rata.

Most censuses are carried out in the spring and may be repeated in autumn. It is important that census work is carried out in a consistent and fair way. Analysis of data over a number of years will provide useful information, such as population trends, deer distribution and sex ratios.

There are a number of ways to count deer, some more practical than others:

Direct counts – vantage point, thermal imaging and spotlighting.
Indirect counts – dung counts and activity index.
Number projections – analysis of cull data.

*The table below is taken from The Deer Initiative best practice guide titled *Census – General* and compares a number of methods:

Method	Information Gained	Specialist Equipment	Relative Accuracy	Pros	Cons
Vantage point	Known minimum number. Estimated total number. Indication of sex ratio and female: young ratio	Binoculars	Good when whole population is on open ground. Tends to underestimate elsewhere. Gives accurate minimum numbers if double counting is avoided	Simple to carry out. Can use local personnel. Can cover large areas on one count	Deer movement susceptible to poor weather. Requires some identification knowledge to avoid miss-classification. Certain age/sex classes may be under/over represented depending on time of year. Can require significant manpower
Thermal imaging	Known minimum number. Estimated total number. Possibility of sample of sex ratio and female: young ratio	TI camera and operator. Vehicle (if required). Rangefinder and compass if using 'distance' statistical analysis	Good when deer show on open ground. Gives accurate minimum numbers if double counting is avoided. In cover 'distance' analysis can give estimate of total population	Useful where population largely nocturnal. Disturbs area less than spotlighting. Can cover large areas in one night	Deer movement susceptible to poor weather. Requires some specialist training of operators. Equipment can be expensive. Best for species that feed regularly in the open at night, such as fallow. In cover, additional range and bearing data is required for 'distance' analysis

Method	Information Gained	Specialist Equipment	Relative Accuracy	Pros	Cons
Spot-lighting	Known minimum number. Estimated total number. Possibility of sample of sex ratio and female: young ratio	Spotlight. Vehicle if not on foot	Good when deer show on open ground. Tends to underestimate elsewhere. Gives accurate minimum numbers if double counting is avoided	Useful where population largely nocturnal. May not be effective where night time poaching occurs. Can use local manpower. Can cover large areas	Best for species that feed regularly in the open at night, i.e. red, fallow, sika and roe
Dung count (FAR method)	Estimate of total numbers	Tape/line marking equipment	Good when used diligently, see cons column	Independent of deer sightings and weather. Useful where deer difficult to see.	Accuracy dependent on estimate of defecation rate and assumption that survey does not change deer behaviour. A thorough survey should include counting in every different habitat, requiring time and resources
Activity index	Index of density (high, med, low)	None	Not a primary means of establishing numbers but with experience can give a broad estimate of deer densities. Good at determining the presence of deer	Independent of deer sightings and weather. Useful where deer hard to see. Can form part of impact survey. Requires little manpower	Needs basic but specialist knowledge
Cohort analysis	Estimate of numbers born in any year leading to projection of population total if sex and young ratios are available	None	Gives accurate minimum count for numbers born in each year if ages are recorded and accurate	Independent of deer sightings and weather. Desktop exercise	Retrospective (at least five years in most cases). Requires fairly precise ageing of dead deer. Requires data from vantage point counts to reconstruct total population

Valuable data can be captured with the use of trail cams

Trail Cams

Through the advance of technology the use of trail/stealth cams, i.e. small portable cameras triggered by infrared sensors, that can be fixed to trees, etc, have become popular in recent years for capturing deer activity. I suspect many are used out of curiosity as much as for census work. They can provide valuable data on activity patterns, which may influence management plans and cull tactics. They are particularly useful at detecting the spread of a species into a previously unpopulated area.

Air Reconnaissance

Clearly the average stalker is not going to finance an operation to put a helicopter or light aircraft into the air for the sole purpose of counting deer on one relatively small area. However, counting deer from the air can be one of the most efficient and cost-effective methods when a landscape scale census is required. Aerial ungulate survey methods have been developed*[32] using infrared and high resolution natural colour images and these have been trialled in the UK by The Deer Initiative. It is likely that the method may be used by forest organisations to survey large areas, especially where there are few internal roads or high risk areas that make ground survey work unsafe.

The use of drones is becoming popular for surveillance work and as technology advances and the equipment becomes more affordable I anticipate their use will increase. Users should make themselves familiar with any current legal and Civil Aviation Authority restrictions on their use, e.g. trespass of the air space, harassment, and use above 500ft. It is likely that the government will instigate a consultation on their use in the future with a view to the consideration of controls where necessary.

Impact Assessment

Fallow possibly have the greatest impact of all species on woodland habitat, trees and agricultural crops and assessment of this should be seen as a barometer and prerequisite to determining the sustainable carrying capacity for the area and

32 Aerial Ungulate Surveys developed by U. Franke, B. Goll, U. Hohmann and M. Heurich

subsequent cull plan. It is arguably more important to determine the cull level based substantially on their impacts than relying too heavily on estimations of population density, which in the case of fallow can be misleading and often underestimated.

It is not difficult to judge the extremes of deer impacts – note the browse line on the holly and total lack of understory

Your observations and experience as a stalker on the ground are valuable. It is not difficult to judge the extremes of damage to woodland habitat or crops. A walkabout in the woodland tells its own story if you know what to look for. Impact assessment is based on just that, but done in a measured way. Provided it is done correctly it should influence stalker activity, investment in habitat protection and management plans. Clearly some experience of recognising the signs and impacts of deer compared to other species is essential and this is elaborated upon in Chapter 10, Crop Damage and Protection.

There are several different methods of assessment. The method recommended is based on the original work of Dr A. Cooke, the detail of which is available from The Deer Initiative website referred to earlier. It should be read together with reference to the associated best practice guides *Habitat Impact* and *Deer Signs*. The method is designed for assessment of woodland and is simple to apply but sensitive enough to provide a broad description of deer impact and activity. However, I would suggest stalkers would benefit from some initial training and practice in using the method, particularly where large scale formal surveys are required. Training courses on impact assessment are available through The Deer Initiative.

Surveys are best carried out during the spring before the canopy becomes too dense. An assessment form is used to record the level of both deer *activity* and *impact* on woodland that you observe. You should cover a good representative area of the woodland to assess the various levels of activity and impact, as indicated on the form. Record simply what you see and be honest in your assessment. Typical *activity* recorded will be the number of deer seen, slots, couches, scrapes, wallows and racks. Recording of *impacts* will include evidence of bark removal or breakage, browsing of woody shoots and grazing of flora.

You should record the distance, area and time taken. The survey should be repeated at the same time each year.

Natural Population Factors

Reproductive Rates

You may assume that up to 80 per cent of adult fallow does reproduce and yearlings will potentially produce one fawn each. The incidence of fawns being served in their year of birth is extremely rare and normally discounted. However, the birth of twin fawns in fallow, whilst not common, has been evident in some areas and as such may require monitoring for future population estimates. A record should be maintained of the number of twins observed and foetuses discovered.

Mortality

Mortality is difficult to determine and will be higher in the young and very old, the former often being the result of fawns being prematurely orphaned or being born late in the season. Deer that die from natural causes are rarely found in the wild; those that become trapped in fences and debris or die at the roadside being more obvious. Many road vehicle collisions go unreported and the evidence of a carcass on the roadside is not always a good guide to the resultant mortality rate. I would guess many more deer are injured and subsequently die away from the roadside, without ever being found.

Emigration /Immigration

This is perhaps the most difficult to determine of all factors affecting population size. The larger the area the less effect this will have; taking it to its extreme landscape scale it has to be close to neutral, particularly where there are natural or man-made barriers preventing movement. The nature of your cull may influence both emigration and immigration; the former may be increased by insufficient culling and the latter increased through over-culling, by creating a void. The problem with fallow is that they often prove your theory wrong and the opposite can occur as a result of the management strategy and activity taking place over the boundary; demonstrating the need for a more landscape approach to their management.

Deer that become trapped and die are more obvious

Level and Type of Cull

Once the carrying capacity is determined a comparison can be made with the actual numbers estimated to be on the ground and from this a cull plan determined. What held well in previous years may not be appropriate for the future and some flexibility is required. There is a tendency for cull requirements to be maintained or raised, but there are occasions when they may need to be lowered if the population is to be sustained at the desired capacity level for the area.

Maintenance Culls

If the number of deer are at, or below, the sustainable carrying capacity, and there are no other factors to dictate that the level should not be maintained, then a 'maintenance cull' should be planned and monitored to ensure stability. Achieving the quota of does should be seen as a priority. If your census indicates an equal balance between the sexes (which is doubtful) then to maintain the status quo will require a cull in the region of 20–25 per cent of the population. This estimate takes account of reproduction by 75 to 80 per cent of the does and mortality at between 5 and 10 per cent (the mortality of adults is estimated at 2 per cent but this will be much higher in the very young and old). Ideally a ratio of 1:1 between the sexes should be aimed for. Achieving this balance with fallow is easier said than done due to their nomadic nature, particularly the bucks. It follows, therefore, that to aim for 70 per cent does and 30 per cent bucks may be a more pragmatic approach. On one well-known estate not one buck was shot for fifteen years in order achieve that parity.

These estimates are not set in stone and you should be flexible in your target numbers to ensure sustainability at an acceptable level. You may have a higher ratio of does to bucks on the ground, in which case your cull figure should be adjusted pro rata taking full account of the increased potential for reproduction. Mortality rates may be higher than the norm as a result of road vehicle collisions or harsh weather. Emigration or immigration could rise as a result of reduction culls on neighbouring ground.

Reduction Culls

Where the estimated population is found to be over the carrying capacity, usually supported by a level of habitat damage that is not sustainable, a 'reduction cull' will be necessary to bring down the number of deer to below the carrying capacity. Such a cull will need to concentrate on a larger percentage of adult females than would otherwise be targeted. Remember, in culling the females you effectively reduce the potential for reproduction many times over the life of a single doe. You should therefore resist the temptation to make up the cull with bucks. The consequences of a substantial reduction in numbers from a previously high density should be noted as this may affect your future cull plans. While the quality of the remaining deer should improve it is likely that survival and reproduction rates will also improve together with a degree of infill from adjacent areas. Accordingly, this 'bounce back' factor should be taken into account. Culls at this level rarely achieve the desired effect in the short term and therefore may have to be repeated over a number of seasons before the carrying capacity is stabilised. The reality is that while an over-population may be viewed by the onlooker as easy to reduce due to the deer's apparent abundance and visibility, once culling starts fallow learn very quickly and the task becomes more difficult as the season progresses.

Welfare and Ethical Considerations

Consideration should be given to restricting or avoiding culling activity during the rut, when only the bucks are in season. Culling bucks at or close to rutting stands serves to educate the does, making them more difficult to stalk when they come into season, which will only be a matter of weeks away.

Quality master bucks should be left alone at this time to get on with their job of serving the does without harassment

There are additional welfare reasons for avoiding disturbance at this time and a valuable insight into the detrimental effects of culling during the rut can be gained by reference to the problems and practices of *Ungulate Management in Europe*, edited by Rory Putman, Marco Apollonio and Reidar Andersen.

An opportunity exists to avoid too much disruption and add substantially to your buck cull by picking off younger bucks, prickets and sorels that have been pushed away from the main rutting stands in the weeks prior to the main rutting activity, i.e. late September into mid-October.

The frustrating trait of mature fallow bucks is their ability to somehow 'disappear' post-rut for a substantial part of the season; appearing to one's annoyance early next season in the wheat during the harvest. This encourages many stalkers to seize the opportunity to cull during the rut; a time when the bucks are easier to stalk as they are more visible and territorial.

If you have to cull surplus mature bucks, or old ones 'going back', at this time of year, then to minimise disruption, it is best done in the latter stages of the rut when a substantial number of the does will have been served by the most dominant bucks. Care needs to be taken here, not only to minimise disruption, but in selecting the right buck to cull. Too much disruption or shooting the wrong buck will lead to the risk of does being served by lesser quality bucks, which will be counterproductive to your management plans in the long term.

It should also be borne in mind that a small but significant number of adult bucks do not make it into winter, post-rut. The effort of a prolonged period of activity during which they rarely eat has the effect of degrading the body condition of the master bucks. A few will not regain condition before the onset of winter and many stalkers report dead mature fallow bucks being found following the rut in November. This cause of mortality is frequently ignored at the cull planning stage, but is an important and potentially significant factor which should be considered.

You should plan to complete your doe cull if possible prior to March so as to avoid shooting heavily pregnant does, which from a welfare point of view is ethically unacceptable to many stalkers. Nevertheless, it may be necessary within the objectives of a reduction cull where concentrating on the females is paramount. Completing the cull by the end of February may also be difficult to achieve for some stalkers whose culling activities may have been restricted by game shooting until the end of January, leaving little time to finish the doe cull.

Cull Principles

Culling deer is not an exact science and there is always a danger of relying too heavily on both scientific assessment and statistical information*[33]. Population management through a process of careful planning, while essential, should not detract from a common sense approach when the need arises to quickly 'change the plan' and by doing so not to add another layer of bureaucracy.

For many stalkers operating on their own and adjacent to fallow sanctuaries over which they have no control, shooting everything possible will never be enough to control a species that knows no boundaries. That is why managing fallow can only be effective when done on a landscape scale that covers their natural range.

33 Examples of cull record formats, population models, etc, are all available through The Deer Initiative best practice guidance available from The Deer Initiative website, www.thedeerinitiative.co.uk

Some broad principles should be held and guide you in your stalking plans:

- Where possible liaise with your neighbouring stalkers or landowners to achieve realistic objectives
- Be prepared to invest the time and resources necessary to achieve the cull
- Resist the temptation to shoot healthy mature bucks during the rut. In doing so, not only is it detrimental and disruptive to mating activity but you educate the does, which in a matter of weeks, will be in season and much harder to stalk as a result
- Welfare considerations should override a desire to cull deer where unnecessary suffering may be caused. You should avoid the risk in early winter of orphaning dependent fawns by culling them before the doe
- Concentrate on culling does in the knowledge that this is the key to reducing and maintaining a sustainable population. But avoid doing so in March, when they will be heavily pregnant, unless a reduction cull is absolutely necessary to prevent serious damage
- Be honest in your cull returns. Providing you have made every effort to achieve the cull, not to do so should not be seen as an embarrassing failure

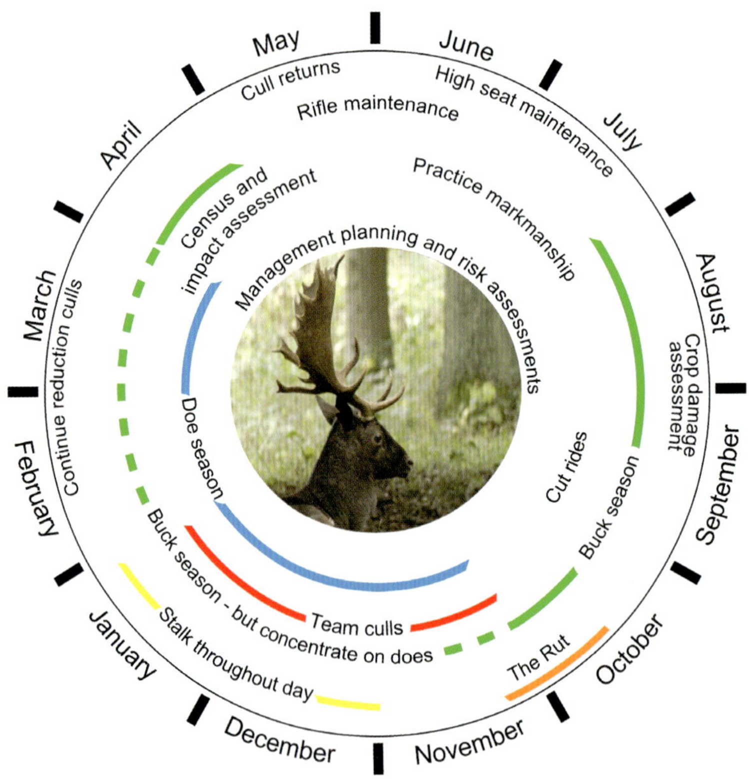

The Stalker's Calendar

Chapter 6

Stalking Techniques

Stalking skills are in our genes; inherited from time immemorial when without such skills we would not have survived. Creeping into your child's room to check they are asleep or entering the house quietly late at night so as not to disturb the family, are evidence of our innate ability to be discreet and avoid detection. It is those latent skills that are revived and developed by the deer stalker, whether stalking with rifle or camera. To be effective, as in any other sport, you must practise and learn from your experiences. If you do not your lack of success at stalking wild fallow will be a constant source of frustration. The deer will see you but you will not see the deer. No matter how many books you read you will not learn the art of stalking by knowing the theory of how to stalk without the ability to put it into practice. There are no short cuts to learning from experience. You have to do it, suffer the disappointments and celebrate the successes.

Many of the best stalkers learned their skills when they were young and this was not by stalking deer. They were out along the hedgerows with their air rifle at dawn and dusk, sometimes crawling to get a close shot at a rabbit or other small quarry. In their teens they were shooting foxes with their .22 centre fires or punt gunning for wildfowl on the edges of the salt marsh. Little did they know that their experiences were to be the foundation for the skills of stalking deer. Effective stalking brings together a number of skills. Use of your equipment, knowing when and where to stalk, learning to use your natural senses and having a good knowledge of your quarry and the ground are some of the fundamentals. In stalking, more than any other sport, patience is a virtue. It can be exhausting and requires total and absolute concentration, often over long periods of time.

Over the years I have been privileged to stalk with, and learn from, some very skilful stalkers, and I continue to do so. I have also stalked with some who are not so skilful and are akin to 'bulls in china shops'. One can excuse the novice, but there are stalkers that have been around for many years that continue to make mistakes from which they seem unable to learn. They are the very stalkers that shun away

from any form of continuous professional development. They 'know it all' and then make up all sorts of excuses for continually 'bumping' deer and failing to achieve their cull targets. Consequently, if you intend to improve your knowledge and skill level through the services of a friend or mentor, then you need to be selective in your choice. Good, safe technique is acquired through continuous training and practice linked to the standards that are now set for both recreational and professional stalker qualifications*[34]. (See Chapter 3, Stalking Opportunities).

While many of the techniques and skills in stalking are appropriate whatever the species, stalking fallow deer in a lowland situation is a far cry from stalking red deer in a remote highland glen. Both are equally demanding but require different techniques. So while you may be adept at one, you may lack the skills in the other.

Knowing your Quarry

A sound knowledge of your quarry's appearance and natural habits are a prerequisite to good stalking technique, i.e. knowing what to look for and where. Fallow are difficult to manage and have a 'bounce back' quality against human intervention. Their senses are superior to ours and they deploy them to keep out of danger and stay alive. They are less territorial than some species and have a tendency to be nomadic, making keeping pace with their whereabouts difficult. In some areas they are arguably one of the most difficult of all the species of deer to stalk. Their whole lifestyle centres on survival with every moment being spent on monitoring the environment for signs of danger. They do nothing without purpose. To stalk them successfully it is essential to recognise their ability to detect danger and the infinite patience they have in doing so. Given an acceptance of their superior senses compared to ours, your stalking technique needs to counter this imbalance.

The range of colours in the pelage of fallow can catch the stalker out in those brief moments when they come into view during a stalk. In many areas there will be a colour typical for the area, in others you may expect to come across any one of the variations, including the occasional white variety. Knowing their habits and how they vary throughout the seasons will directly influence your stalking plans. These are all covered in Chapter 1, which provides an insight into their natural history. Putting theory aside, there is much to learn out there on the ground and getting to know the location of stands during the rut, where they go to keep warm in the hard weather and the crops they like to eat is essential information in their management.

Choosing When and Where to Stalk

The weather is a key factor in dictating deer behaviour and this will influence your

34 DSC1 & 2. admin@dmq.org.uk Best Practice www.thedeerinitiative.co.uk

decisions of when and where to stalk. Fog, mist, heavy rain and high winds may postpone your stalking plans. The difficulty with the former conditions is one of safety in ensuring both adequate identification of your quarry and backstop. The weather can change during the day, particularly the wind's strength and direction, so adapting to changing conditions will increase your chances of success. In frosty or dry conditions finding a quiet route may be difficult as the leaf litter underfoot will be noisy and you will find it like walking on cornflakes. Keep an eye on the weather forecast for the area and any likely changes that may ultimately influence where and when you stalk.

Although fallow, together with the other species of deer, are crepuscular by nature, to restrict your stalking activity to dawn and dusk when they should be

Left: Fog and mist can make identification of both quarry and backstop difficult – these are not fallow deer and the shot would be unsafe

Below: High winds may postpone your stalking plans in woodland

most active may not always be the right decision. During the short, cold winter days they may be active throughout the daylight hours. Indeed, I have experienced considerable success in the middle of winter days when the temperature has risen. Most animals enjoy the warmth of the sun and fallow are no exception. When the sun suddenly bursts out during an otherwise dull day do not be surprised to find the deer have left their beds suddenly and popped out on the woodland edge, perhaps giving you the opportunity of a midday stalk. On the other hand, like many other creatures, they do not like strong winds, which reduce their ability to detect you. When everything is moving around them it is more difficult for them to spot unusual movement. Their hearing is also impaired through the noise of the wind. They become nervous and, knowing they are vulnerable in these conditions, will often disappear to the safety of dense cover, giving you the impression that they have become extinct overnight. When they do venture out into the wind to feed they are often difficult to stalk as they are constantly on the alert. In the stalker's favour, a strong wind can mask the noise and movement of an approach and scent is restricted to a fast narrow channel, making a quiet approach on the edge of the wind possible.

Fallow are quick to learn the patterns of stalking behaviour that are repetitious. Times and places that are linked to potential danger create a response and their own behaviour will change to avoid this. You are, by your very stalking activities, effectively educating the deer each time you stalk. It is important, therefore, not only to vary the times you stalk, but also the routes you take. By contrast, they are also quick to adapt to conditions that present no perceived danger to them, e.g. farm operations and ramblers. It is not uncommon to hear from the tractor driver or casual walker that they have encountered numerous deer, seemingly unperturbed at their presence or activity. The deer distinguish between this behaviour that presents no danger and that of the predatory stalker, moving cat-like through the undergrowth.

Whenever you plan to stalk, be it early or late, there are a number of considerations to be taken into account, not least notifying those that need be aware of your intentions. It is important from a safety aspect that someone has knowledge of where you are stalking and when you intend to return. If you are not the owner or occupier of the ground then routinely informing them of your visits can be useful as they may inform you of forestry or agricultural work that may affect your plans. In addition, if they hear a shot they will not suspect poaching. There may also be other residents in the area that would benefit from knowing you are about. If you change your vehicle make sure all interested parties are aware of the type and registration number of your new vehicle.

The Wind, Scent and its Effect

With the knowledge of a fallow deer's ability to pick up your scent at considerable distances in excess of your shooting range, the wind direction is a key factor that will influence your chosen route. You must therefore endeavour to stalk directly into the wind or at an angle to it ensuring that your scent does not carry into areas where you are expecting to find deer. However, you may set out with the wind in your face but sooner or later realise it is in the back of your neck. It is almost impossible to have the wind in your favour at all times. On hilly ground trying to beat it is almost impossible as the gradients create swirls, troughs and uplifts of wind that are not always predictable. This is a constant source of frustration on this type of terrain but, given the experience of different wind directions and strengths, you can lessen the detrimental effects by changing your route. Wind direction should also be taken into account when using high seats, as elaborated upon later.

When deer detect human scent their anti-predator instinct brings an immediate and dramatic response, which is far more pronounced than if they see or hear you. It will often stop them in their tracks. Once your presence has been detected by scent you are beyond suspicion. If this is linked to a quiet, predatory-like, stalking activity then nothing will be left to chance and the deer will depart quickly. In many situations when you are caught out by the wind you will not even know they were ever present. They say, 'the onlooker gets more of the view' and I have had those embarrassing occasions when, having failed to defeat the wind, the local farmer or walker has told me of deer departing at a gallop from the woodland I have been in.

There are a number of ways to determine wind direction and you should not rely entirely on the weather forecast. You should check it out when you first arrive at your stalking ground. On many occasions you do not need a device to help you determine its direction. The wind in your face and its effect on the trees around you will be enough of an indication. In calmer conditions, when the wind gently drifts rather than blows, assessing wind direction is more difficult and the use of a device may be helpful. I have seen many ingenious methods used, some being quite amusing. One of my stalking friends, who can be militaristic at times, uses a puff of fuller's earth and another blows bubbles into the air. A puff of talcum powder can also work. For many years I have used a simple cigarette lighter, which has the advantage of being small and quick to use. Its disadvantage is the slight noise made on ignition. Remember, you may have to use it at regular intervals during the stalk so whatever you decide to use should be practical and small enough to be carried in the pocket.

Stalking Woodland

Stalking fallow within their natural habitat can test the most skilful of stalkers and stalking on foot through woodland has to be the most challenging aspect of the sport. This calls for not only an awareness of the wind, but a quiet approach, using your eyes and binoculars to their best advantage. Your clothing[35] should be both quiet and the right colour to blend into your surroundings. I would recommend boots rather than wellingtons for woodland stalking as they are quieter and provide better control when placing your feet. They also give better grip and are safer on hilly ground. Remember,

35 See Chapter 4, Stalking Necessities – clothing

having a mobile phone is useful for emergencies but when stalking can be a distraction so ensure you put it on silent mode or simply switch it off.

Wild deer have a number of distinct advantages in woodland compared to open ground. Firstly, they have the advantage of concealment through their natural camouflage. This, combined with their ability to remain completely motionless for an infinite period of time, makes them difficult to detect without them having some awareness of your presence first. Their patience outstretches our own and this adds to their ability to remain undetected. Your aim should be to detect them before they detect you. The latter usually results in their rapid departure, denying you the opportunity of a shot. Where the woodland canopy and undergrowth is sparse due to excessive grazing by deer, stalking can be particularly challenging as the deer will be quick to pick up your movement at considerable distances.

An insight into the effect of your intrusion into their woodland world will provide you the opportunity to forward plan and hopefully avoid some blunders. Birds and animals within the canopy are the deer's messengers and effectively provide them with an early warning system that rarely fails them. If you have stood quietly, hidden in woodland and observed the effect of someone moving towards you from a distance you will appreciate my point. Blackbird, wren and nuthatch are some of the worst of the 'telltales'. Their alarm calls, warning of danger, are picked up quickly by the deer and they will be on high alert, turning their eyes and ears in the direction of the potential danger. This knock-on reaction can be most annoying at times and adjustment to a slower pace is often necessary to minimise the disturbance. If there is a game shoot on the ground early autumn stalking can be particularly frustrating, with pheasants continually running ahead of you. If you cannot avoid them your only option is to stalk extremely slowly until you are out of their home range.

If you intend to stalk during the morning you should plan to be in your selected area at the best time, i.e. as the light emerges when visibility is good enough to ensure you are able to identify your quarry and confirm adequate safety of a backstop. It can be a mistake to enter woodland too early, particularly if there are many roosting woodpigeon. The clatter they create in leaving their perch prematurely will alert deer and move them on ahead of you, ruining the chance of a shot. Having assessed the wind direction and decided upon your route, commence your stalk carefully and remain alert to the possibility of an early chance presenting itself. Do not be surprised if you feel somewhat awkward and noisy as you set out, particularly if you have not stalked for a while. Concentration is vital as you begin to use your own natural senses to their maximum potential. You will experience a period of settling into the woodland scene and the sooner you can tune in to the environment and melt into the surroundings the better. Move very slowly until your confidence builds and you begin to move more quietly and feel less conspicuous.

How you place your feet is important as continually cracking twigs will alert deer to your presence. Looking for the quietest route ahead and dropping your gaze to the ground will ensure you avoid most obstacles by careful placement of your feet. If you have chosen to stalk along a ride you may find the grassy edge quieter than the centre. If there are no rides, look for the natural paths used by the deer and use them to avoid making unnecessary noise. In heavy undergrowth you may have to rely on detecting obstacles under the soles of your feet by feel and there are a number of techniques to achieve this. You can try placing the boot to the ground at a side angle or heel first and then on contact rolling the boot in. I find balancing and keeping the weight on the back foot as you test the ground with the front foot to be most effective and this can help avoid the pressure of cracking twigs or stumbling on to something noisy. If you do make a noise or a pheasant is flushed suddenly try to remain completely still for a while until the woodland has settled down.

The conditions and topography will dictate the pace. In dead ground, i.e. ground that you can see is clear with your physical presence hidden due to the gradient or cover, you should be able to make quicker progress as long as you are quiet. As you look ahead to plan your route you may be able to take advantage of obvious cover, be it canopy or high vegetation. You may occasionally have to crawl to negotiate overhanging branches or climb down a steep gradient, in which case you may have to unload for safety reasons. If you have a guest with you it is important that you have a safe system of operating, as outlined in Chapter 12.

Binoculars are a key piece of equipment and as useful in woodland as on the hill. However, the best optics you possess are those that are permanently with you – your eyes; so use them. Many stalkers in woodland over-use their binoculars and in doing so restrict their wider view. The eyes are the initial scanning equipment, focusing quickly on the distant canopy edge while checking the foreground, with at times hardly a movement of the head. This should be supplemented by use of the binoculars to check out the darker corners or the unusual colour or movement of anything remotely like a deer. Your movement in bringing the binoculars up to eye level should be in slow motion. Only time spent observing deer will provide you with the skill to pick up the colour of coat, the swish of a tail or movement of an ear or antler quickly.

Binoculars are as useful in woodland as they are on the hill

Only time spent observing deer will provide you with the skill to see them before they see you

In places likely to hold deer your pace may have to be painfully slow, giving you the opportunity to check out all areas before moving on. Be careful not to restrict your focus to what is ahead, check out the flanks as well as occasionally taking a glimpse behind you. Occasionally, waiting for a few minutes in attractive spots can be effective, especially if you have some cover. Use your hearing too and listen for any sound of deer movement around you. Pigeon that appear to be moving prematurely out of the wood may be a sign that deer are moving ahead and this should instigate a check on the wind and route.

Be prepared to freeze at any moment and remain completely still should you detect what may be deer. If you do 'bump' deer be prepared for a quick shot if they settle back in range and give you a second chance. If they disappear out of view without having confirmed the danger you may get a second chance if you move quickly to a vantage point. However, you should resist the temptation to play cat and mouse. Trying to catch up with deer in this way is usually futile and should not be attempted. Better to assess the ground spoilt and amend your route accordingly; there will usually be another chance and you should remain patient.

When you do find deer, restrict your movements immediately. If you can only see one, expect others to be close by. You will know if the deer are suspicious by their reactions. They may take a few robotic type steps towards you, moving their head up and down in an effort to detect the danger. Prickets will often do this during the rut, perhaps in fear of what may be facing them. Does with fawns at foot will take on a protective stance and stamp a front foot. This behaviour is usually accompanied with an uplifting of the tail. If they are staring straight at you it may be you have been detected and a mistake now will cost you the opportunity of a shot. In this situation any movement in preparation for a shot will have to be done with the upmost stealth. If you remain completely still the deer may settle back down and perhaps begin to feed, giving you the chance to plan your next move.

If you think you have not been detected and they are not too close then use your binoculars to assess what deer are present prior to deciding if a shot is on. A stalk into a closer or safer position for the shot may be necessary. You must now plan your route carefully and take advantage of the cover available. A crawl may be required or simply keeping a low profile may be enough. Do not make your move until you are satisfied that you have not been detected. Plan your route to a shooting position by using trees, bushes or dead ground to shield your presence, but remember you must be in 'stealth mode' and move like a cat. If the deer are feeding make your moves when their heads are down and be prepared to wait for the right moment to move on. You must move slowly and quietly. If the deer are close you should restrict your movements and use your eyes rather than binoculars. Your selection of quarry, taking the shot using your sticks or taking advantage of a natural lean are dealt with in the next chapter (7).

If the deer is close you should restrict your movement and use your eyes rather than binoculars. This young doe has detected the danger!

The Sixth Sense

There is one sense I am almost reluctant to mention for fear of ridicule, a sixth sense, with which some stalkers may relate. In my early stalking days I dismissed this as nonsense and put it down to my imagination. There have been numerous occasions where my success in locating deer has been enhanced by an unexplained awareness of being in close proximity to them, well before I have seen or heard anything. Whether this is the combination of a number of unrecognised physical factors bringing about a psychological response, I am not sure. When I have experienced this sensation I have stopped and remained completely still, putting myself on high alert, and deer have appeared suddenly as anticipated. I could, of course, be the victim of a self-fulfilling prophecy but it has happened now on too many occasions for me to dismiss it as fantasy.

Stalking Open Ground

If the location and topography of your stalking ground is that of open ground, away from or adjacent to wooded areas, then this will call for additional techniques to those of stalking within the woodland. If not disturbed, fallow are quite content to live out in the open fields where the acreages are vast. They will also travel considerable distances seeking out the most attractive of crops that provide them with both food and cover. They feel safe from predators and, provided they have the grazing, will remain in the locality for long periods. Where the acreage is extensive with little or no culling taking place their numbers will build up. In some parts of the country, e.g. Lincolnshire and parts of southern England, it is not unusual to see herds of between two and three hundred fallow grazing in these vast fields. The areas where no culling takes place become sanctuaries for the deer and left uncontrolled allow for a disproportionate increase in the population, creating a problem for adjacent landowners through damage to vulnerable crops and woodland.

Reconnaissance over a wide open landscape will be necessary and this is one of the few occasions when the use of a telescope will be an advantage in identifying deer over greater distances than the norm. If the ground is predominantly flat then locating deer can be difficult as they are easily screened by crops and hedgerows. You also have the added difficulty of ensuring an adequate backstop when the opportunity of a shot arises. In this situation the installation of carefully sited high seats has to be a serious consideration (See Chapter 9).

Getting to know the feeding habits of fallow and the crops in the area will be essential in terms of determining their movements. Where they have been under management pressure through culling, those movements from the preferred safety of the woodland to their feeding ground in the open may be restricted to the hours of darkness. Their forced nocturnal habits may mean the only chance you have of intercepting them will be at first or last light. If you are unable to use high seats then positioning yourself at a safe vantage point in advance of any movement may yield a result. Where the pressure is not so great it is often possible to locate deer throughout the day time. When you do there is usually time to plan your stalk according to the prevailing wind using whatever cover presents itself, be it hedgerow, crop or field margin. The conditions faced in stalking open ground are such that the average range for taking a shot is usually greater, and sometimes double that in the woodland. However, that is no excuse for taking shots in excess of your capabilities. (See Chapter 7, The Decision to Shoot.)

Knowledge of the topography of the land will assist you in making quick decisions on how best to commence a particular stalk. Trying to approach fallow in the open by using woodland can be hazardous, particularly if your approach is from the very woodland from which they have emerged. They will pay careful attention to the woodland, which they see as a source of potential danger, as opposed to the open ground around them, from where they do not expect to be approached without early warning. This explains why they will sometimes seek the refuge of a big open landscape when disturbed in woodland. There will be occasions due to the wind and nature of the ground that you have to make an approach via the woodland. As with

The average range for taking shots on open ground is usually greater than in woodland. Note here the stalkers have made use of the cover provided by the grass along the fence line

stalking on foot in woodland referred to earlier, the wildlife around you will be alerted quickly to your presence, particularly your predatory technique of creeping along the woodland edge or just within it. Therefore, a steady approach is necessary to minimise any disturbance likely to be transmitted to the deer.

Crawling

There may be occasions when, due to the prevailing wind, there is no cover or dead ground that can be used in your approach. Your options will be limited to either waiting for the deer to move ground or attempting an audacious approach in the open. This will mean a crawl if you are to stand any chance of a shot. You may be surprised with what you can get away with provided you keep low and quiet. Done carefully with the wind in your favour, the deer will have difficulty detecting you. Crawling into fallow in open ground can be very successful and the technique is reminiscent of my early wildfowling days when punt gunning. It can also be just as muddy. Many of the same principles apply. Keeping as silent as possible and maintaining a low profile are essential. You will quickly realise the unforeseen benefits that can be made of slight undulations of the ground and minimal vegetation to conceal yourself while crawling. If the land provides sufficient gradient to provide dead ground rapid progress can be made as you can switch quickly from a crawl to a crouched walk and back to a crawl as necessary.

The art of crawling is not difficult if you are reasonably fit. We all learnt to do it before walking. Crawling, while carrying your rifle safely and with binoculars around your neck, is an acquired skill that can be practised. Muzzle awareness is paramount both in terms of avoiding blocking the barrel and ensuring the safety of a companion, see Chapter 12, Safe Stalking. There are a number of different crawling techniques that you can adapt to suit your physique and carrying capacity. An army-type crawl will move you quickly while keeping you as close to the ground as possible. The use of your forearms and elbows rather than your hands to push forward will help to lift your torso off the ground and help in safely carrying your rifle along. Your rifle should be held in a forward position just clear of the ground as you progress. Binoculars can be a nuisance unless you have them on a harness that helps keep them tight to your chest. On occasions I have moved them out of the way on to my back and this prevents them getting damaged or soiled. Move each limb individually forward to move across the ground. A typical sequence would be:

- Right elbow/forearm forward
- Left knee forward
- Left elbow/forearm forward
- Right knee forward.

High Seat Techniques

The use of a strategically placed high seat or deer hide to enable you to wait for deer to appear can be a productive option against that of actively stalking on foot. Their use is generally best served during the early morning or evening when deer are on the move. Getting your preparation, timing and technique right will maximise your chances of success.

Your choice of deciding to use a seat to wait for deer will be influenced by many factors, as outlined in Chapter 9. Their use is particularly effective for the late afternoon, when stalking on foot can be difficult due to the failing light. If you are participating in a collaborative team cull, stalking on foot is normally prohibited and you will have no other option than occupying your allocated seat (See Chapter 11).

If you decide to occupy a seat your first consideration will be your clothing, to which you should give careful thought. Sitting for long periods inactive and in an elevated position can be a cold affair at any time of year. The onset of hypothermia has the potential to affect your shooting and ability to remain alert. See Chapter 4 for advice on clothing and keeping warm while in high seats.

Timing is an important factor in high seat use and one that your local knowledge of deer habits will influence. There are no hard and fast rules and on occasions you may decide to go to a seat at an unconventional time of the day to catch out deer. Generally though if you are to occupy a seat in the early morning you should plan to be in your seat in the darkness, ideally approximately fifteen minutes before the first light appears. It may then be half an hour before you can see well enough to identify deer and shoot safely. If you plan to sit in the seat towards the end of the day then allowing for a two-hour wait up to darkness is sensible. Arriving too late in a seat increases the chance of disturbing deer that have already emerged, so extra care should be taken in your approach. If you are a visiting stalker you should not embark to a high seat in the darkness that you have never been to before without a very clear and concise brief from your host of its location and safety. Ideally you should be taken to your seat.

You should not assume that by using a high seat you avoid the problem of leaving your scent. While the higher position will help keep the drift of scent high on the wind it is still a factor to be considered, both on your approach to the seat and while you remain in it. The weather conditions and topography of the land around the seat will govern the dispersal of your scent. Initially, your first consideration will be the wind direction. Can I get to the seat without my scent clearing the very ground where I expect to see deer and, once in the seat will the wind be to my advantage?

The solution is to have a number of seats across your stalking area providing you with a choice dependent on weather conditions. You should stalk into your chosen seat, moving quietly and carefully, even in the darkness. There should be no need to use a torch as your eyes will adjust to the poor light sufficiently for you to make your way safely. The value of clearing a path to and from the seat previously will now be appreciated. Your aim should be to get into the seat undetected. If you are approaching the seat in good light then you should take care to check the ground around it as you get close. It is not unusual in these circumstances to see deer on the approach and providing it is safe you should not dismiss the opportunity of a shot before getting into the seat. I have on many occasions crawled to the base of the seat to get a shot in these circumstances, using the rungs of the ladder as lean for the shot.

Assuming you have arrived at your seat without incident you should first ensure it has not been tampered with and appears safe and rigid. Even in the darkness you should be able to see sufficiently to check this quietly without creating any disturbance. If you intend to put on extra clothing, do so before climbing the ladder. Make sure you remove any bullet in the chamber of the rifle prior to climbing with a visual and physical check to confirm. Whether you remove the magazine or not is a matter for you so long as the rifle has no bullet in the chamber when you climb. Your rifle should be carried up the ladder in such a way as to provide you with both hands for climbing using the safe system of three points of contact on the ladder at all times.

This is a technique that can be practised when not stalking. A thin rope or cord can be used to haul up equipment to the seat if necessary, including the rifle. The rifle should not be hauled up without the protection of a cover and, of course, you must ensure it is unloaded.

As soon as you are in the seat and settled you should load immediately and make safe. You should remain alert from the offset as you may see deer within seconds. Do not sit there without first going through a number of preparatory techniques. Check that the shooting rail is secure and if it is one of the adjustable types quietly move it to suit your shooting position. Check out shooting distances and different firing positions you may need to assume. If necessary adjust the focus of your telescopic sight to a mid-range setting. In the early morning you will note your safe area for taking a shot will increase as the backstop becomes clearer. In the evening the opposite will occur as the light fades and areas that you could see into are no longer visible. You should also note windows of shooting opportunity in which branches or low cover may obstruct the path of a bullet. While these may be avoidable in good light they will be less obvious later as the darkness comes and care should be taken to ensure they are avoided if there is a late opportunity for a shot.

Use your binoculars to check out the outlying areas. Look hard and listen. The late Arthur Cadman, admired for his knowledge of fallow deer, often reminded me of the words carved in a New Forest seat: 'Sit still, look long and hold yourself quiet.' This advice holds as good today as it did all those years ago. Fallow can move like ghosts but in woodland with thick canopy around you may get a heads up by the sound of a cracking branch. If you hear the movement of deer you can usually determine the direction of travel and position yourself in readiness for the shot. Be patient, both in the waiting and once deer are spotted. In woodland focus your attention on areas behind the canopy where you may detect early movement of a deer.

In many seat locations you may have observation around the seat of almost 360 degrees and concentrating on a wide spectrum is tiring. Try to keep as still as possible and minimise movements of your head by moving your eyes to their extreme peripheral vision. This should give you a 40 per cent field of view without moving the head. Do not ignore the ground behind you and have a plan to deal with this by practising a safe shooting position should a chance from behind present itself.

A key factor in the success of high seat use is one of maintaining optimism. The psychological effects of waiting immobile for long periods can bring about a feeling of doubt that you are in the right place at the right time. A feeling that you should be elsewhere may induce a decision to leave too early. So continually exercising some routines and maintaining a constant watch are essential. When deer do emerge, especially into open ground adjacent to cover, they will be on high alert with all senses tuned to detect the first sign of danger. So keep calm and restrict any initial movements to a minimum. If the circumstances permit, give the deer time to settle. Fallow, unlike muntjac, once settled will stand and gaze, walk about and perhaps feed, giving you the opportunity to select a suitable animal to shoot. You may also have your thoughts on additional animals to be shot if the opportunity presents itself should this fit within your cull plan.

Occasionally deer may emerge too close to the seat and this can make both remaining unobserved and the subsequent shot difficult. In seats adjacent to steep ground deer will pick up your movement in the seat very quickly where you appear at eye level to them. There can also be a risk of deer picking up your movement in seats that are positioned on a domed area where their approach is from dead ground below as you will effectively appear on their horizon. Where deer emerge too far out you may have to be patient and wait for them to move closer. If they remain at a distance it is a matter for you, given the individual circumstances, to decide whether you are confident enough to take on the longer range shot. Taking the shot techniques and follow-up are covered in Chapter 7.

Ensure you unload before you descend

When you do decide to leave your seat you should unload before climbing down. Having sat quietly for a long period of time you should leave your seat with the same care as you stalked into it. This is important as leaving the seat in a noisy manner will educate any deer in close proximity. There may even be an opportunity for a shot on departure as deer may be nearby and previously unseen from the seat.

Guest Stalkers

High seats are a good safe option when entertaining guests providing you ensure they are equipped adequately for the cold and they are able to find their allocated seat. In the dark this usually means taking them to it.

The techniques I have suggested are drawn from my own experience of success and failure over the years. With hindsight I, like many before and after me, have broken all the rules of good stalking techniques and on occasions still been successful – or should I say perhaps just lucky. I vividly recall one such occasion spent in a high seat in Shropshire, some twenty-five years ago. At the time I was hosting my German friend, Jochen, and had arranged for him to stalk with my nephew, Mike, then a young, enthusiastic forestry ranger with a good knowledge of fallow deer. The intention was to get Jochen a shot, hopefully at a fallow buck.

It was late October and with the rut still in full swing, our hopes were high. Mike had arranged to 'park' me out of the way in a high seat on the periphery of the ground. He was to accompany Jochen and take him to the chosen seat, where he was confident of a buck presenting itself for the German guest. That was the plan.

That morning we were out of our beds in good time and set off in the darkness. It felt cold for the time of year and there was a threat of rain. Typical, I thought, just when I wanted everything going for us. I was anxious for Jochen to get a shot so success, I thought, hinged on Mike's plan.

When we arrived at the wood we walked quietly together for some distance. I had no knowledge of the area and so Mike escorted me to my seat. I remember the brief, 'Shoot any deer in season, John, as there is a problem with the neighbouring farmer. But you may see nothing here.' Fine, I thought, as long as Jochen gets a chance.

I was happy to sit with a half-chance of seeing something of interest. My seat was a free stander at the junction of two main rides within an area of mixed plantation. I climbed the seat as it started to rain and prepared for the wait, hoping to hear a shot from my friend. I had been in the seat for perhaps fifteen minutes before the first light of the day slowly gave me a view along the rides.

I went through my usual ritual of imagining what may appear and where; assessing safe areas and good leans from differing angles in the seat. I had three areas of interest, a ride immediately in front, one from behind and one to my right. I found myself constantly turning my head in desperation so as not to miss anything. Suddenly, on checking the ride to my right, a fallow buck, almost ghost-like, was stood motionless and broadside at about 75 yards. Typically, I had not seen him emerge. I had the impression it was a sorel. I turned slowly, engaged the buck and took the shot. There was a good reaction and the buck leapt forward and disappeared into the trees. I let things settle down. In those days I was not using a sound moderator and I felt the shot had disturbed the entire wood. I let a few minutes pass but could not resist going to look for the buck and went to the point of shot. The light was still poor and looking for blood seemed pointless. I went in among the trees and found the buck quickly. It was a sorel and I decided to do a quick field gralloch. I left the beast and returned quietly to my then wet seat.

I settled back into the seat and a further fifteen minutes went by when I sensed there was something moving close and below my seat. I moved too quickly and spooked what turned out to be a muntjac buck that had emerged in my blind area. I had never shot a muntjac and the opportunity had gone. But I was to be proved wrong as a few minutes later, crossing the ride behind me some 100 yards away, was another muntjac. Behind it emerged a second one, which was a buck. It paused for a moment and I was quick to get a shot off. My first muntjac dropped at the shot and, keen to have a look, I left the seat immediately. There it lay, a young buck, that at the time I suspect had its mind on other things. I did a quick gralloch, not much different to paunching a rabbit, I thought. I left the muntjac on the ride. It was now 7.30 a.m. and the rain had stopped. I returned to my seat again to sit it out to the end of play, planned for 8.30 a.m., at which time Mike and Jochen would appear hopefully with a story to tell. But I had not heard a shot. I remained optimistic, thinking they may be out of my hearing zone.

I had been back in the seat for perhaps a quarter of an hour and was feeling pretty pleased with myself; after all I had shot a sorel and my first muntjac. Looking down the ride ahead, out to some 200 yards, there was a movement. It was a fallow pricket and it was on the move and crossing the ride from left to right. It never hesitated and disappeared into the right hand block of woodland. I had a hunch it could appear on the ride to my right, perhaps where I had shot the sorel. I prepared myself for such an opportunity and waited in anticipation. Two minutes passed and the pricket emerged and stood in exactly the same place as the sorel. I took the shot as it stood broadside. The reaction was good and I left the seat yet again to find the pricket lying alongside the sorel. I duly gralloched the beast.

I took my time returning once again to the seat. It was now 8 a.m. and, having convinced myself that it was all over, I relaxed into the seat. I was praying for the guest to have been successful as there was now the potential for considerable embarrassment. I casually observed the rides that earlier had demanded my absolute attention. Some ten minutes passed and there was a movement ahead of me. To my amazement a roe buck appeared on the ride ahead of me at 40 yards. It stood broadside for a moment facing to the right. I never hesitated and shot immediately. The buck swerved and turned at the shot, dashing back into the trees from where it had emerged. I was happy with the shot and decided to remain in the seat to await the arrival of Mike and Jochen.

When they arrived I was deliberately coy as it became clear they had not heard my shots. I asked how they had got on. To my dismay and embarrassment Jochen had not had a shot and neither had they seen a deer! I disclosed I had had a shot and walked them out to the fallow bucks and muntjac. I saved the story of the roe buck until last. They were in disbelief and I sent Jochen into the canopy to find the buck. He went in like an African guide. I had attempted to lessen the experience by intimating it was just a young buck but I'm afraid Jochen came out dragging a good strong six-pointer, which remains on my wall today – just in case I need a reminder of that October morning.

I often cast my mind back to this experience that taught me a thing or two about high seat techniques and entertaining guests. I had broken all the rules that morning and left my seat repeatedly, but still had the opportunity to shoot deer. I realised that when deer appear too close they present problems of engagement, as referred to earlier. Muntjac, being small, are conscious of aerial predators and will pick up your movement or noise from a high seat quickly. Fallow are not immune to this either. I also realised it is never over until you have unloaded and left your seat for good, so you must always be prepared for a shot. The noise from shooting on a number of occasions, even without a moderator, will not necessarily spoil your chances of seeing and shooting more deer. With regard to entertaining guests, you may think twice about taking your own rifle with you. And finally, be specific when briefing individuals over what they can and cannot shoot as shooting 'any deer in season' may involve more than one species. I am not sure to this day whether Mike actually meant what he said. No doubt many stalkers will have had equally memorable successes when using high seats. What matters is that you learn and benefit from the experience.

Chapter 7

The Decision to Shoot

Your stalking technique has enabled you to get in range of the deer, and a shot is possible. Your actions now are crucial to success in converting the chance. Even before the beast is selected you will have made an assessment of the range, safety of the shot and how to maximise the opportunity to shoot additional animals, if this fits in with your cull plan.

Assuming you have the tool for the job, i.e. the rifle of your choice and suitable ammunition in which you have total confidence, there should be no reason why a safe and humane shot should not be possible. You select your point of aim, squeeze the trigger and within an instant the shot is away, almost by surprise, if your technique is good.

Sounds straight forward does it not? The reality is that to cull deer consistently in an efficient and humane way requires precision and a focused mind to execute; a skill that is not acquired overnight. As with any other discipline, being physically and mentally fit, using the right equipment and adequate practice are all necessary for a successful outcome. I have been fortunate indeed over the years to have benefited from the advice and guidance of some first class stalkers. However, no one is perfect and they would all admit to making the odd mistake, such as taking a potentially unsafe shot or wounding a beast that then required a follow-up.

As emphasised in Chapter 12, stalking is much about learning from experience. It is also about taking the responsibility to shoot safely and humanely. That means taking account of animal welfare, best practice and continuous development of your skills. If you cannot shoot to a consistent standard at an artificial target on the range with the luxury of no time constraint, then you will have no chance when out of breath and faced with the opportunity to take a shot within seconds at live quarry. If you are not fit enough and confident in these circumstances you should not be venturing out with a high-powered rifle to shoot deer. It's as simple as that. Gaining the knowledge to identify your target correctly and practice in field conditions is therefore essential. It follows that newcomers to stalking should be encouraged to achieve the basic deer

stalking qualifications (DSC1 & 2) as described in Chapter 3; these being seen as the first stepping stones to becoming fit and competent. Best practice courses linked to marksmanship are also available through The Deer Initiative and are of great benefit to both novice and experienced stalker.

Techniques

Practice makes Perfect

A prerequisite to accurate and humane shooting is to maintain your rifle and scope in good condition. Regular practice and checking your rifle's zero to ensure the scope is calibrated to the point of aim are important in maintaining your skill level. For many stalkers the availability and convenience of suitable land to do this is a facility not easily acquired. However, there is usually somewhere you can go, away from your stalking area if possible, and efforts should be made to secure it.

You should check your rifle zero:

- Whenever you lose confidence in its accuracy
- If the scope or rifle has suffered a knock or damage
- If you change or use a new batch of ammunition
- If the rifle has not been used for a long period of time
- You have experienced an unexplained miss.

While the basic stalking qualification (DSC1) assessment attempts to simulate field conditions, i.e. taking shots prone, kneeling and standing (with the use of sticks), and at short range without support, it should be recognised that there is a certain amount of added psychological pressure in taking a shot at a live target. 'Buck fever' – the curse of those that become overly excited and nervous when taking the shot – can be a real problem, often leading to a misplaced shot. Therefore, the more you are able to practise in simulated field conditions where you can introduce time constraints and the like, the better you will be when it comes to the real thing.

Assessing Range

Your ability to judge distances is also a key factor in the decision to take the shot. The greater the distance, the greater becomes any error by the shooter, compounded by the effects of adverse weather, e.g. wind. Judging distance is something you can practise and use modern technology to test yourself. Carrying the equipment to determine range, be it incorporated within your binoculars or not, can be an asset but also an incumbent. In many woodland situations if you are to convert the half-chance of a shot you will not have the time to start determining range other than by your own judgement. In any case, at relatively short distances it is a pointless exercise as it should make little difference to your point of aim. Even at distances over 100 metres most deer legal cartridges will deliver their bullet well within their trajectory to hit the vital organs of a deer, so normally there is no need to make elevation allowances. What matters is that you know how your rifle performs at a given distance. This is important, not only for shots over the normal distance, but also for a shot at close quarters, e.g. humane dispatch situations.

When you are not stalking you should practise judging various distances out to 200 metres, this being the longest distance from where even an experienced stalker should attempt a shot. There will be places on your ground where you see deer regularly that present the opportunity for a shot – the hot spots. Determining the distance from these potential shooting locations to certain points adjacent to where you see the deer is a useful exercise in preparation for stalking in the months ahead. This can also be done from high seat locations and known distances recorded on the seat itself as a reminder.

Rifle Rests and Using Natural Supports

Once a rifle is zeroed correctly with ammunition that performs consistently, then it will be your own technique that will ultimately determine its accuracy in field conditions. Shooting accurately depends on many factors, not least the stability of the rifle at the point of taking the shot. Your physical position, how the rifle is held and your trigger technique all have a bearing on stability. You only have to observe the target shooter to realise this is a key factor. Shooting at targets, with all the trappings of sandbags, bench rests and the like with no time constraints, is distinctly different to most stalking situations, where you may be cold, out of breath and have only seconds to convert the chance with or without suitable support.

Making use of a natural support

The equipment available and its use to aid accurate shooting are described in Chapter 4. There will be occasions where natural supports can be used that may provide for a more stable position in which the rifle can be held. Undulating ground will often provide both suitable cover for the stalk and support from the prone position for a shot, as will the use of trees, branches and fence posts in woodland situations. On steep wooded ridges I have often found good shooting positions on protruding tree roots overlooking the ground below.

When the opportunity arises for a shot, suitable support to enable the rifle to be held steady should be sought quickly. Much depends on the circumstances of the stalk and topography of the ground. If you are on open ground and have a fitted bipod you will need to get prone or into a kneeling position to facilitate a steady aim. In a woodland situation where there may be no close natural supports, e.g. the side of a tree or fence post, then you will need to use your sticks. The skill of bringing them quietly and quickly into use is one that is acquired through practice, not necessarily while stalking.

Taking a shot off the shoulder without additional support should be restricted to close encounters and the urgent necessity to dispatch an injured or diseased animal that is mobile and likely to escape.

Above: Practise the skill of using your sticks

Below: A pricket in the corridor of uncertainty. You need to wait for him to turn clear of the branches

Safety Considerations

Whatever shot placement you decide upon, it must not only achieve a swift and humane death, but be ultimately safe. That means not only ensuring a safe backstop but an unobstructed flight path of the bullet. Safe backstops are elaborated upon in Chapter 12, Safe Stalking. Shots taken with a solid earth backstop safeguard and reduce the risk of ricochet and striking an unintended target. You cannot assume there is a safe backstop; you have to be able to see it. This is particularly important in woodland situations, where the lower canopy may obscure hidden dangers. You should also be careful to ensure there is no vegetation, branches or twigs at any point between the muzzle and target. If there is you may have to move position or wait for the deer to move and present a clearer view.

Close obstructions are not always seen through the scope, much to the surprise of those that have shot holes through their car bonnets when using

them as rests for zeroing or blown apart nearby branches and the like. If a high speed bullet is in any way obstructed it is likely to break up or deflect depending on the circumstances, calibre and type of bullet. This presents a risk to public safety and the possibility of wounding a beast.

It is only when you have confirmed there are no obstructions and the sequence of alignment is correct that you should make a controlled and deliberate trigger release. In the heat of the moment you must also be mindful that with most rifles, having taken a shot and reloaded, the safety catch will remain off and require resetting, unlike many shotguns that have automatic safeties.

Safeguarding Deer Welfare through Best Practice

Deer welfare should be foremost in the minds of all who manage deer. Stalkers have a clear duty of care to ensure shooting is carried out in such a manner so as to minimise stress and suffering, and so their objective should be to achieve a swift and humane kill with the first shot.

In 2005, the British Deer Society (BDS) initiated a research project*[36] into the shooting performance of stalkers with a view to improving standards and their success rates when shooting deer. The aim was to establish a scientific basis for refining the instruction on BDS Deer Stalking training courses and improve advice to deer stalkers with a view to safeguarding deer welfare during culling. What is significant about the study are the factors associated with missing and with wounding an animal.

While the findings largely confirmed previous best practice teaching they provide several clear pointers for improving welfare by maximising the chances of a quick and certain kill and minimising wounding. These are summarised as follows:

- Choose a comfortable shooting position
- Avoid shooting off elbows or freehand, use a support (e.g. sticks, bipod)
- Aim at the chest or lower neck *(points of aim are covered later)*
- Use bullets heavier than 75 grains *(The research found a higher rate of wounding of roe shot with the smaller calibres and lighter bullets – see Chapter 4 for details of legal requirements)*
- Avoid shooting when there is insufficient time
- Shoot a distant animal only if there is sufficient time
- Shoot an animal when it is stationary
- Avoid shooting an animal that is heavily obscured or in thicket

36 Authors: Aebischer, N. J., Wheatley, C. J. and Rose, H. R. (2014) Factors Associated with Shooting Accuracy and Wounding Rate of Four Managed Wild Deer Species in the UK, Based on Anonymous Field Records from Deer Stalkers, PLoS ONE 9(10): e109698. doi:10.1371/journal.pone.0109698. Details of the research can be found on the BDS website www.bds.org.uk

- Take extra care when the ground is not well known
- Even when experienced, avoid attempting risky shots
- Carry out shooting practice at least once a month.

Target Selection

Having stalked in range of deer and positioned yourself for the shot, selecting which deer to shoot will be your next priority. If the deer have become suspicious this will have to be done quickly, a skill that only comes through the experience of observing deer regularly. Choosing the right sex, age and condition will have to be considered if culling selectively. This may be an informed decision based on your cull plan. Deer that are diseased, injured or in poor condition should take priority in your decision to shoot, whatever your cull plan may dictate. You have a responsibility to ensure venison entering the food chain does not present a risk to human health through disease and therefore the initial observation of the animal before the shot should be noted automatically, prompting further investigation if the animal's behaviour and appearance does not appear normal.

While injuries causing lameness can be spotted quickly, disease may not be so obvious and therefore a routine inspection of every carcass is required as described in the next chapter on disease identification by veterinary Peter Green.

Fallow in poor body condition are not too difficult to pick out for the trained eye. The photograph below shows a fallow pricket in very poor condition. This should prompt not only a decision to cull but further investigation as referred to earlier. You will note the bone structure of the animal is more obvious with the top of the tail and rump area appearing angular. Further examination would reveal the outline of the ribs and spinal column.

Note the poor condition of this pricket in its overall appearance, particularly the rump region between the wings of the pelvis and tail head. The pelvic contour indicated is concave. This will be convex on an animal in good condition, as can be seen in the following photograph that shows a comparison between the good and poor condition of two fallow bucks.

Deer in poor condition, diseased or injured should take priority in your decision to shoot. Note the poor condition of this pricket in its overall appearance, particularly the rump region

Note the more pronounced bone structure and concave pelvic contour of the buck on the left

As referred to in Chapter 1, assessing the age of deer through observation in the wild can be difficult. This can be done more accurately in relation to bucks as the appearance of the antlers should indicate an approximate age at least sufficient to determine young bucks (up to four-year-olds), middle aged and old. The does will be more difficult and you may only be able to judge the young (fawns and yearlings) with any certainty, the older does tending to be longer in the face than the young.

If you are pursuing a reduction cull it will be important to maximise the opportunity to shoot additional animals. With the exception of bucks at certain times of the year, fallow are rarely alone, so although you may only be able to see one beast, it is most likely there will be others close by and therefore you should resist the temptation to shoot whatever deer first presents a clear shot. If you have not been observed and the deer are not suspicious, then patience is a virtue in this situation. Wait and look carefully for the movement of other deer. If others emerge then weighing up your chances of shooting additional animals will influence which deer you shoot first and where you place the shot.

Shot Placement and Reaction

Having the ability to hold the rifle steady and squeeze the trigger is only part of the art of taking the shot. To execute a humane shot requires two distinct skills – being able to shoot to the point of aim and having the knowledge of where that point of aim should be on the animal to bring about a swift and humane death. The wise saying, 'You do not shoot at a deer, you shoot into and through it' tends to highlight the fundamental principles of shot placement. Knowledge of a deer's anatomy together with an appreciation of the angles of shot is essential in achieving a humane shot; consequently the position of the animal at the point of the shot is a key factor in ensuring a clean effective kill.

There are three key areas to place a shot that will bring about a swift humane death, the head, neck and chest (heart lung area). However, these require some explanation and some caution with regard to the exact aiming point. Shots at a beast directly facing to or away from you should be avoided in the knowledge that if you wait the animal will turn and provide you with a safer humane shot; the exception being the attempted dispatch of a wounded beast.

The reaction to the shot provides the stalker with valuable information that may suggest where the bullet has struck. This may prompt an immediate second shot in the case of a suspected wounded animal or help to confirm a fatal strike with the animal being found dead within a short distance.

A description is given below of the advantages and disadvantages of each shot together with the typical reactions you may observe as a result of both accurate and misplaced shots. This is not an exact science and you should be aware there will be occasions where no reaction to the shot is observed and no bullet strike is heard, but nevertheless the shot is a fatal one and the deer will be lying dead nearby. You should also note that deer, under stress through being injured or aware of the presence of a predator (you), are likely to run faster and further following the shot when compared to deer shot that are unaware of your presence. A further factor affecting reaction to the shot will be the calibre, muzzle energy and weight of bullet used and the range over which the shot is taken.

Head Shots

The ethics and practicalities of head shooting are a political hot potato within the stalking world, creating heated debate over their use. It is accepted that a shot to the head that destroys vital areas of the brain and brain stem will cause instantaneous loss of consciousness and death. It is without doubt the most humane of shots and I know many experienced stalkers who regularly practise it; encouraged by game dealers willing to pay a higher price for an undamaged carcass. Why then should best practice guidance state that head shots should be avoided except for humane dispatch?

Well the reason is that there are very few stalkers who are capable of consistently dispatching deer humanely by head shooting. Those that do usually know their limits, being selective in its use and choosing to opt for an alternative shot placement if the distance is too great or they do not have a rock steady hold when taking aim.

Consider the basic facts. While the head might appear to offer a reasonably large target, the brain itself is very small; no bigger than a tennis ball in fallow deer; in the young considerably smaller. While there may be some compensation for error through the damage done by an expanding bullet, if the shot is not reasonably accurate there is a high risk of the bullet failing to hit the brain area located high in the head towards the back of the skull. Add to this the fact the head is a part of the anatomy that is highly mobile and capable of turning in an instant then you have a recipe for disaster.

Most stalkers will have the skill to shoot a 4in group at 100m under range conditions and indeed prove so when achieving their DSC1 qualification. However, this is no guarantee that while stalking they are capable of shooting within a 2in group required for a head shot when subjected to the added pressures of the effects of wind, distance and time. In addition to the skill required to shoot to this tolerance there is a high risk of failing to hit the head in exactly the right place, resulting in a lost animal that, unless found, will suffer a slow painful death. Typical of inaccurate head shots are injuries to the lower face and jaw. So, unless you are an extremely confident and accurate shot, it is not a shot to contemplate taking.

If you have any doubt over the matter you should consider undertaking the 'orange test' as described by a trusted stalking friend, David Brown, one of the best rifle shots I have had the pleasure to stalk with:

The Orange Test

This is designed to test yourself or a fellow stalker and provoke thought in respect of the risks associated with head shooting. It will also dispel the myth that stalkers can achieve the same accuracy and consistency while stalking as they can in a zeroing type situation. You should appreciate that practice is different to zeroing!

1. Prepare a number of targets from empty four pint milk containers and skewer a small orange into each. The container represents the head of a fallow and the orange is the brain within it.
2. Position the targets on sticks in a safe area of woodland at varying angles at distances from 25–120m to facilitate shots to be taken from the prone and standing position. In addition, include a target to be shot using a fence post or tree rest.
3. Take your friend for a simulated stalk and, as each target comes into view, put them under pressure to shoot quickly from the different positions. They must, of course, ensure a safe backstop exists on each occasion.

Not many stalkers will hit the orange within the container every time and they will be able to draw their own conclusions about the potential outcome and how this may influence future shot placement.

If a head shot is necessary a shot from behind is the preferred position, the point of aim being at the back of the head in the area of the atlas joint on a vertical line between the ears. In humane dispatch situations at close range, a shot to the front of the head or from any angle may have to be taken. Care needs to be taken with a head-on shot, especially when a beast has its head up looking down its nose at you.

The shot must be high up in the head to avoid the nasal cavity. The point of aim on the horizontal should be on an imaginary line between the eyes and base of the ears. From a full profile position the point of aim should be below the ear and towards the back of the head.

Reaction

The reaction to a well-executed head shot will be an instant collapse and instantaneous death. If the shot is misplaced then the animal may react in a similar way by collapsing but will not be dead. It may then quickly get up and run, particularly if disturbed, thus making it very difficult to dispatch with a second shot. This reaction may also be observed from a fallow buck if the bullet strikes part of the antler. Alternatively, there may be no discernible reaction as the animal turns and runs. A moribund deer may twitch and paddle post mortem but should cease after about thirty seconds.

Above: The point of aim on a wounded buck

Right: An attempted head shot, the bullet passing through the antler

Neck Shots

In my early stalking days I was encouraged to take neck shots, this being the preferred shot placement. Today, it is still a shot that I will occasionally take when the right circumstances exist and I am confident of a humane shot. It is practised by many stalkers motivated by the extra premium paid by the game dealers for a clean carcass. However, best practice guidance suggests it should generally be avoided and this again is because of the high risk of wounding.

A neck shot will prove fatal if the spinal cord (vertebral column) is severed. But beware, as with head shots, unless executed correctly it is not the most humane of shots and may result in a wounded animal that will be very mobile and difficult to dispatch. If the animal is not found a slow death through enforced starvation or asphyxiation is a likely consequence of a poor neck shot.

The risk of wounding is high as the target area, the vertebral column within the neck, is relatively narrow and there is a risk of the bullet missing this and travelling through the flesh below where the windpipe and oesophagus lie. As with the head, the neck is also a very mobile part of the body and may move as the shot is about to be taken, resulting in a clear miss or wound. There is also a risk that if the shot is high in the neck a miss may hit the lower head region, such as the jaw, and this will not be immediately fatal. For this reason, placing the point of aim lower down the neck where there is less movement can be a safer option. The enlarged neck of a fallow buck during the rut is a great temptation on which to consider placing a shot but remember the vital killing area remains the same; it is the non-fatal zone that has increased in size.

Point of aim for the neck shot. This will vary according to the position of the animal

Reaction

The reaction to a well-placed neck shot will be an immediate collapse and death. If the shot is misplaced an immediate collapse may also result, followed by the animal remaining either immobile but still alive or immediately regaining its feet and running, in which case an immediate second shot should be taken if safe to do so.

Chest Shots

The chest shot is the commonly accepted shot in most circumstances and provides for the largest target, giving a greater degree of latitude than the head or neck shot. It is also likely to be the most static area of the body and even where the vital organs are not hit, major blood vessels will be severed causing a rapid loss of consciousness as the blood circulation ceases.

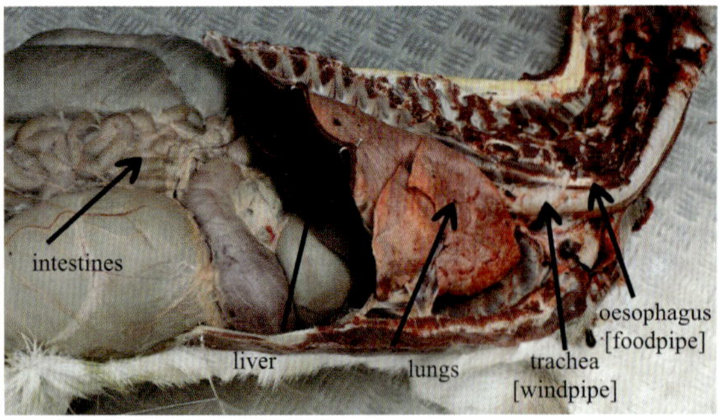

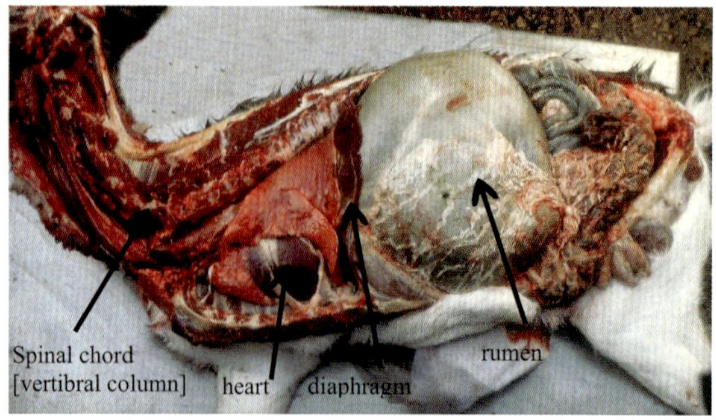

The preferred shot to the chest is a horizontal aim at the deer stood broadside, a third to halfway up the chest cavity area and ideally just behind the shoulder. This position on a fallow will appear just below the horizontal midline of the main body of the animal. Many stalkers will use the vertical line of the foreleg as a guide.

The research commissioned by the BDS referred to earlier found the highest success rate in shooting deer was achieved through chest shot placement as opposed to head and neck shots. It is the shot recommended within the best practice guidance and through DSC1 qualification teaching, both of which are endorsed by the British Deer Society (BDS). However, it is not without its problems if due care is not taken in shot placement (the point of aim). This is particularly important when the animal is not facing perfectly broadside, which is often the case. In this situation a thorough understanding of the deer's internal anatomy is essential to be able to place the bullet so that its internal passage through the body coincides with the vital organs.

Above and right: Knowledge of a deer's internal anatomy is essential

Below: Deer clock chart

To provide an insight into the path of a bullet when shots are taken from varying degrees to the 90 degree angle a useful 'deer clock' is shown within the best practice guidance available from The Deer Initiative*[37]. This is based on the 'elk clock' theory used by Swedish hunters that provides a diagrammatical insight into the extent to which the killing zone (chest/lung area) is exposed at varying angles to the stalker's position. A simplified version of the deer clock is shown.

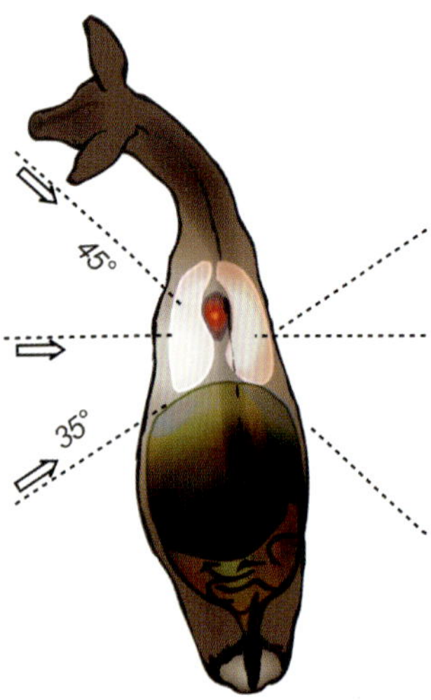

In studying the clock shown you will appreciate that the 'angle' of shot as it enters the body of a deer is a key factor in achieving a lethal shot. In consequence, the point of aim will vary according to the angle at which the animal is positioned to you. You will note the extent to which the point of aim must be adjusted when a beast is stood at an angle to you, be it facing towards or away from you. For shots outside these angles the point of aim will have to be adjusted but will inevitably result in the path of the bullet passing through the rumen and diaphragm if facing away and conversely if facing towards you. Therefore these shots should be avoided with the exception of attempting to dispatch a wounded animal.

37 www.thedeerinitiative.co.uk/html/bestpractice

This point of aim will achieve a humane shot without contamination of the carcass as the bullet will pass in front of the diaphragm. However, it will damage both shoulders and many stalkers will be tempted to take the point of aim further back to minimise this. In doing so the bullet is likely to pass through the rumen and any error may result in a wounded beast. It is better to wait for the opportunity to take a cleaner shot when the beast turns and presents at a wider angle.

Above: This shot will be lethal but damage both shoulders

Left: The debatable point of aim for the chest shot

This point of aim for the chest shot will achieve humane dispatch of the animal by destroying vital organs*[38]. It also provides for some margin of error and a clean carcass unless a shoulder is caught. Many experienced shots will take a point of aim just off the shoulder but ensuring the shot is still well forward of the diaphragm. Taking the point of aim slightly higher will also be fatal and increase the margin of error of a low shot.

38 Details of shot placement and the positioning of vital organs can be found on The Deer Initiative Best Practice website, www.thedeerinitiative.co.uk/html/bestpractice

In discussing the topic of shot placement with deer consultant and stalker Patrick Faulkner, he described an excellent teaching tool – a polystyrene beaker that, when pierced through with a needle to mimic the track of a bullet, provides an inside view of a cavity representing that of the inside of a deer. This simple but effective means of viewing angles provides for the novice stalker an insight into the path of a bullet through an animal. This theory can be built on by the careful examination of the insides of shot deer, examining both the entry and exit of the bullet. Not all bullets, of course, will exit and some will break up and be lodged on the opposite side of the entry wound or elsewhere. A thorough examination of a carcass comparing your recollection of the circumstances of the shot and the perceived position of the animal at the time is a valuable learning experience. This experience is often the proof that what you thought was a deer stood perfectly broadside actually turned out to be one stood at an angle when the shot was taken.

Reaction

The reaction to a fatal chest shot is likely to be a leap or lunge forward followed by short run and collapse. If the beast was alert and about to take flight as a result of your

Above: Patrick's beaker demonstrating a three-dimensional view of the angle of shot through the body

Right: A leap or lunge forward is a typical reaction to the chest shot presence just prior to the shot, the run before collapse may be considerable. I have known this to be in excess of 60m, but generally you should expect to find the beast within 30m.

If the shot is very low it is likely to pass through the heart, resulting in a leap forward, often with a kick back, then a short fast run and collapse.

If the shot is too high and has touched the spine an immediate collapse may result with the animal alive but paralysed, requiring a further shot to dispatch it.

A shot slightly forward where the bullet strikes through one or both shoulders will usually be fatal and may result in an immediate collapse or a short run before collapsing.

A shot too far forward runs the risk of wounding in the front shoulder, top foreleg or brisket area. The animal may stagger or collapse at the shot but regain itself and run, even on three legs. A further shot will then be required.

A shot too far back behind the diaphragm in the area of the liver or stomach will not be immediately fatal and the animal may move off slowly and hunch up, requiring an immediate second shot. If the shot is low and back (low gut) the deer may run a considerable distance before couching up and require dispatching. (See photograph of fallow doe found dead on page 155 and pricket on page 95.)

Reaction to a Clean Miss

A clean miss at an undisturbed animal may result in no more than an inquisitive stare or a sudden head up and short run, standing again with head up in a 'ready for flight' mode. If a fallow shows no reaction to the shot and pronks away and stands, this normally signifies a clean miss. The trait of pronking is described in Chapter 1.

There is a danger of being too prescriptive with regard to the reaction to any particular shot. On many occasions I have failed to notice any apparent reaction to a shot and, not hearing a strike either, assumed a miss only to find a dead beast close by with the shot placed perfectly. So you should always keep an open mind and never assume a miss or be fixated by where you think the bullet has struck. On occasions the experience of stalking fallow has a habit of proving us all wrong.

Taking Additional Shots

In maximising your opportunity to achieve your cull you may have decided prior to the shot to attempt to shoot more than one animal from the same group and this may influence your shot placement and choice of the first beast to be shot. Taking a neck shot in the knowledge that the deer will fall instantly is a distinct advantage when attempting to shoot additional animals, which following the shot may remain for long enough for you to shoot. In this situation taking a chest shot may result in the beast running a short distance and spooking others into flight, making it difficult to shoot additional animals. But to do this you must be confident of the first shot killing cleanly. If you are not, it may be better to opt for the safety of the recommended chest shot in the hope that an opportunity will still present itself for additional shots. Try not to be too ambitious and be satisfied with one humanely shot deer if that is what results. As they say, you should 'cut a stick when you see it' and this is very relevant to the culling of fallow that may not be there to be shot on the next occasion.

Extra care is required when additional shots are taken to ensure adequate backstops are present and that the target deer is stood clear of other animals that may otherwise be wounded accidently through the bullet's continued path. This is just as important as taking the correct point of aim. In taking the decision to shoot you should be mindful of the risk of orphaning fawns that, while they may no longer be totally dependent on the dam, nevertheless will not do as well without her protection. In these circumstances, early in the doe season, your intention should be to shoot the fawn first, even if this aggravates the chances of shooting the doe immediately after.

Follow-Up

In the vast majority of cases if you have taken care with your shot placement the deer will have died instantly from the shot, albeit it may have run a short distance before collapsing. It is always useful to follow a shot deer visually and mark its position where it drops against a recognisable feature. Having climbed down from a high seat or negotiated a ditch you may find the view somewhat different in the follow-up.

Even if you are confident of a fatal shot, you should never assume such and care should be taken when going forward to find the beast. Always be prepared to take a further shot on the approach if it is not dead and it is safe to do so. As outlined above, the observed reaction to your chosen shot placement will provide you with valuable information on which to judge whether the shot is a fatal one. If the reaction is one that indicates a possible wound, then a further shot will be necessary. If this has not been possible and the deer has run off into cover and disappeared then care needs to be taken with any follow-up action.

It is good practice to wait for a few minutes following any shot taken, longer if you suspect the animal to be wounded (at least thirty minutes). The old stalkers would light a cigarette and when smoked would make their move. While I would not encourage any stalker to smoke, waiting a short while is a good tactic; allowing for other deer to depart and giving yourself the opportunity to take note of exactly where the deer was stood, the direction taken when last seen and (before you leave it) the place you took the shot from. This latter point is of particular importance in woodland situations where the cover may be dense and you require a reference point when searching. A piece of white tissue wrapped around a branch at head height is sufficient.

Examining the Strike Area

Where the beast has run off and cannot be seen, and you are not confident of a fatal shot or suspect a complete miss, careful examination of the ground and vegetation in the area of where the beast stood is vital. Evidence of blood (sometimes referred to as paint) and its depth of colour may suggest where the bullet has struck, e.g. bright red being arterial, light and frothy indicating the lungs and dark blood may be the liver area. You may find hair (pins) that may give a clue as to where the bullet has struck the body. If the bullet has grazed the beast then this will often result in copious amounts of cut hair being scattered around. Tissue and bone may also be found and the size of fragments may indicate the strike area. Be prepared to search and search again for evidence until exhausted. The absence of evidence of a strike has to be viewed with some concern but by no means should you assume a miss.

Following a Blood Trail

If you find blood there may be sufficient to determine a blood trail that you can follow, moving quietly and carefully as you look for the deer ahead, checking out anything suspicious with your binoculars. You should consider turning the magnification down on your scope and refocusing in preparation for a possible close range shot. If the trail runs out and the deer is not found within a reasonable distance then it is better to use a dog at this stage and resist the temptation to go on searching endlessly. If you do not have a dog immediately available then postpone your search until you have arranged this.

Below left: Examine the ground and vegetation carefully for blood

Below middle: Snow on the ground makes finding blood far easier

Below right: Do not restrict your search to ground level. The blood at head height on the tree trunk was the result of shooting the injured sorel from a high seat, as featured in Chapter 6

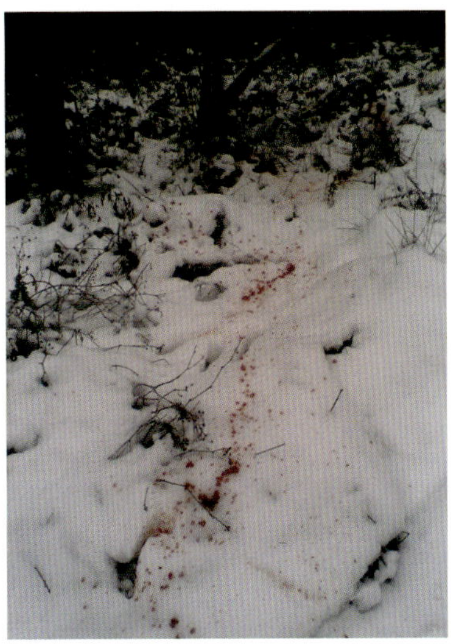

Once you have the dog there it should be used to track from the original strike area. Ideally you should have some assistance in this operation, enabling one person to track and control the dog and the other to be close and available to shoot a wounded animal if necessary.

Great care should be taken with tracking in this situation as you are likely to suddenly come up close to the injured beast lying down but with its head up and alert. Your tactic should be to spot it well in advance, enabling you to stalk in as close as necessary to assess the backstop and take a careful head or neck shot to dispatch it. Be extremely careful not to stalk in too close because if the animal sees, scents you or hears you it may spring to its feet suddenly and run. This is one reason that I have never supported the desire for any stalker to possess a pistol for humane dispatch. It is simply unnecessary and more likely to create a problem than solve one. Where it is necessary to take a shot at very short range ensure you place your point of aim high enough to compensate for the increased angle of alignment between barrel and scope. You will only know this allowance if you have practised on artificial targets at varying short distances. If the beast is stood, a shot to the chest should be taken if possible and if moving, providing a safe backstop is assured, any shot likely to dispatch the animal should be taken.

Shot placement should be to the head or neck when dispatching a wounded beast in these circumstances

Where the beast appears dead your approach should again be a careful one, checking constantly for any signs of life and in a state of readiness should there be a sudden movement and the need for a further shot. Once you have confirmed the animal is dead through the eye reflex test it should be bled and gralloched immediately in line with best practice*[39], making sure you have made your rifle safe in the first instance.

39 www.thedeerinitiative.co.uk/html/bestpractice

Never assume a miss even when there is no evidence of a strike. My advice is to never give up on a search until it has been exhausted, ideally with the assistance of a tracking dog. As a general rule, it is always better to wait than to charge in. A wounded deer, un-chased, will soon couch up. Adrenalin will subside and a planned follow-up after perhaps an hour is more likely to produce a successful outcome.

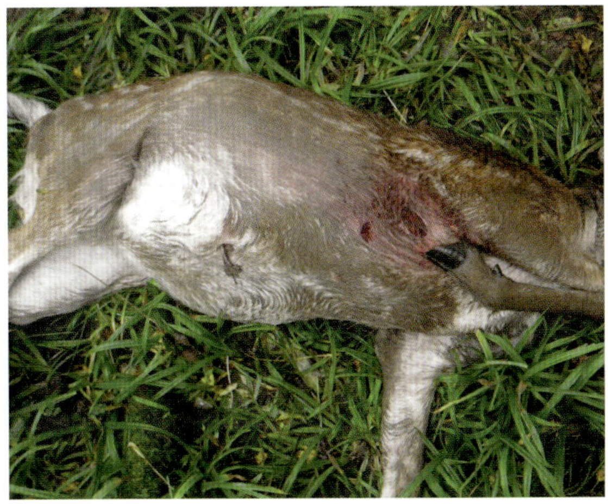

The result of a shot low and back. The stalker had no dog and failed to find this doe on the day it was shot

Chapter 8

Identifying Disease by Peter Green, BVSc Cert EO MRCVS

In the last chapter John took you as far as the shot. You have stalked carefully in to the deer, made certain of a safe backstop, found a secure rifle rest and waited for the deer to turn into a suitable position to make a clean humane shot. But how do you know this deer is healthy and well? And when you have culled the deer and you get up to the carcass, how can you assess whether or not the venison is safe to eat? Certainly, there is a widespread belief that venison is a 'healthy' meat; we are told that it has less fat than domesticated red meat and it goes without saying this wild deer will have received no chemicals, medicines or additives that might be undesirable. On the whole, all this is correct: wild deer in the UK are generally very healthy – but there are some exceptions and although 99 per cent of the fallow deer on your patch may be in blooming good health, you cannot take for granted that every single animal will be free of disease.

Before the Shot

So let us start at the beginning: looking at the individual deer that you are watching through your scope or field glasses – how close can you get to it? We sometimes need to be careful about being too proud of our field craft. We might be pretty impressed with ourselves that we have managed to creep up to this deer to within 30m: what outstanding skill! How quiet and stealthy and well camouflaged we must have been. But wait a minute, the truth is that if you have managed to get within 30m of a wild adult fallow deer, you ought to be thinking: is there something wrong with this animal?

Lesson One is simple: deer behave in a predictable way. Before you shoot the deer, try to get into the subconscious habit of checking it is behaving normally. Most experienced stalkers find themselves doing this without thinking about it; having seen so many normal and healthy deer, and seen so many fallow disappear at the faintest rustle of clothing or snap of a twig, alarm bells begin to sound when a deer appears to ignore what ought to spook it. Of all the UK deer, perhaps with the exception of sika in dense woodland, fallow are probably the cutest when it comes to picking up the presence of the stalker. If an individual deer stays behind when all others flee, or stays couched when every other group member is up and alert, you should question its healthiness.

Lesson Two is similar: deer move in a predictable way. Even though you may not be able to see its legs because of understory, or crops or long grass, you can tell if a deer is lame by watching the way its body moves. Is it hopping, or limping, or moving in a way that seems, well … just odd? Can you see any wounds or apparent deformities? Are its antlers symmetrical? Is its back end soiled by diarrhoea? All these factors may give you clues before the shot that the deer is somehow compromised and will alert you to be vigilant when you are dressing it out.

This is important because of a very obvious fact: if there are a hundred fallow deer on your patch and one of them is diseased or disabled, the likelihood of you finding this deer in a shootable situation is far greater than for the other ninety-nine. If you have a problem in your herd with a particular infection, or with a heavy internal parasite burden, it will be the worst affected animals that unwittingly self-select for culling. These are the ones that will be under the weather, slightly depressed, sluggish and off their guard. These are the deer that will linger last when all others have bounded off over the hill or into the thicket, so be alert to unusual behaviour or appearance before the shot.

Before the Gralloch

Let us assume all is apparently normal as you stalk, spy and then cull the deer. You wait until the others have moved away before showing yourself and then you make your way to where the deer has fallen. Having confirmed death it is good practice to 'stick' or bleed the carcass, irrespective of your shot placement. If it is properly chest shot, a deep stab wound into the thoracic cavity between the base of the neck and the end of the sternum (breast bone) will probably yield little blood because the deer has already bled out into the chest cavity and there is no continuing circulation. But if you neck shot it, or head shot it, sticking it is essential because the heart may beat for many minutes and you want to drain the carcass of blood as soon as possible.

Look at the condition of the animal: is it emaciated? Can you feel the backbone and pelvis through the skin? Unless it is a buck that is really badly 'run-up' from the rut, an emaciated carcass should sharpen your attention to look for the reason why. Make sure you check both sides of the carcass. You will want to have the deer lying on its right side for the gralloch because the rumen and forestomachs are on the left; this will be the upper side as you remove all the internal organs. It is far easier to roll out the rumen without puncturing it if it is closer to you while you are working. Even if the deer is already lying on its right side turn it over on to its left side, check it and turn it back. Look at the coat: are there any obvious bare patches that you would not expect? If the light is good and you are not battling against falling twilight (a reason for preferring morning stalking), what external parasites can you see? As a rough guide, tiny speck-like parasites that move slowly are lice; larger, darker insect parasites that move quickly through the coat are keds and blob-like parasites that are stuck to the skin are ticks. Lice are small, less than 3mm in length, and are usually buff coloured or grey. Keds get on to the deer by flying and then shedding their wings; lice are transferred by direct contact, or rarely, by flies. Ticks get on to the deer by grabbing the hair as the animal moves through vegetation.

In some parts of the country all the deer have some external parasites. Moorland and heathland habitats tend to harbour

Above: Get into the habit of checking over the deer before starting the gralloch

Above left: The gralloch should be carried out with the beast lying on its right side

Left: Keds are large insect parasites that move quickly through the coat more ticks. Some external parasites are not a cause for concern but a very heavy tick infestation or a carcass crawling with lice may be a sign of debility from disease.

Check for abnormal discharges like diarrhoea from the anus or mucous or pus from the vulva. Apart from a small amount of soiling around the anus that sometimes occurs in bucks during the rut, the area under the tail should be clean in both sexes.

Before proceeding any further, check the ears for any ear tags. Deer are occasionally culled after being involved in a research project; rarely it may be an escapee from a deer farm (deer park deer are not tagged) or may have received dangerous drugs at some stage. The tag may give instructions about reporting the cull: if you have killed the deer on land where you are lawfully stalking, don't be concerned about making such a report, it will assist the research and you will not be criticised. If you find a tag that says EAT NOT, then do not eat the carcass or feed it to the dogs.

Dealing with a Carcass that is Obviously Unhealthy

If the deer lying at your feet is quite clearly abnormal, what should you do? It depends to some extent on the nature of the obvious abnormality. Concentrate on the body of the deer, not on the limbs. Broken legs, amputated legs, deformed legs, overgrown hooves and other leg problems are all quite common and generally do not affect the health of the deer, nor the suitability for human consumption.

If the body of the deer is abnormal, you should be more concerned. Perhaps it is severely underweight, even emaciated; perhaps it is abnormally bloated; perhaps there is an obvious wound, other than your bullet wound; perhaps there is profuse diarrhoea or a stinking discharge from the vulva. In such cases, you should make up your mind there and then not to eat the deer or sell it on for human consumption. That is the first and most important decision, irrespective of your anticipated income, the need to fill the freezer or the venison promised to a friend.

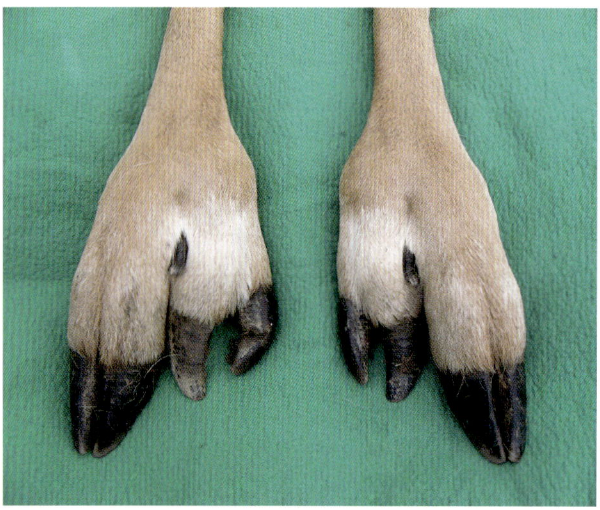

A rare abnormality known as polydactyly does not affect the health of the deer

Whether or not you decide to proceed to investigate the problem, detecting something that has affected the body of the deer to that extent is enough to indicate that it is safer not to eat it. If you do decide to open it up to have a look, proceed cautiously, wear gloves and open it up somewhere away from your larder or cold room.

Encountering Something Unusual Inside a Deer

Your culled fallow deer may appear perfectly healthy, or it may be obviously diseased. Whatever the case, from time to time you will encounter unusual things as you are gralloching or butchering. It is not your job to make a diagnosis or to identify specific diseases, although many stalkers become experts in recognising the more common conditions seen in UK deer. The foundation of the EC Game Meat Regulations, by which wild venison enters the food chain, is the reliability of 'trained hunters' to inspect and then certify the health of the deer carcasses they are handling. This does not mean all deer stalkers have to be pathologists because the mainstay of this arrangement is not the diagnosis of disease, but is the recognition of what is not normal. Your best tool in the recognition of something unhealthy is your knowledge and experience of what is healthy and normal. You may not know *what* is wrong, but you need to recognise that there is *something* wrong, because it is different from what you know to be normal.

The Lymph Nodes

You should be able to find the basic suite of carcass lymph nodes: the submandibular, retropharyngeal, bronchial and mesenteric. You might even recognise the mediastinal nodes in between the lungs and the portal nodes next to the liver. Your DSC1 and 2 qualifications will have trained you in this skill. Make it a routine practice to find them, look at them and know what is normal. Lymph nodes are the indicators of disease nearby; they become enlarged or abscessed when infection is present. As a good rule of thumb, if you are looking in the right place and you can't find them, they are normal. If they are large, be extra vigilant; if any of them are abscessed, stop dealing with the carcass and go no further. As we discuss below, any abscess is a potential case of TB and should be reported.

Later, if you are butchering the carcass you may come across the pre-scapular node in the muscles in front of the shoulder. This lymph node is always very big and may look alarming compared with the nodes in the chest and abdomen – don't worry, it is meant to be up to the size of a walnut in fallow deer.

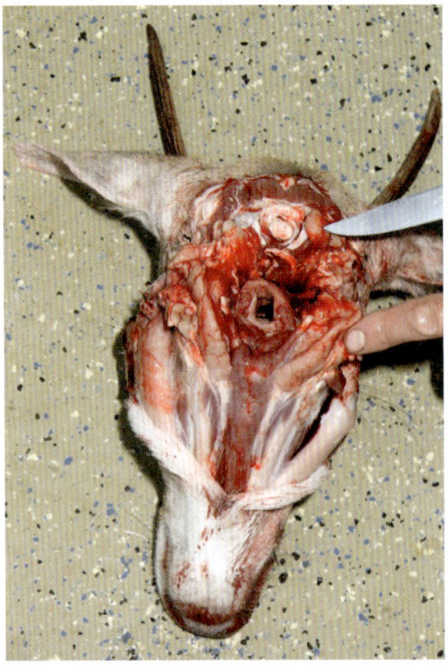

Fig 1

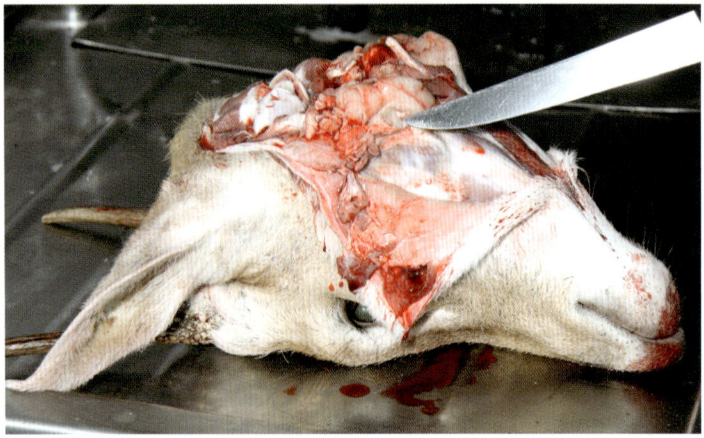

Fig 2

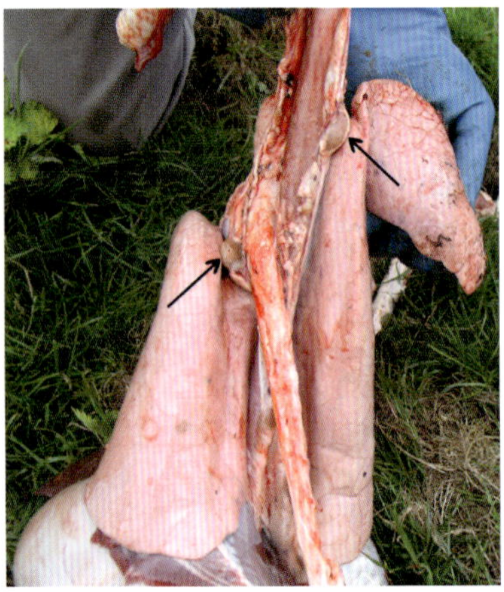

Fig 3

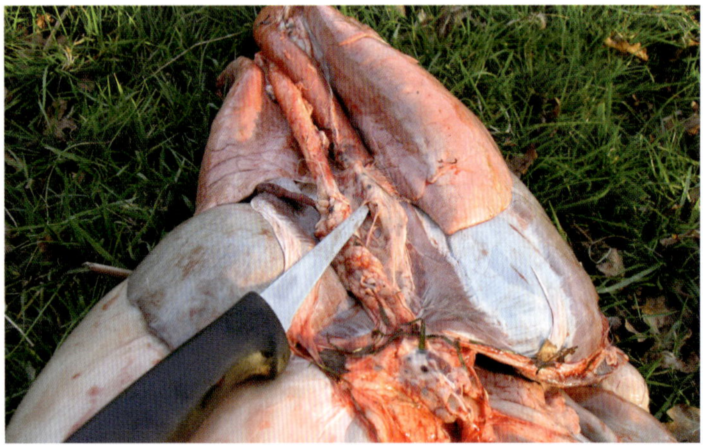

Fig 4

The suite of lymph nodes
Fig 1 Retropharyngeal
Fig 2 Submandibular
Fig 3 Bronchial
Fig 4 Mediastinal
Fig 5 Portal
Fig 6 The mesenteric lymph nodes in a circular chain within the coil of the spiral colon

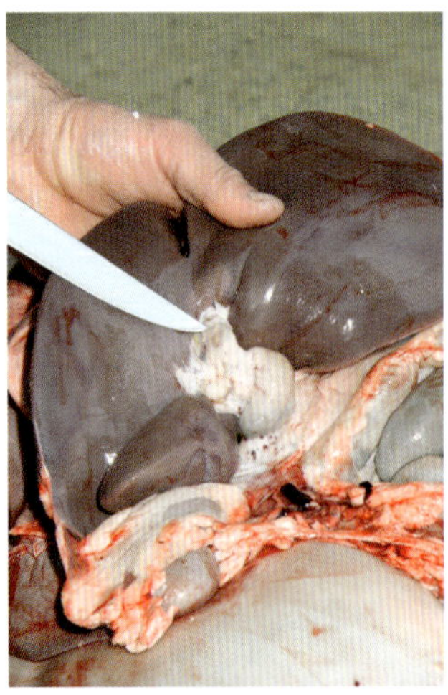

Fig 5

Fig 6

Disease Terminology

It will help to understand the basic terminology used to describe diseases and injuries in all mammals.

Inflammation is a term used when any tissue is pathologically stirred up. Classically, in living tissue, the signs of inflammation are reddening, swelling and heat because of increased blood supply and increased fluid between cells. In a deer carcass signs of inflammation are usually limited to the surfaces of the internal organs, particularly the guts and membranes of the abdomen. If any of these are angry looking, bright deep red or livid, the affected part can be described as inflamed. Extensive inflammation is a reason to bin the carcass.

An adhesion is an abnormal sticking or fusing together of parts that should normally be separate. The most common sites for adhesions are between the lungs and the internal chest wall and between different parts of the bowel. Adhesions are a legacy of inflammation that was present long ago. An adhesion of the lungs to the chest wall may be evidence of pneumonia or a penetrating rutting wound several years before. As the disease or injury healed the affected tissues alongside each other became stuck together with scar tissue. Adhesions are rarely an indication of current disease, unless there are also other abnormalities. A simple adhesion is no reason to condemn the carcass.

An abscess is a lump with a wall of fibrous tissue and a centre filled with pus. Abscesses come in all sizes and can be found in any tissue. The pus may be liquid like milk, it may be thick like custard or even firm and rubbery like cheese. But if you come across a lump with white, grey or yellow contents, it's an abscess. Sometimes abscesses are only discovered when they are incised accidentally; sometimes the lumps are obvious before they are opened up. In some diseases, like tuberculosis, the abscesses are usually seen before they are cut open; in others they are not so obvious. All abscesses are the result of infection, although in long-standing abscesses the infection may have died. Internal abscesses are a reason to reject the carcass, irrespective of the nature of the infection.

Adhesions on the left side of the internal chest wall – note the old injuries to the ribs 7–10 indicated

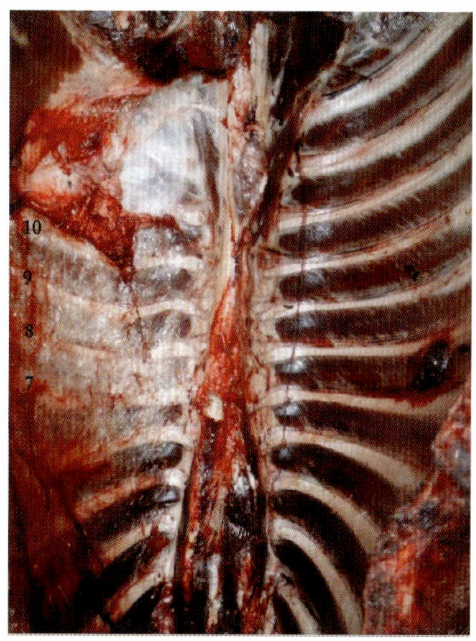

A cyst is an internal balloon filled with fluid that is usually more or less clear. Cysts tend to deflate when they are cut and the fluid is released because they usually have thin flimsy walls, in contrast to the firm walls of abscesses. Cysts can be caused by some parasites, or they may be the result of other, non-infectious disease processes.

A tumour is a lump of dense, living tissue. Strictly speaking, a tumour just means a swelling, but the term has come to mean a lump of abnormal tissue and hence a lump of cancerous tissue.

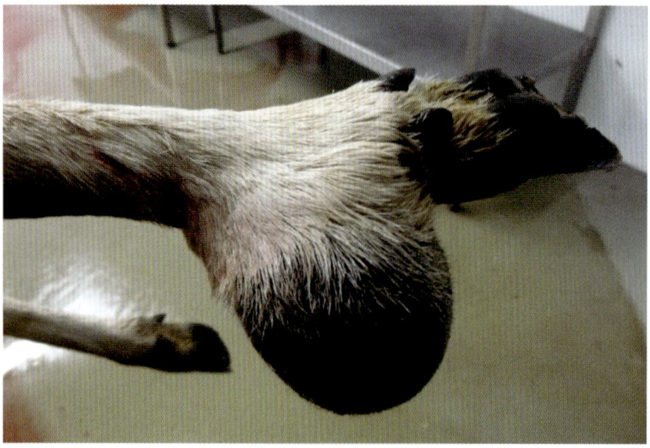

A tumour of the skin on the side of the lower limb

The cut surface of a tumour looks like a jumble of disorganised tissue; tumours are usually firm and they can occur anywhere, both internally and externally. If a tumour represents a malignant cancer, there may be further patches or lumps of abnormal tissue in the lungs, liver or other internal organs. Many tumours are benign and solitary; a single hard lump or nodule of tissue is no reason to reject a carcass, especially if it is in or on the skin.

A nodule is a small, rounded, firm lump of tissue. The term is usually employed to describe something that has been felt with the fingers or seen with the eyes, but not investigated. A nodule might turn out to be an abscess, or a tumour.

Traumatic injury comes in all forms and most stalkers will be able to recognise the after-effects of such damage. The bullet and wound channel is itself a traumatic injury, with associated bleeding, bruising and disruption of muscle, bone and internal organs. Rutting injuries, road traffic accidents, entanglement in fences, illegal sub-lethal calibres and other such traumas may leave lasting evidence such as healed limb fractures, internal adhesions and obvious repairs. Trauma is not a basis for condemning the carcass, although best practice would require that all bruised, damaged or blood-stained meat is discarded. See Chapter 4 for examples of injuries caused through sub-lethal calibre.

Specific Diseases of Fallow Deer in the UK

As we noted at the beginning of this chapter, fallow deer are generally very healthy. There are a few conditions that turn up fairly regularly and are interesting but not serious, and a very small number that are less common but more important.

Internal Parasites

Fallow deer commonly harbour a variety of internal parasites. The most common is a kind of lungworm that causes small, pea-sized nodules in the lungs. The worms are very small and are difficult to distinguish from the surrounding lung tissue when the nodules are cut open. You cannot usually see this lungworm infection on the surface of the lung, but you can detect the tiny lumps when you squeeze or roll the lung tissue between finger and thumb. There may be a grey or black stain on the surface of the lung above a worm nodule close to the surface. The worms belong to the group known as the metastrongyles. They do not cause significant disease and can be ignored.

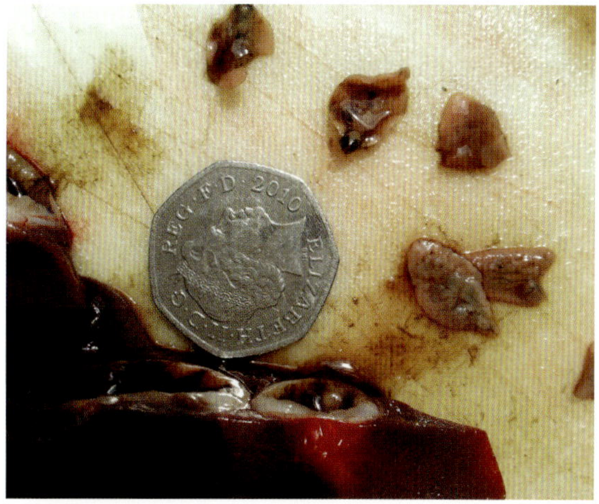

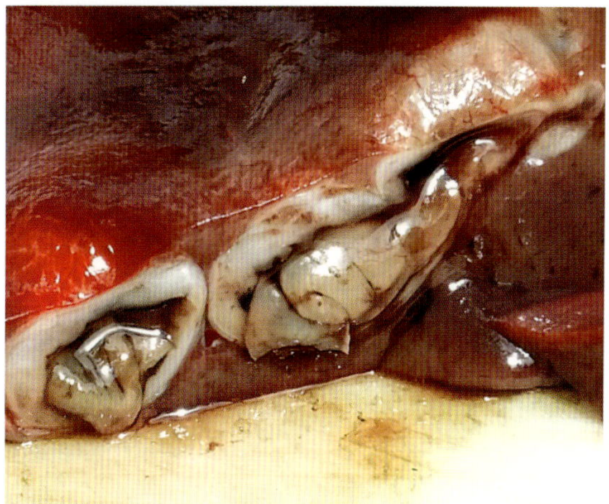

Liver fluke

Liver fluke (*Fasciola hepatica*) is regularly seen in fallow. Affected livers have dense white or light brown patches that are tough to cut. The flukes can often be squeezed out of the bile duct tubes inside the liver; they are leaf-shaped and about the size of a 5p coin. This fluke is exactly the same species that infects farm animals. Deer with liver fluke are usually in good condition; only in very severe infections do the flukes affect the animal. Flukey livers should be discarded but the venison is safe to eat.

Tape worm cysts are sometimes seen on the abdominal or thoracic organs. They are usually thin-walled balloons that range from grape sized to grapefruit sized and represent the intermediate stage in the life history of tapeworms (*Taenia hydatigena*) that live as adults in the bowel of dogs, foxes, badgers, stoats and weasels. The cysts are called 'hydatid cysts'. They are not serious and the carcass can be used for human consumption, but the offal should not be fed to dogs. A much rarer form of tapeworm cyst (*Echinococcus granulosus*) consists of tennis ball-sized cysts embedded in liver, lungs or other organs. The cysts have lots of little internal compartments. Affected carcasses should be discarded.

Occasionally fallow deer are infected with a 'bot' that lives in the pouches at the back of the throat or in the oesophagus. They look like large maggots and are the larvae of a parasitic fly called the nose bot fly (*Cephenemyia*).

Internal Infections

Tuberculosis (TB) is caused by a bacterium. It is a legal requirement to notify the authorities of any suspicion of TB. The disease affects fewer than 1 per cent of UK wild deer, but some areas have a higher prevalence in fallow herds. TB causes internal abscesses; these can assume a wide variety of forms, from multiple small abscesses in lungs or in the mesenteric lymph nodes to single large abscesses almost anywhere. You should therefore *treat any internal abscess in a deer as a possible case of TB* and notify DEFRA by contacting your divisional veterinary manager (DVM). Stop processing the carcass; put it somewhere out of the reach of scavengers and cover it up. The DVM will tell you what to do.

Above: A sorel in poor condition. This animal was suffering from tuberculosis

Right: Overgrown hooves, often caused by infection in the joints of the toes

Other notifiable diseases include foot and mouth disease, bluetongue and epizootic haemorrhagic disease. These are all very rare in deer and are unlikely to occur unless there is an outbreak in farm animals, in which case you would be alert to the possible occurrence in deer. In the event of such an outbreak, details of what to look for in deer would be widely publicised.

Johne's disease (paratuberculosis) causes inflammation and thickening of the bowel wall and diarrhoea. Deer can be infected for a long time before they show clinical signs, but if you find a deer with very loose faeces and thickened guts, it is one of the possible causes.

Septic arthritis is common in fallow deer. It is usually caused by a bacterium called Yersinia. Affected deer have swollen joints, which may lead to lameness and deformation of the limbs. Incised joints are thickened and may contain pus rather than clear joint fluid. If the bottom joints of the toes are infected, the hooves may grow long and curled into 'Aladdin's Slippers'. Yersinia can also cause diarrhoea, especially in fawns.

Non-Infectious Diseases

Fallow deer can succumb to illness caused by things other than infection. Deer that gorge on cereals, sheep feed or other concentrates can become very sick and die from rumenal acidosis. Affected deer are dull and may have diarrhoea. The rumen will be full of the unnaturally rich food.

After top-dressing crops or grass with high nitrogen fertiliser in the spring deer may be affected by the compounds used and may be encountered in a poor state, lying about, depressed or even found dead. This is especially the case if there has been a drought after the fertiliser was applied and the deer have grazed the crops before any rain has dissolved the nitrogen granules. There are no specific internal signs.

Female fallow may carry mummified fawns in the uterus without appearing sick. If the cervix remains closed the dead fawn does not become infected and may shrivel up; if the cervix opens and infection enters, there will be pus and the doe is more likely to be ill.

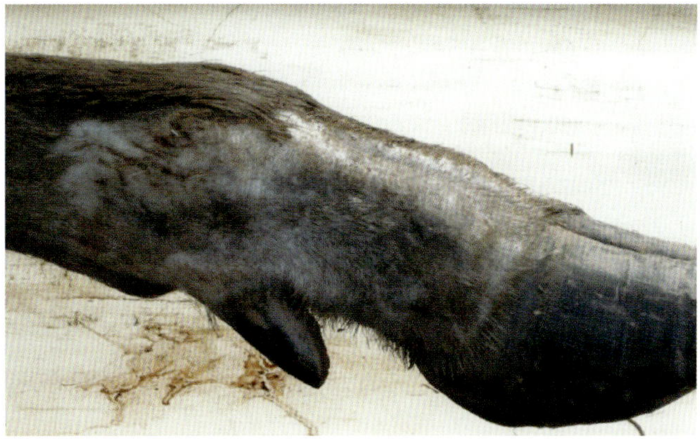

Digital dermatitis of the lower limb in a fallow buck

Skin Disease

Apart from external parasites, fallow deer are encountered regularly with warty tumours of various sizes. These are called fibromas and are not serious. Occasionally the lower limbs get a crusty bacterial infection, which leads to areas of baldness above the hooves; again, this can be ignored.

Conclusion

Think of every gralloching exercise as a post-mortem examination. Just like deer in life, you can learn to spot unusual things in deer after death. You may not know what you have found, but you can be so familiar with what is normal that you pick up the abnormal when you come across it. The European Game Meat Regulations provide stalkers with an immense privilege: you can produce meat for human consumption without it passing through an abattoir and without it being examined by a professional meat hygiene official. Under the so-called 'hunter's exemption' stalkers are trusted to check carefully for signs of disease or illness in the deer they cull both before and after it is killed. This is a great responsibility and should not be taken lightly. It is not just a matter of the health of the deer but also a matter of the hygiene of the gralloch and the handling of the carcass. Hopefully all of us would discard a carcass that is obviously diseased, but it is easy to spoil a perfectly healthy carcass by bad gralloching technique or bad carcass management. If in doubt about the suitability of a carcass for human consumption, make the safe choice and bin it.

Learn to remove the bowels and rumen without leaving a trace of faeces or bowel contents on the carcass. Carcasses should be cooled and hung properly. If you skin a carcass, the outside of the skin, the fur side, should not touch the meat at any stage.

Hopefully all UK deer stalkers maintain great respect for the deer they cull. This respect will influence our shooting, so that we do not take risky shots that cause non-fatal wounds. We must respect the carcass and deal with it efficiently and hygienically; this is because we have respect for the people who will consume and enjoy the venison we are producing. It's a great privilege, but a job well done brings great rewards.

Chapter 9

The Waiting Game

Stalkers spend a considerable amount of time waiting for deer to come to them. When they do, the stalker is usually in the pound seat with the odds in his favour, particularly if 15ft up in a high seat among the trees.

In recent years the use of high seats in the UK has become increasingly popular commensurate with the rise in deer numbers of all species, particularly fallow. This rise has emphasised the need for active management through culling in targeted areas of vulnerable habitat and crops, where high seats can be most effective. Their use in helping achieve culls safely and humanely, especially in areas of high usage by the general public, has been recognised by The Deer Initiative (D.I.). In collaboration with the Forestry Commission, both steel semi-permanent and aluminium portable high seats have been provided to support landowners and managers in areas across England and Wales where high deer impacts are of concern. The use of high seats has also been incorporated within the D.I. best practice guidance and all stalkers should familiarise themselves with this, details of which can be found on the D.I. website[*40].

High seats have been popular with hunters on the Continent for many years. As you travel through some countries in Europe you will notice high seats are a common feature within the rural landscape and sometimes even within the suburbs of major towns. One of the reasons for their popularity has been their use in the management of wild boar populations, where shooting from high seats is a most effective method. Wild boar are often driven to waiting rifles and so, for good observation and safety reasons, the use of high seats has distinct advantages. You will also note that many of these seats in Europe are substantial constructions; usually made out of wood and with a roof on to keep the occupant warm and dry. Many are designed to enable the user to stand in as well as sit, thus providing a distinct advantage in the technique of shooting at running boar where the feet can be positioned appropriately.

Some Continental seats amount to elaborate tree houses and are quite luxurious if you have had the privilege to occupy one. In the UK many of the seats used and built

40 www.thedeerinitiative.co.uk

by the Forestry Commission are of substantial construction and similar to those built by our European neighbours. Over-elaborate seats may raise the question of whether you may incur liability for planning consent and advice is given in this regard later on page 177. However, the vast majority of seats used by recreational stalkers are pretty basic by comparison, offering little or no protection against the elements. They nevertheless serve their purpose provided they are correctly sited and used, even if they are not always well received by our foreign guests.

A seat in Germany (a Hochsitz) used by the author in severe weather conditions

No stalker should doubt the effectiveness of high seats or the skill required in their use. They can be an important management tool in helping you to achieve your cull. Shooting from high seats is not stalking in the true sense of the word but nevertheless many of the techniques of stalking need to be deployed for a successful outcome. The tactics of when, where, and how to use high seats can be a sporting challenge. Many stalkers including myself enjoy this challenge. Success depends on a number of key factors, not least your ability to be patient and, on occasions, tolerate the cold. I have found that being ultimately successful extends one's patience and with the availability now of superior clothing compared to my early stalking days, much can be done to mitigate the cold.

Advantages

Shooting from a high seat offers so many distinct advantages, not least from a safety perspective. They provide for unhurried, accurate shooting, with the advantages of angled trajectory into safe backstops. They allow you longer periods of observation and, as the quarry is often undisturbed, this enables you to be more selective when shooting. They also have the advantage of reducing the curse of your scent being carried directly at ground level to your intended quarry, although you must still take account of the wind and the potential for scent to be carried. Used against fallow, high seats can be most effective if deployed in the right place at the right time. So they have their time and place in the stalker's calendar, albeit many of us prefer the challenge of actively stalking our quarry on foot. However, there is no reason why you cannot combine the two tactics, particularly in the winter months where fallow can be stalked throughout the day. The techniques of both are dealt with in detail in Chapter 6 on Stalking Techniques.

We should, of course, acknowledge the ancillary pleasure that can be derived from sitting quietly up a high seat in the countryside. On almost every outing there is something of interest to observe. Seeing the first light emerge in the early morning as the countryside awakens and the fading light of late afternoon, each throwing an amazing contrast of changing colours, adds to the mystique of dawn and dusk. In a high seat you are in the equivalent of an observation hide, so even if you don't see a deer it is a great opportunity to see wildlife.

I have witnessed many fascinating encounters with all manner of birds, mammals and insects. If you sit quietly and well hidden in the countryside for a long period of time you will see nature as it is; undisturbed in its true environment. Harrier and barn owl endlessly hunting the woodland margin, hobby in pursuit of bats in the darkening and nightjar emerging are but a few of the privileged sightings I have witnessed. One evening, on my stalking ground at Hereford, I was privy to a tawny owl's attempt to take a weasel. A fierce battle ensued among the dead leaves below the woodland

View from a high seat in the Brinsop Valley in Herefordshire

Check the interior for unwelcome guests – a hornet's nest in this case

canopy with the owl eventually giving up the challenge and the weasel living to fight another day. So no matter whether you encounter your quarry or not, when in a high seat there is always something of interest to pass the time of day.

Not all encounters with wildlife are as pleasurable as those described. I know of one forestry ranger who recounted an alarming experience of his own. He had climbed and entered his chosen seat in the darkness of a late summer morning. The seat was of the Thetford style with a roof with enough room to place the rifle alongside him while waiting for the light to come. Having settled down he became aware of the increasing intensity of the noise of buzzing insects. They were hornets. They had nested on the underside of the roof space and he had entered their living space! The hornets attacked and the ranger, having been stung a number of times, literally jumped out of the seat to the ground, breaking his ankle as he did. Lying on the ground injured and badly stung he passed out but fortunately regained consciousness and managed to get to his vehicle. His rifle, which had remained in the seat, was recovered later. The experience highlights the need for the checking of this type of seat for unwelcome guests at the relevant time of year.

Interesting experiences in high seats are not restricted to wildlife and occasionally life can become interesting when sat quietly 15ft up among the trees. The activities of other countryside dwellers can at times provide remarkable and memorable events.

Take for instance the woodland jogger who decides a call of nature is imminent and drops his shorts nearby without realising he is being observed from above. This happened recently while I was waiting for a fallow buck and my feeling was one of frustration at the time. I had stalked into the seat and taken up my position in a quiet, careful manner so as not to scupper the chance of seeing the buck. It was, after all, private woodland, and I had invested considerable time and effort to get into position. Not only that, the effect of his deed lingered on somewhat to spoil the ambience of the woodland. Despite this untimely disturbance the buck appeared within ten minutes of the jogger's departure and, who knows, he may even have moved the buck to me without realising it. I will not venture to relay some of the sexual encounters I have witnessed; no doubt your imagination and own experience will satisfy any curiosity. These situations when they arise may require early announcement of your presence if you want to avoid being accused of voyeurism. Needless to say there is more to sitting up a high seat than culling deer. However, not all public interventions are pleasurable or acceptable. Outright confrontations with individual members of the public can and do occur for a variety of reasons. How you should react to such confrontation and the consequences of actions taken are outlined later.

Assessing the Need and Location

You may consider high seats are essential in a client-based stalking enterprise where some control measures may be necessary to ensure safe shooting or where collaborative team culls are undertaken. On the other hand, you may be against their use for personal reasons or it may be that the owner of the ground does not wish them to be erected, in which case you will have to honour their wish. Not everyone appreciates their value and some see them as eyesores or likely to attract unwarranted adverse publicity. Some owners may object to seats being attached directly to trees for fear of possible damage to the tree itself, which is somewhat ironic since the seat is often required as a means of tree protection. With modern ratchet straps and a regular check on growing tension there should be no need for crude nails or screws to secure the seat and so damage to the actual tree can be kept to a minimum.

You should not discount the use of a ground level seat, often referred to as a doe box or deer hide. If the ground is high enough to give a panoramic view over a chosen area then there is no need to go higher. In this situation a seat may not be necessary at all if you consider the ground can be stalked in the conventional manner on foot. However, a doe box does afford you the option of spending a long period of time overlooking such an area in relative comfort with the advantages of a high seat situation should deer emerge. If you are unable to use high seats then you will have to concentrate yours efforts on other techniques to achieve your cull. If you see their use as an essential tool in your management plans then, given the freedom to use them, there are some key factors before you erect a seat that may influence your decisions and ultimate success.

A useful old doe box

If you are taking on new ground or reviewing an area you have had for some time an assessment of whether to invest the time and expense to erect high seats or change existing ones should be made. This will be based on your experience and knowledge of the ground and the success or otherwise of achieving your cull. If it is new ground your first consideration should be to consider whether a high seat is necessary and whether you can stalk and shoot effectively from ground level. Many stalkers tend to be too eager to put high seats in at every corner without due consideration of deer activity and consequently much time and effort can be wasted in having to relocate them. So take your time to study the habits of the deer in your area before embarking on the options of using high seats.

Assessment of the frequent comings and goings of fallow and their impact within your area are essential factors in deciding both the need and location. Seats should be located with some thought given to where you anticipate deer emerging to feed from, such as woodland edges and rides or travelling between areas of woodland and arable ground. You may know, through the experience of stalking the ground, that in certain areas it is difficult to approach discreetly on foot. This may be due to a lack of cover or simply that the topography renders the area unsafe to shoot into from a standing or prone position, having no backstop. You will find these are often the very places deer frequent for the reason that they have safe vantage points and you do not. That is why they are there. Try and see it from their point of view and you will quickly realise why they survive so well in the wild. These are the areas therefore to consider and give priority to, i.e. those areas that are flat or domed and where either the sighting of deer or the provision of a safe backstop is difficult.

The positioning of high seats can also help concentrate your efforts in vulnerable areas where the potential for crop damage is high. In addition, the forester or owner of the land can see from the position of a high seat that efforts are being made to resolve and prevent damage. So the key areas to consider will be those overlooking vulnerable crops, conservation areas and new plantations. Seats can also be particularly useful where high vegetation, such as bracken in early autumn, severely inhibits your ability to see enough of the quarry. Where a number of seats are to be used in close proximity, e.g. as in collaborative team culling, then further consideration should be given from a safety point of view to ensure they do not overlap potential shooting areas. This is elaborated upon in Chapter 11 on collaborative and team culls.

The view from a woodland edge seat positioned to protect crops overlooking an area where deer emerge. Some pruning is necessary

Having decided on the general area for a high seat now look for a position that provides a clear safe shooting distance to your intended quarry. Remember, it is the assessment of deer activity that dictates the area for the seat position. Walk about and survey the area, taking a number of views from differing points. You do not want to be too close to what I would refer to as the 'hot spots' or, conversely, too far. Your ideal range will be between 50 and 150 yards with an acceptance that deer at times may emerge very close to a seat or alternatively suddenly appear on the extremity of your chosen area. Both situations can be difficult to deal with, as elaborated upon in Chapter 6 on stalking techniques.

Ideally the position should provide you with some cover while in the seat and on its approach, enabling you to get to it discreetly. The position also needs to afford some clear sight lines. If the seat is overlooking crops, a woodland edge or open area there may be little to be done apart from pruning off a few branches around the seat or nearby. Remember, the slightest twig or vegetation can cause a bullet to deflect from its true course and so time spent in cutting back is not wasted. If you are placing the seat within woodland then more substantial clearing work may be needed to ensure you have sufficient clear areas to enable deer to be seen and to provide safe backstops. Dependent on the time of year, you may need to take into account the effect of the potential growth of the woodland canopy which may blank out key observation areas. If substantial clearing is to be done you should first ensure this is acceptable to the owner. Don't be put off a site in woodland on the basis of a restricted view from a standing position. Look up and try to visualise the view from higher up above the canopy. Usually the higher you go the more of the view you get.

A seat positioned in woodland to take advantage of the opportunities presented following selective thinning of trees and canopy

Selecting a Seat and Erection

The area chosen will dictate the type of seat, be it portable or permanent, i.e. a lean-to, free-stander or ground level doe box. Whether the seat is of metal or wood is a matter of personal choice, perhaps influenced by availability and cost. Wooden seats do have their advantages and in a woodland setting can look more in keeping. The majority of manufactured seats are of sensible height; 9 to 12ft to the seat being adequate. There is generally no advantage to go higher with a seat as this exposes the user to greater risk as well as expense and effort.

If there are suitable trees available then a lean-to type will be preferred since, when positioned correctly, they are less obvious, afford better cover and are cheaper to buy. But remember, in selecting a tree you must make an assessment to ensure it is safe to use. Check the tree is in good condition, is not rotting and is strong enough to provide a reasonably static position even in a good wind. No tree will stay completely still and most will move even in a moderate wind. The stronger the tree the less movement there will be when taking a shot. If the seat has to be removed immediately after use then a portable one will be most practical. Where there are no suitable trees available, in young plantation areas for example, your only choice will be a free-standing seat. If the seat area is not enclosed you will need some form of cover around the seat to mask your appearance and movement.

Below left: Where a seat has to be removed after use a portable seat is more practical

Below middle: Before erecting a seat assess the tree to be used from a safety point of view. In a gale all trees can move but if rotten they may fall

Below right: Freestanding seats may be your only option in plantation areas

Planning Permission

Some wooden free-standing seats are substantial constructions with windows and door giving the appearance of tree houses. As such they raise the question of whether planning permission should be sought from the local authority. This is somewhat of a grey area with regard to size and permanency but generally planning permission will not be required if the high seat is of sensible proportions and associated with forestry or agricultural protection. However, unusually large seats may turn the head of local planners or be inappropriate for the location selected. There becomes a point at which the sheer size and footprint of an over-elaborate seat may be viewed as development requiring planning permission. The vast majority of seats do not raise such concerns but if you intend to build something really big it may be wise to seek advice from your local planning authority.

Erection

Ideally you should seek assistance with the transport and erection of all but the light portable seats. In addition, I can assure you from experience and a little embarrassment at times, that two minds are better than one when it comes to on-site construction of some designs. Transporting the chosen seat can be a tiresome chore without mechanised transport, particularly if the ladder is all one piece. If the ground is not too wet you may be able to get close to the location with a trailer. If this is not

An ATV can make transport of a seat to the chosen site easy but awareness of the width is required if woodland rides are to be negotiated safely

possible an ATV can be used but, as there will be a considerable overhang, care should be exercised within woodland. The ladder on the majority of manufactured steel seats will be in two sections, which makes light of an otherwise awkward job. If the location is within woodland the last few yards or more will inevitably involve a physical carry.

Having decided on your position the seat should be erected and your final judgement made from it in situ. You will need to have a selection of tools to hand:

- Tool for constructing the seat e.g. Allen key, spanner
- Grease (copper slip)
- Ratchet strap or rope long enough to pass around the trees girth (lean-to)
- Pipe insulation with plastic ties for shooting rail
- Security chain and lock (optional for lean-to)
- Spade
- Pruning tools including long reach pole saw
- Brushcutter/strimmer
- Appropriate warning notice and fixings (see photograph on page 182)

Both feet of the ladder require a stable footing

Using the necessary tools, construct the seat on the ground and apply some grease to the fixings, screws and bolts to prevent corrosion and facilitate dismantling in the future. In erecting the most common lean-to type seat the ground at the immediate base of the tree should be cleared of any debris and if necessary a flat area prepared with the spade to support the feet of the ladder. If the ground is particularly wet you may need some form of ballast or membrane to prevent one or both feet sinking too far into the ground. Both feet of the ladder require a stable footing; if one sinks the ladder will tilt and be unsafe. On good ground the slight sinkage of both feet will be sufficient to provide a safe anchor.

Check the area of the tree where you estimate the back of the seat will rest and cut any branches off that may obstruct. Some seats can be heavy and the initial lift up into position is best done with some help. While still horizontal, place the feet in their approximate position on the ground first. Then, with assistance and using the ground as the fulcrum, lift the top of the seat up first above your head and walk it in towards the tree using the ladder rails as you go. Once the seat is upright and leaning against the tree minor adjustments to its position can be made.

You will appreciate the safety benefit of your assistant 'footing' the ladder while you climb it for the first time to secure the necessary strap or fixing to the tree. You will need to set the ladder at the correct 'rake' or angle to the tree. Too vertical a position will make climbing more difficult and the seat will be at an uncomfortable forward tipping angle. Conversely, if the ladder angle is too great stability will be lost and the sitting position will be tilted too far back. An angle of around 75 degrees is recommended. Use the one in four rule (one unit out for every four up). When the seat is secure, sit in it and make your final assessment. If you are not happy with it, particularly from a safety point of view, then find another place.

Once you are confident with the seat's position carry out any further work required to the actual seat. Fitting a security chain and lock will prevent the opportunist from interfering with or actually stealing the seat. The shooting rail is an important feature; its stability should be checked. On some designs the shooting support rail height and lateral position can be adjusted. If this is of galvanised steel or similar hard material I would advise you soften the surface in some way. Pipe insulation is ideal, although occasionally it may be damaged by birds and require replacing. It will provide you with a more comfortable and quiet lean, and reduce the potential for damaging your rifle or scope. It will also prevent any icing up in the winter months.

If the seat is of the plastic moulded type make sure there are some drainage holes in its base to prevent water retention. Cut any branches or foliage around the seat that are in your way or obstruct your view. Now have a good look around and visualise the opportunities you may have. There may be some obvious obstructions that restrict your view and their removal is best done by directing your assistant with the cutting gear to the offending branches or obstructions while you remain in the seat. If you are erecting a seat in the winter months you should bear in mind the view from the seat will change with the seasons. Account should therefore be taken of the increase in cover that spring will bring. The route to and from the seat should be cleared to ensure a quiet approach and departure can be made. Finally, as referred to later with regards to health and safety in areas of public access, a notice warning against unauthorised use should be placed in a prominent position on the ladder. Further steps to prevent misuse in certain situations may have to be taken to mitigate your liabilities and these may include the fitting of a shroud/guard to prevent climbing. In some locations removing the seat after use may be a sensible option.

Health and Safety Considerations

The use of high seats presents an obvious risk of injury to both stalker and others. As elaborated upon in Chapter12 Safe Stalking, if you are engaged in an 'undertaking' to manage deer then the health and safety laws apply to you. You are therefore responsible, not only for your own safety, but also that of others and this may even include someone who is not authorised to use the seat. High seats should therefore be well documented in any risk assessment. In adhering to best practice*[41] much can be done to mitigate the risks involved. As outlined earlier, care should be taken to ensure their location affords unobstructed views and safe arcs of fire with good backstops. It is ironic that their very use in some areas is in itself a control measure to minimise risk, i.e. shooting from an elevated position to achieve a safer trajectory of the bullet in an area that, to shoot from the ground, would be unsafe. Risk assessments should also consider the inherent dangers of inclement weather. Icy conditions can make climbing into a seat hazardous and high winds may affect safe shooting and personal safety through the risk of falling trees.

The Health and Safety Executive (HSE) has produced extensive guidance on safe working and in particular working at heights on which legislation exists*[42]. There is also guidance on the safe use of ladders*[43], which is relevant to the use of high seats.

The only specific HSE reference to high seats is contained within its leaflet Gamekeeping and Deer Farming, and this is quoted below:

> ***Deer Stalking – High Seats***
> *High seats should be carefully sited to give an unobstructed field of shooting and a solid backstop – preferably earth or some similar material which won't cause ricochets. The rungs of wooden ladders should be properly secured and not just supported by nails or screws.*
>
> *Wherever there is public access always detach the ladder after use or fit a cover to it to deter children from reaching the seats. Make sure rifles are completely unloaded before climbing up or down the ladder.*

41 Deer Best Practice Guides: culling: high seats published by The Deer Initiative

42 Work at Height Regulations, 2005

43 HSE leaflet – Safe use of Ladders and Stepladders. See also http://www.hse.gove.uk/pubns/indg455.pdf

Design and Inspection

Periodic safety checks should be made to ensure seats are secure and fit for purpose. This seat has slipped due to poor installation

Seats should be of sound construction; using safe materials and design. The height should be reasonable and no more than is required for the job. The higher the seat the more safeguards should be built in. Once erected, they should be well maintained and inspected prior to each use. In practice such inspections amount to a visual and physical check as to stability prior to climbing the ladder. Recorded periodic safety checks should be made and these should be frequent enough to ensure any deterioration defect can be remedied. The guidance on the use of ladders includes the risk of over-reaching while on a ladder. To mitigate this risk it recommends keeping the body centred within the ladder and maintaining three points of contact while climbing. The guidance also covers measures to take against the risk of slipping, e.g. keeping the rungs clean and in good condition, non-slip footwear, fitness and training. These measures, aimed at the working environment, are equally relevant to the high seat user.

Guarding Against Unauthorised Use

Account should also be taken of any site specific risks and these should be documented within the risk assessment together with the control measures to mitigate the risk. These should be proportionate to the risk involved. Where possible, seats should be sited in sensible safe areas away from public rights of way. An overriding principle of the legislation is that you must take account of any risk assessment carried out and do all that is reasonably practicable to prevent anyone falling.

Areas that are known to have high public access will require additional or more stringent control measures within the risk assessment. In certain areas the use of portable seats, erected late in the day before shooting and then removed following shooting, will be appropriate. In more remote areas of woodland I think it reasonable for them to be left in situ provided they are signed adequately and their construction does not suggest special measures or present an obvious danger to the legitimate user, or indeed a trespasser. Special provisions should be made for those that are left in situ where children are likely to play, even if the seats are safe and well maintained. In this situation fitting a cover to prevent climbing would be seen as a minimum requirement. If the seat is of substantial construction of the Thetford style, locking the door to the seated enclosure at the top of the ladder without some measure to prevent climbing would not be sufficient. In addition, ropes or chains should not be left loose and hanging from seats. The legislation states you must be prepared for children to be less careful than adults and consequently extra measures need to be taken to guard against their use.

There is no specific legal requirement to place warning signs on high seats. Some stalkers view their use as ineffective and counterproductive since they draw attention to an otherwise unnoticed structure. Others view conspicuous signs warning of the danger of unauthorised use as a control measure that may deter the casual passer-by or youngster. In many situations signing may not be necessary with the risks being minimised through other control measures. However, in areas of open public access and where rights of way are used regularly it is good practice for appropriate signs to be used.

The use of signs is recommended in areas where the public have access

Occupier's Liabilities

In addition to the Health and Safety legislation for safe working there are legal responsibilities for owners and occupiers that you should be aware of and these will apply in all cases where high seats are not removed after shooting*[44].

The definition of 'occupier' can be quite wide and may include the stalking tenant responsible for the installation and maintenance of the seats. The legislation imposes a common duty of care to all visitors and this also includes those that may be there without authority. This means you must take such care as is reasonable in the circumstances to ensure the visitor's safety while on the land. In practical terms this means if there are potential dangers on the land you must take reasonable steps to safeguard the visitor from the danger. High seats may be viewed as a potential danger. Hence the advice given in respect of preventing children from climbing the ladder. You should ensure seats are safe to use both for the legitimate user and the inquisitive, unauthorised onlooker. The test in respect of unauthorised use would be whether a person with the knowledge, ability and resources of the occupier could and would take steps to protect trespassers from any danger on the land. There will be many situations with stalking licences and permissions where legal liability may fall in part on the owners as well as the stalking tenant. Contractors operate at their own risk to a degree. However, should there be an accident any investigation would centre on the owner's responsibility to ensure adequate training and awareness of the risks was in place and was monitored frequently. They should be able to show their role has not been merely passive. The owner needs to be able to demonstrate intervention to ensure control measures were implemented – rather than just written.

Public Interference and Confrontation

In addition to the obvious risks posed by the use of high seats, there is also greater potential for public interference and confrontation than in other stalking activities. Not all public interference is confrontational. Some activities, albeit frustrating and annoying at the time given your efforts, have to be ignored. In areas where ramblers have equal rights, better let them pass without a word in the knowledge that deer have an uncanny sense that they present no danger. You are quite likely to see deer emerge just after they have passed by provided their dog has not self-hunted the entire wood. The occasional walker in places where they should not be may need to be made aware of their 'wrongdoing', but in a polite manner. That 'wrongdoing' is civil trespass, a tort in civil law and, on private land not subject to public access, it is actionable per se. You are in your rights as an owner or occupier of the land to politely require a trespasser

44 The Occupier's Liability Acts, 1957 and 1984. The Occupier's Liability (Scotland) Act, 1960

to leave by the shortest route to the public footpath or other highway. Reasonable force can be used to achieve this should they refuse. However, while the common law of trespass allows this, the decision to force someone to return to the highway or footpath when you are in possession of a firearm is fraught with danger and best avoided. It may bring about a reaction that is disproportionate and one that may fail to achieve your objective of getting the person to leave the area.

The psychology of human interactions has been well studied and it is often the case that your initial approach to someone's presence affects their reaction to you and so the cycle can spiral out of control if you get off to a bad start. In psychological terms, this interaction is sometimes referred to as the Betari Box. So getting off to a bad start may dictate how the exchange progresses, resulting in dispute. The reverse applies; an initial polite approach is usually best and can defuse an outright confrontation.

Where someone takes issue with your stalking activity care needs to be taken not to escalate the situation, particularly if they are not trespassing and have an equal right to remain. If they are on a footpath or other public highway then they have a right to pass and re-pass as a means of communication along the path. If they are on land with free public access they have a right to roam. If these rights of access, be it on the footpath or otherwise, are abused then the individual may forfeit the protection provided by legitimate access and effectively become a trespasser. This doctrine is supported by case law*[45]. Abusing such rights may take many forms and includes committing unlawful acts. Disrupting someone else's lawful sport or activity such as stalking would amount to an abuse and this is catered for not only at civil law but also criminal law*[46]. There are also specific activities that are prohibited in open access areas such as moor and heath land and these are outlined in access agreements and relevant legislation*[47].

If you are in the high seat when challenged you should unload and make it clear to the person that you have done so. Climbing down the seat is an option to be decided upon dependent on individual circumstances. It may just make matters worse. A polite explanation of what you are doing may be all that is necessary. If it becomes clear that the individual is not prepared to accept your explanation and leave then you may decide to alight from the seat if you have not done so. You should be willing to produce identification and written authority, together with a brief explanation of your activity. In the majority of cases this will suffice and there will be no need to take any further action. Further harassment or threats may incur the potential risk of criminal offences being committed. You must be careful not to react in any way that will render you liable to counter-claim. Harassment, verbal abuse and threats

45 Harrison v Duke of Rutland, 1893

46 Criminal Justice and Public Order Act, 1994

47 Countryside and Rights of Way Act, 2000

of physical violence are all matters that can be pursued by the police if the offending person(s) is known. If you think it appropriate to take the matter further and involve the police you should make a note of what took place, including a description of the individual(s) involved. You have no power to demand someone's name and address in these circumstances. High seats also suffer from vandalism, which amounts to the offence of criminal damage. Where seats are removed or totally destroyed offences of theft will be committed. If you have evidence of those responsible you should report the matter to the police immediately.

Best practice events run by The Deer Initiative have featured high seat risk assessment and these have included dealing with public confrontation. Many stalkers have been able to practise their interpersonal skills in a safe environment by role playing both stalker and irate member of the public. Interpersonal skills can be improved upon if you are prepared to accept constructive feedback from others. As the poet, Robbie Burns, put it, 'Give us the gift to see ourselves as others see us.'

Chapter 10

Crop Damage and Protection

For the individual stalker the identification, assessment and prevention of crop damage has to be a key objective within their management philosophy.

An increasing deer population with no natural predators, in a country under pressure from a rising human population, has created a climate in which deer are constantly in the news. On many occasions incidents involving deer occur in urban environments where their welfare is compromised. They are involved in road vehicle collisions, become trapped in fences or just find themselves in the wrong place at the wrong time, often with dire consequences. In a country with a reducing green belt, a programme of planting many young trees and preservation of special sites, news stories tend to centre on the problem of too many deer causing too much damage.

Despite these problems deer have a much valued aesthetic value and bring benefits within the wider biodiversity of the countryside. A balanced and managed approach to their control is therefore necessary. After all, it is man's very action of introducing additional species of deer, then restricting their range through various means, that is ironically partly to blame for unacceptable deer densities in some areas.

The culling of deer for the sole purpose of protecting crops is a long established practice in the commercial world of forestry. In recent years this practice has extended to a need to protect the wider natural environment, particularly in conservation areas.

A recent government forestry and woodland policy statement confirmed the commitment to protect, improve and expand England's woodland. In order to achieve these commitments, the sustainable management and development of our current and future woodland resource will therefore rely upon continued and active management of deer populations.

The problem of deer affecting both flora and fauna adversely has been given considerable publicity, with support for action from a number of nationally established bodies. Culling has become more widely accepted by the public, particularly in areas where there is an overabundance of deer and culling is seen as a last resort; albeit a minority remain vehemently opposed.

In some areas there has been such an increase in the fallow deer population that the damage to habitat has reached unsustainable levels and many stalkers now see their role as one that fulfils both a sporting and conservation role. Owners of commercial forest areas where extensive felling and restocking has taken place are requiring stalkers, who are granted licences, to be focused on control and damage limitation, rather than stalking for sport. Woodland Improvement Grants (WIGS) require deer management plans to be in place and impose conditions to ensure the necessary culling takes place, e.g. minimum stalking outings per year; the emphasis clearly being on control. Where culls are not achieved financial penalties may be imposed, adding to the pressure on the deer manager/stalker to do a job of work rather than treating the task as recreational. Whether or not in years to come an alternative humane means of reducing the deer population will be found, and how this will affect the sport of stalking, remains to be seen.

Stalkers should appreciate that the presence of deer is not necessarily detrimental to our natural environment. Deer activity, e.g. what they eat, should not automatically be viewed as causing 'damage'. In many situations their presence is beneficial, so maintaining a balanced, sustainable population of deer should be an overriding strategy in the management of our countryside. Deer have always been an important species within our woodland, where they have helped create, through their selective grazing and browsing, diversity of both flora and fauna.

Deer in commercial forestry on both the Public Forest Estate (PFE) and private ground can provide cost benefits in terms of guided and leased stalking, venison production and wildlife watching. While some landowners may tolerate a certain amount of damage on the basis of a return on the sporting revenue, for it to be totally ignored by the stalker may result in not only unsustainable damage to the natural environment, but a loss of stalking rights or non-renewal of licence.

Types of Damage

Woodland

Fallow deer are predominantly grazing animals but also commonly browse trees and shrubs. It is the tender young shoots of trees and plants that are preferred; particularly at risk are the valuable lead shoots of trees. Most trees are eaten, especially the broadleaves such as cherry, ash and willow. They will also damage the bark of trees by stripping and eating it or by the bucks rubbing it with their antlers (fraying). Both bark stripping and fraying can result in the ultimate death of the tree. This will be inevitable where the damage affects the entire circumference of the tree, effectively destroying the cambium layer essential for it to live. Identifying damage and the culprit is essential if you are to remedy the matter.

Above: Woodland damage – note the distinctive browse line and lack of ground flora

Bark Stripping

Bark stripping by fallow is not as common as with red and sika deer and where alternative food is available you may find no evidence of this within the woodland. By using their teeth fallow will peel and eat the bark off trees. They tend to prefer the smooth barked trees such as ash and willow. The bark is chiselled off in an upward movement using the front incisors. It is then gripped against the upper dental pad, torn off and eaten. The analysis of bark suggests there is some important nourishment value in it, even when compared to mid-quality grasses. It has been suggested that one of the causes of bark stripping may be the need for roughage or possibly certain minerals and carbohydrates that bark contains (De Nahlik, 1992).

Identifying the cause of bark stripping can be difficult and careful examination should be made not only of the tree but the surrounding area, which may provide evidence of tracks or droppings. The time of year should be taken into account together with the height of the damage, which is an important factor in confirming the identity of the offending animal.

Below: Typical bark stripping by fallow. Note the weather conditions in the left photo, which may have been instrumental

Livestock, squirrels, rabbits, hares and rodents will all strip bark, particularly in severe weather conditions.

When bark is stripped teeth marks are not always evident. Where they are, and are broad and running vertically up the peeled stem with torn or broken bark hanging at the top, it is likely that deer will be the culprit. Sheep can inflict similar damage but their teeth marks will tend to be diagonal, as will the damage caused by horses. Rodent and squirrel damage will show narrower teeth marks. Badgers will use the trunks of trees as scratching posts, inflicting considerable damage to the bark with their front claws. Scratch marks will usually be obvious. Some areas of the country may now also suffer tree damage from wild boar as they continue to breed and extend their range. They will bark strip trees and roots as well as uprooting small trees.

Tree Fraying and Thrashing

Damage to trees and bushes occurs from two distinct activities of the fallow buck. Tree fraying, where the tree bark and small branches are damaged by the buck rubbing and striking his antlers against them, is most common in the autumn when they are shedding their velvet, as elaborated upon in Chapter 2. This is a cleaning process in which the tree is used merely as a means of applying pressure to rub off the remaining velvet. If not disturbed, a buck will spend some time cleaning in this way at the chosen tree. Isolated young whippy trees are often selected and if you look carefully in the area you usually find evidence of previous years' fraying on trees that have survived the damage. Fallow bucks will fray at varying heights of at least 100cm or more, determined by the nature of the tree, antler length and their effective level of head and neck movement. You may also find fraying damage just prior to the casting of antlers in the spring. Quite why this occurs is not generally known; it may be simply the result of a sense of irritation of the impending loss.

Tree fraying caused by a buck rubbing off the dying velvet from his antlers

The wanton thrashing of trees, overhanging branches and bushes by the buck's antlers is an activity that can cause considerable damage. It is not restricted to the woody elements of habitat either as bracken and similar foliage is likely to fall victim to the treatment. It can also lead to entanglements with fencing and debris, as described in Chapter 2. Territorial dominance, an upsurge in testosterone levels and scent marking via the sub-orbital and frontal glands appear to be the main motivators for this activity, which is most noticeable in late autumn leading up to the rut when territories are being marked and defended.

On occasions fallow bucks will also damage tree protection guards or tubes by fraying and thrashing. If these are not substantial and well staked they are likely to be destroyed together with the tree therein. There is some anecdotal evidence that fallow are more likely to damage certain colours of guards, e.g. red tubes rather than white (D. B. Barnes, 2015). There appears no logical explanation for this and the matter would certainly lend itself to further research.

Bucks will wantonly thrash trees, bushes and other foliage leading up to the rut

Ground Flora

In addition to trees a wide variety of ground flora can be damaged, both within the woodland and the surrounding areas of open ground. Where deer densities are too high heavy browsing within woodland prevents natural regeneration of many plant and tree species and reduces the abundance of palatable plants and structural diversity of the ground vegetation. Consequently, many SSSIs (Sites of Special Scientific Interest) and ASNW (Ancient Semi-Natural Woodland) habitats are in a declining state. The problem is that these impacts often occur over time and their significance is not always spotted quickly enough for serious damage to be prevented.

As with damage to trees, close examination of the type of damage is important in determining the cause. Deer damage will be most noticeable in the spring as new growth emerges. The browsed stems will show the typical rough, shredded surface. This tell-tale sign is the result of the manner in which the foliage is severed; as deer lack upper jaw incisors it is gripped between the lower incisors and upper dental pad/gum and torn away in a sideways movement leaving the jagged edge. Fallow will browse commonly up to 1.8m. (F.C. Practice Note 1999) and on occasions will stand on their hind legs to reach choice foliage.

Agricultural Crops

The impact of large numbers of deer feeding on farm crops can be significant. Fallow will spend many hours away from woodland in adjacent agricultural fields, where they will feed on pasture and arable crops, sometimes causing thousands of pounds' worth of damage. In recent years farmers have experienced small profits (2–3 per cent) on the overall production of some crops and this is at risk from excessive numbers of herding deer such as fallow. It is not just what they eat that causes concern; it is their physical movement through some crops and habit of lying up (couched) that can cause considerable damage. The attraction is clear – a safe place to be, providing cover to rest and palatable food readily available throughout the day.

Fields of ripening wheat are particularly vulnerable, with the previously untouched ears of corn being eaten at will. The flattening of cereal crops by lying up and trampling to and fro causing as much, if not more, damage than the amount eaten. Flattened cereals deteriorate and become difficult to harvest. Rape, beans and linseed suffer from this type of damage too; as dense crops they provide ideal habitat for fallow on warm sunny days. The deer's movement through these crops as they ripen also knocks out the seed heads (known as shedding), causing damage by reducing yields and unwanted seed dispersal. Rape will have been visited some months previously when, in its earlier growth stage, the flower heads formed and became an attractive browse. Beet crops and kale also attract the attentions of fallow, particularly in hard weather. Once harvested, fallow are very partial to the dying green tops of beet left on the ground. Even following some rotovation of the surface, when you would think there was nothing there to eat, they will seek out the remaining leaf tops amongst the tilth.

Above: Fields of wheat damaged by fallow

Right: Confirmation of the culprits

Such is the efficiency of modern farming methods that it is rare for the ground to remain uncultivated for more than a few days after the crops are harvested. However, fallow

The myriad of tracks and lying up areas of fallow deer can be seen in this aerial view of a field of rape

are quick to graze rape, bean and cereal stubble, clearing up any crop remnants. However, the main attraction is the emerging growth of grasses and plants amidst the stubble. This can be a productive time in coming to terms with some cull bucks that have suddenly been deprived of their late summer habitat.

Effects on Wildlife

Damage is not restricted to trees and vegetation. Too high a density of deer can effectively destroy the understory of woodland up to the browse line below the lower canopy of the trees. The reduced field layer resulting from heavy grazing reduces the abundance and diversity of invertebrates and small mammals dependent on the shrub and ground layers for food and cover (e.g. Hill, 1985; Putman, 1986) and thus may in turn reduce the diversity of raptors or mammalian predators (e.g. Tubbs, 1974, 1982; Putman, 1986; Putman *et al.,* 1989; Petty and Avery, 1990).

Many wild birds can be affected adversely through loss of habitat, e.g. lack of shelter, food and suitable nesting sites. Not all these effects are entirely negative (Putman, 1996). Research has shown some species actually benefit from such heavy grazing, e.g. wood warblers, pied flycatchers and redstarts (Stowe, 1987; Mitchell and Kirby, 1990). Having recognised that a certain level of grazing can benefit some species of flora and fauna some conservation bodies have introduced controlled grazing on many conservation areas. So deer in sustainable numbers have their part to play in the overall picture of biodiversity.

Assessing the Damage

Clearly where damage is severe you do not need to resort to detailed scientific methods to tell you the obvious. In woodland, where damage is not severe, it is not so easy and a more measured scientific approach by periodic impact assessment is required. This should form part of your management plans in providing an overall picture of the current state of habitat and deer densities from which realistic cull targets can be set. Monitoring damage in this way also helps to identify potential problems at an early stage, enabling control measures to be taken and serious damage prevented. And prevention is better than cure, particularly when it comes to the well-being of our woodlands.

There are a number of well-practised methods of assessing damage within woodlands and these are dealt with in detail in Chapter 5. Assessing damage to agricultural crops is a different matter. If this is done through an estimated loss of yield it is somewhat akin to 'closing the door after the horse has bolted', albeit this may be relevant to a compensation claim.

Determining long term damage to some crops can be difficult, e.g. grass and the early growth of cereals. These types of crop can recover. It is well known that a certain amount of grazing can be beneficial and results in additional side growth (tillering) being stimulated. Gardeners and foresters know well the benefits of selective pruning and deer grazing, and browsing can sometimes have the same effect. So decisions as to what constitutes serious damage causing a commercial loss are not straightforward, as referred to later in respect of out of season culling.

Control Measures

Even if it was possible, the complete removal of deer on a landscape scale to prevent damage would not be an acceptable control measure. It is clear that shooting on its own in an effort to reduce deer density and limit damage is not sufficient. Any management based exclusively on reduction of population densities is unlikely to prove effective (Putman, 1996). A combination of habitat protection and maintenance of a sustainable population of deer must therefore be central to any damage management strategy. With regards to agricultural crops, these tend to be targeted when the natural food sources diminish and diversionary feeding is a control measure rarely exploited. The mowing of woodland rides in midsummer to promote regrowth has been successful in reducing damage by fallow to growing and maturing cereal crops in adjacent farmland (B. Mayle).

Habitat Protection

Fencing

Well-maintained fences, constructed to the required specifications, can provide an effective barrier against deer but the costs can be high and disproportionate. Fences can also exclude non-target species, cause injury to wildlife and are not pleasing to the eye. Where large areas are fenced there is also a risk of deer being fenced in and where this is likely provision should be made to enable them to escape without re-entry. Ideally, entire woods should not be fenced.

Considerable research has been conducted into the most effective types of fence and minimum heights, mesh size, strengths and durability for fallow have been determined*[48]. Deer behaviour at fences varies between the species. Fallow when faced with such barriers approach in a consistent and measured way. Bucks will tend to jump a fence if possible without attempting to push through, whereas does will test a fence by prodding and pushing with their head in an attempt to seek a way through or under. Only where this is unsuccessful will they attempt to jump it*[49].

A minimum fence height of 1.8m and a maximum mesh size of 200cm × 220cm are recommended for fallow. Clearly where smaller species are present mesh size will need to be reduced (down to 150mm for roe and 75mm hexagonal for muntjac) (Putman, 1999).

Fallow prefer to go through or under fencing rather than having to jump

48 Practice note H. Pepper, Forest Research 99.

49 Forest Fencing – Technical Guide, R. Trout and H. Pepper (2006)

These specifications should take account of the area to be fenced and the need/desire for deer to penetrate the fenced area. The greater the need for access by deer, the more secure the fence will have to be. If small areas are fenced and the deer have choices and can easily walk around to other feeding areas they may not attempt breaching the fenced area, even where this is able to be penetrated due to inadequate specification. While fencing may keep deer out initially, with the passage of time and a lack of maintenance all fences become breached and deer will then readily gain access. In areas where this occurs they may find themselves trapped and excessive damage can occur as a result.

Tree Guards and Shelters

Protecting individual trees by the use of shelters or guards is a much cheaper option compared to fencing, although tree guards are not suitable for all tree species, e.g. conifers. They have the advantage of providing a more natural landscape together with avoiding many of the problems associated with high fences. The disadvantage is that the ground flora and shrubby vegetation are not protected and will be vulnerable if deer densities are high. In this situation, where there is a risk of serious damage, further action will be necessary to reduce deer numbers to a sustainable level; alternatively complete exclusion by fencing is the only option.

Where fallow are present, guards or tubes should be fitted using substantial stakes that will not easily be pushed over by deer or damaged by the wind, particularly in exposed positions. They need to be 1.8m high to ensure the tasty tops of emerging trees are not eaten out. Spiral type guards have been found to be ineffective against deer and are not recommended. As referred to earlier, fallow bucks will sometimes damage tree guards by fraying or thrashing and periodic inspection should be made to ensure this is kept to a minimum. Stalkers can help landowners and foresters in this respect by being vigilant and bringing vulnerable trees to notice. Often it is simply a matter of repositioning the guard and renewing a cable tie and if you are stalking and able to do this in passing then relationships can be enhanced.

The crown of this young tree has been eaten by fallow. Resources are wasted if guards are not of sufficient height, i.e. a minimum of 1.8m

Deterrents

Historically, a number of deterrents have been tried and tested in an attempt to deter deer, some ingenious ones too, where treasured plants in gardens have been at risk. Lion dung, human hair and a variety of chemical substances have all been used with varied success. The application of chemical repellents to anything other than small numbers of trees or garden plants is only a temporary measure and not really suitable for large areas of woodland or plantations. Acoustic and visual deterrents can work on a temporary basis at specific sites, but deer are quick to learn they do not present a danger and eventually ignore them. I have shot fallow regularly next to game release pens where radios play full blast in a bid to deter foxes.

I recall in my early days of stalking in Herefordshire that Steve, my stalking companion, came up with one such acoustic deterrent. He was called to a meeting with an elderly lady and her somewhat eccentric partner. They lived in Wood Cottage, an idyllic little property with a view of the Black Mountains of Wales. Little did we know then, but this cottage would later become our 'base camp' for all stalking activities on the nearby estate. Earlier that week the couple had been shocked to find that half their treasured roses had been eaten during a night-time raid of fallow deer; the tracks were evident. They feared their remaining roses would suffer a similar fate and wanted something done about the deer. To them, this was as serious as ten acres of crop being damaged on the neighbouring estate. Shooting the deer on site was not a safe option and Steven rigged up an elaborate tripwire connected to a biscuit tin in which he had placed some stones. Being a rather Heath Robinson contraption, I was initially sceptical as to whether it would work, but the following night there was action in the garden. The couple were awakened by the enormous clatter of the tin and the sound of fast running deer, who were never to return to the garden again. The roses had been saved and as a result the hospitality at Wood Cottage was established and has continued to this day.

In small areas electric fencing can provide a short term deterrent but it has been found to be less effective against deer than livestock. It requires regular checking and maintenance and, together with the risks to deer welfare and to other users of the countryside, its use is limited. It appears the majority of deterrents are either not suitable in the long term or have not been developed sufficiently to a point where they can provide an effective alternative to the physical means of tree protection described earlier.

Reducing Deer Density

Managing deer by controlling their numbers through culling is one of the most effective means of preventing unacceptable levels of damage. But, as mentioned earlier, this needs to be achieved on a landscape scale for it to be effective. There is little point in shooting deer to reduce damage if their loss in numbers are merely compensated for by an infill from adjacent areas. This supports the need for Deer Management Groups as promoted and encouraged by The Deer Initiative together with the practice of collaborative team culls as described in detail in Chapter 11.

In addition to increasing deer management activity a monitoring process should be introduced together with considering woodland management options that may be available within the various schemes offering financial assistance. A combination of careful management of deer numbers and the physical protection of habitat has to be the key to crop protection with the acceptance that deer have their place within our woodland ecosystem.

Preventing damage to agricultural crops can become a seasonal challenge for the stalker, who needs to demonstrate a willingness to prevent it. One of the problems with fallow is that of cereal crops being harvested long before the fallow does come into season, and so shooting as a means of crop protection can be relatively ineffective, as only the bucks are in season. While there are benefits of culling some bucks early in the season, the fallow does learn quickly from experience and begin to restrict their visits to the hours of darkness. Educating the does and fawns in this way can be counterproductive. By the time the does come into open season the fields are bare and no longer provide the tempting buffet they did when covered by standing crops.

Care needs to be taken when extracting carcasses from standing crops

Stalkers should also take care over extraction of carcasses in standing crops, which if not done carefully can cause as much damage as the deer that has been shot. In responding to crop damage by targeting offending deer, full use should be made of high seats, as outlined in Chapter 9.

Culling During the Close Season and at Night

The fact there are large numbers of deer, creating concern over the damage they may be causing, is no excuse for an abuse of the legal exemptions to shoot deer out of season or at night. I fear at the present time there is considerable abuse of these exemptions in the UK but only a small number of such cases have been brought before the courts. There is no substitute for well-structured deer management practices capable of achieving an effective cull, both within the open seasons and daylight hours. However, there are circumstances in which the shooting of deer out of season or at night can be justified.

As a stalker you have a responsibility to react to concerns over crop damage.

Where damage is obvious and potentially serious, action should be taken quickly to prevent further damage. In countries such as Germany, to turn a blind eye to damage may render the stalking tenant liable to a considerable compensation claim. Where serious damage is being caused to agricultural crops or new plantations your response may have to be immediate, even if it is out of season. In these circumstances you need to be fully aware of your liabilities*[50] should there be a legal challenge against your activities.

Legislation – England and Wales

The Deer Act, 1991, provides for the taking of deer in certain situations during the close season for the purpose of crop protection. It also allows for the conditional use of shotguns.

Under Section 7(1) provided you are **authorised** you are only entitled to rely on the defence of shooting out of season during the daytime if you are able to satisfy three important elements:

1. That you have reasonable grounds for believing that deer of the **same species** were causing or had caused damage to crops, vegetables, fruit, growing timber or any other form of property on the land, and
2. That it was likely that further serious damage would be caused and any such damage was likely to be serious, and
3. That your action was necessary to prevent it.

The Act does not define the meaning of crops and clearly anything grown on the land that can be quantified would appear to fall within the definition. Pasture used for grazing of livestock has value and could be classed as a crop but difficulties may arise in proving the potential for serious damage as a certain level of grazing could be argued to be beneficial. Where other forms of property are damaged each case would have to be judged on its merits as to determining the nature of the damage and its value. It would ultimately be for the court to decide as to whether they were satisfied that damage was being caused and the action was necessary to prevent it.

For the purposes of the Act an 'authorised person' means the occupier of the land where the shooting took place, their employee or resident member of the household (authorised in writing by the occupier) and someone with the rights to shoot deer or any person acting on their written authority.

50 Risks and liabilities associated with deer management are dealt with in detail in the book *Deer Law and Liabilities*, published by Quiller Publishing

Restrictions as to Where Deer are Shot

Stalkers shooting deer under this exemption should be aware they are not entitled to shoot other than the place where the damage is occurring. Shooting deer in a location remote from the damaged crop or intercepting them en route may negate the legal exemption and put you at risk of prosecution. Case law provides a precedent.

In the case of Traill v Buckingham, 1972, it was stated that damage was being caused to crops on Buckingham's land. It was believed that the deer responsible were to be found in a wood adjoining his, but occupied by Traill. The wood had previously belonged to Buckingham's father, who sold it but retained the right to shoot deer there. During the close season Buckingham, having the right to shoot the deer in the wood owned by Traill, entered the woodland and shot a red hind. The court on appeal decided he was only entitled to deal with marauding deer on the land where the damage was being caused and not, as in this case, on adjoining land.

Use of Shotguns

Authorised persons may use a shotgun that would otherwise be prohibited for the culling of deer provided the above conditions are met, i.e. under section 7(1). The shotgun must be not less than 12-bore calibre. The ammunition used is restricted to either AAA shot or single rifled slug of not less than 350 grains (non-spherical bullet); the latter requiring the authorisation of a firearms certificate. There will be circumstances in which the use of a shotgun is appropriate and perhaps the safest option at short range, but generally I do not recommend their use for the welfare reasons that justified their prohibition in our deer legislation.

Licences to Preserve Public Health and Safety, Natural Heritage and to Prevent Serious Damage to Property

While a specific licence is not required under the general exemption for crop damage, provision has been made under Article 4 of the Regulatory Reform Act, 2007, amending the 1991 Act, to confer a power to grant licences for other reasons than those specified above.

This allows for the shooting of deer in the close season and at night for the purpose of preserving public health or public safety, and conserving the natural heritage. An additional provision exists for a night licence for preventing serious damage to property, of which there has to be evidence in the year preceding the application.

I should stress that the granting of such licences is exceptional. They will only be granted where there is no satisfactory alternative to culling and a serious risk to public health or safety, or serious damage to natural heritage or property, exists. The culling required would have to be shown as unlikely to have a significant impact on the conservation of the species of deer to be culled. The applicant will have to satisfy a number of conditions. A licence will only be granted where other preventative measures have been shown to be ineffective or impractical, e.g. open season shooting, fencing, etc. Licences are granted by Natural England, in relation to any land in England, or the Welsh ministers in relation to any land in Wales.

Legislation – Scotland

The Wildlife & Natural Environment (Scotland) Act, 2011 (WANE Act) made a number of changes to the Deer (Scotland) Act, 1996. These changes, which covered the close seasons and owner and occupier's rights to prevent damage, mean any deer shot in the close season requires authorisation from Scottish Natural Heritage (SNH). This effectively means that no one in Scotland is able to cull deer out of season or at night without authorisation, with the exception of relieving suffering of injured or diseased animals or a deer that is starving with no reasonable chance of recovering. Occupier's rights to cull deer to prevent damage in season on enclosed woodland and improved agricultural land remain.

A general authorisation is issued (under section 5(6) of the amended Act) on an annual basis and does not have to be individually applied for or possessed by stalkers. The principle is similar to that of general licences issued for the control of pest species. It allows occupiers suffering damage to improved agricultural land or enclosed woodland to control deer in the close season during the daytime, i.e. one hour before sunrise to one hour after sunset. The exception to this, at the time of writing, is that the authorisation does not allow the culling of female deer over one year old of any species between the period 1 April to 31 August. If, however, an occupier is suffering damage from female deer between these dates a specific authorisation may be applied for from SNH. The authorisation therefore allows the shooting of fallow does between the following inclusive dates: 16 February to 31 March and 1 September to 20 October.

Those operating under the general authorisation must have read and understood it and carried out any control in accordance with the conditions listed. You should be aware the conditions may change from year to year. The authorisation allows for 'occupiers' as defined below to cull deer where no other means of control, which might reasonably be adopted in the circumstances, would be adequate in the following circumstances as outlined in Section 5 (6) of Deer (Scotland) Act, 1996:

a) the taking or killing is necessary –
    i) to prevent damage to any crops, pasture or human or animal foodstuffs on any agricultural land which forms part of that land; or
    ii) to prevent damage to any enclosed woodland which forms part of that land: or
b) the taking or killing is necessary –

i) to prevent damage to any unenclosed woodland which forms part of that land; or
ii) to prevent damage, whether directly or indirectly, to the natural heritage generally; or
iii) in the interests of public safety.

Persons authorised by the general authorisation include the following:

- The occupier suffering damage to those interests outlined
- Any of the following classes of person authorised in writing by the occupier suffering damage:
  - The owner in person
  - The owner's employees
  - The occupier's employees
  - Any other person normally resident on the land
  - Any other person approved in writing by SNH as a fit and competent person*.

*This approval is gained through application to SNH to be entered on the Fit and Competent Register. The qualifications and experience currently accepted by SNH as meeting the required standard for entry on the register is as follows:

- The Deer Stalking Certificate 2 (DSC2), or
- The DSC1 together with providing details of two referees that you meet the required standard. One of the referees must hold the DSC1 qualification.

The definition of 'Fit and Competent' is currently under review and you should check the latest position prior to shooting. For more information relating to qualifications see Chapter 3 on stalking opportunities.

Enclosed land is defined by the Deer (Scotland) Act, 1996 as meaning enclosed by a stock-proof fence or other barrier, and unenclosed shall be construed accordingly. It is for those operating under the general authorisation to satisfy themselves that the land is enclosed.

Under the Deer (Firearms, etc) Order, 1985 authorised persons may use a shotgun that would otherwise be prohibited for the culling of deer provided the above conditions are met. The shotgun must be not less than 12-bore calibre. The ammunition used is restricted for any deer to a single rifled non-spherical slug not less than 380 grains, or SSG or larger cartridge. For roe deer a cartridge loaded with AAA shot or larger is permitted.

Any requirement to shoot out of season to prevent damage to unenclosed woodland, the natural heritage or the interests of public safety requires a specific authorisation from SNH, as would any requirement for culling at night.

Best Practice

The authorised person must comply with The Deer (Firearms, etc) (Scotland) Order, 1985, the Deer (Scotland) Act, 1996 (as amended) and best practice as published by the Wild Deer Best Practice Partnership and available on the Best Practice website*[51]. Occupiers should be able to demonstrate that other appropriate means of control, including liaison with others who control deer on the land and on adjacent lands or, where appropriate, the local Deer Management Group, have been explored before undertaking control under this authorisation. Occupiers must provide details of deer killed under this general authorisation to the owner of the land.

Legislation – Northern Ireland

Article 20(6) of the Wildlife (N.I.) Order, 1985, as amended, allows for the culling of deer during the close season on cultivated land, enclosed pasture, enclosed woodland or garden grounds, provided you can satisfy a court that you are authorised and had reasonable grounds for believing that deer of the same species were causing, or had caused, serious damage to crops, pasture, vegetables, fruit, growing timber or any other form of property on the land. You also need to show there was a likelihood of further serious damage and that your actions were necessary to prevent it.

Deer can also be culled during the close season in accordance with the conditions of a licence granted by the Department of Environment, for the purpose of:

a) preserving public health or public safety,
b) conserving the natural heritage, or
c) preventing serious damage to property.

Authorised persons and the use of shotguns to prevent crop damage are as defined for England and Wales.

Advice on Taking Action

Prior to embarking on shooting deer for the purposes of crop protection you should give some thought to how you may defend your position should you be challenged and required to justify your actions.

You may anticipate some searching questions and an independent inspection of the damaged crop. If you are ignorant of your obligations you may fail to convince

51 www.bestpracticeguides.org.uk

those requiring an explanation that your actions are bona fide and this may trigger further enquiries and involvement of enforcement agencies. At best you may incur some embarrassing publicity, at worst a conviction for criminal offences, undermining your credibility as a stalker and suitability to hold a firearm certificate.

It is essential that in taking action to prevent crop damage you do so with the full support and authority of the landowner or occupier of the land. If you possess the licence for the deer stalking on the land in question you must ensure any conditions with regard to shooting within the close season are not breached. A site visit, ideally with the landowner, occupier or forester, to assess damage and the potential for further damage before taking any action would be good practice. Photographing the location and damage would mean you would be in a position to provide valuable evidence at a later date. With the majority of mobile phones having inbuilt cameras this should be achieved easily.

In providing *reasonable grounds* for taking action you would be expected to show what other means of prevention had been taken or considered previously. The legislation is so framed that one would expect damage to be evident and although not explicit in terms of when the damage occurred it would be reasonable to expect there to be evidence of recent damage. In a recent case on which I advised, evidence was given by an independent expert that the damage was more than a year old and likely to have been caused by a different species of deer to those shot. A conviction followed.

What is important is that you do not shoot deer on the basis of a 'hunch' that damage is likely to be caused if you do not take immediate action. To do so may render you liable to prosecution.

Compensation for Crop Damage

In circumstances where the tenant of an agricultural holding suffers crop damage from deer and is restricted from culling them, e.g. the stalking rights are vested in the owner or other third party, a claim for compensation can be made under the Agricultural Holdings Act, 1986, or in Scotland the Agricultural Holdings (Scotland) Act, 1991.

To claim compensation, a tenant must give his landlord written notice within one month of the damage becoming evident and give him the opportunity to make an inspection of a growing crop before it is harvested or, after harvest, before it is removed from the land. A written notice of a claim is then sent to the landlord within one month after the expiry of the end of the year in respect of which the claim is made. Where the shooting rights are held by a third party, e.g. a stalker with the licence, the landlord is entitled to be indemnified by the third party against such claims, which may be settled by arbitration under the Acts.

An anomaly exists in respect of the situation where the landowner, not being a tenant, does not own the stalking rights and therefore cannot control the deer that may be damaging his crops. A claim for compensation would not be possible under this legislation and the owner may have to resort to a civil remedy. However, legal action to prevent the damage could be considered under the Agriculture Act, 1947 and Agriculture (Scotland) Act, 1948. This legislation makes provision for Agricultural Departments to serve a notice*[52] requiring any person having the responsibility to do so to take, destroy or prevent the escape of certain pest species including deer, which are not on Schedule 1 of the Wildlife and Countryside Act 1981.

Fallow can be made to feel unwelcome

52 The purpose of the notice is to prevent damage to crops, pasture, foodstuffs, livestock, trees, bank, hedges or works on any land

Chapter 11

Collaborative and Team Culls

Deer stalking is generally regarded as a solitary affair, conducted by a single stalker. In recent years there has been such an increase in fallow deer numbers that traditional methods of deer management in some areas have failed to reduce the population to a sustainable level. Where they are in such high densities and a large cull is required to prevent serious damage to the flora, woodland or crops, a collaborative cull involving the use of a team of stalkers may be an effective option. Shooting is usually restricted to high seats with stalkers acting strategically as a team to achieve the cull. Deer are sometimes moved through the woodland towards the waiting rifles to increase shooting opportunities.

The term 'collaborative cull' is used here to describe both single team culls conducted on one estate to several teams that may be operating in unison on a landscape scale over a number of neighbouring estates. There is a distinction here between this type of organised cull, in which high seats are almost exclusively used, to that of small scale manoeuvres between stalkers where deer are moved quietly between them. This is elaborated upon later. Whatever the level of collaboration the principles of safe and effective shooting remain and these should be central to how they are organised and assessed, bearing in mind the risks involved.

In recent years collaborative culls in targeted areas have been highly successful in reducing the population of fallow deer, a species known for its wide ranging habits and lifestyle. Many of these culls have involved small teams of stalkers operating on private country estates, charity and publicly owned woodland. These team efforts have made a major contribution to the national cull of fallow deer. Many have involved the co-ordinating work of The Deer Initiative in bringing together major landowners and stalkers on a landscape scale.

Collaborative team culls are not a new strategy. Their effectiveness has been tried and tested over many years by some major landowners, e.g. the Forestry Commission, that has within its overall deer management plans, brought together its forestry rangers for team culls in targeted regions. Modern day team culls have progressed from the deer drives of old where inappropriate firearms were used and deer were shot on the move, resulting in a high rate of wounding. Elsewhere in Europe collaborative culls have long been established, particularly as a means of dealing with wild boar populations. In my experience, while these are very well organised and efficiently run, their approach to deer welfare is distinctly at odds with our own, as shooting moving deer along with wild boar is commonplace in some areas.

Collaborative culls elsewhere in Europe have long been established, particularly as a means of dealing with wild boar. Jagermeister Jochen Algermissen places a tree sprig in his hat, having been congratulated on shooting the most boar; this being part of the traditional ceremony to respect the quarry

Deer Welfare

In our desire to protect the wider environment and biodiversity of our woodland perhaps we should remind ourselves continually of the need to safeguard animal welfare. Culls carried out too frequently and over too long a timescale can have an adverse effect on deer welfare. High levels of stress can be caused to deer that are harassed continually. They become disorientated and will run in panic seeking refuge. When they are seen panting with tongues hanging out it is a clear sign they are under too much pressure. In these conditions deer may become nervous, secretive and difficult to stalk. They may also be displaced into areas of unfavourable habitat where no control is possible, resulting in environmental damage and road safety concerns.

Fallow will seek refuge when pressurised. Huddling together in the open is a defensive reaction to the threat of predators

Moving deer to waiting marksmen should be achieved by moving quietly through the woodland with the least amount of disturbance as possible so as not to panic the deer. Often just the presence of a walker on the ground is enough to alert the deer and produce the desired effect.

In many areas collaborative culls supplement traditional deer management practices and the resident stalker can be left with the difficult task of 'picking up the pieces' in the months to follow. So account needs to be taken of not only deer welfare but also the needs of individual stalkers responsible for local deer management plans. Where large scale collaborative team culls take place in which deer are moved purposely, two days of culling should be sufficient. Ideally the days should be split within the season. They should not take place too late when the does will be heavily pregnant.

Many areas where team culls take place have, in addition to the fallow, resident roe populations. The roe's desire to remain or return to their territories quickly following disturbance makes them vulnerable to overshooting; unlike the fallow that may travel long distances and not return to their previous habitat for some days. So during a collaborative cull there may be a need to monitor and restrict the numbers of roe shot, particularly adult does that tend to be targeted when a number of roe come through together.

The manner in which deer are shot is an important welfare consideration for those setting the ground rules. Rifles should be of an appropriate legal calibre and the ammunition should reach satisfactory energy levels to achieve humane dispatch. Deer should not be shot on the move unless wounded and then only if safe to do so. Briefing as to bullet placement needs to be defined clearly, i.e. chest shot placement only. Stalkers need to be competent and arrive with their rifles in good order and zeroed recently to ensure accurate and humane shooting. As referred to later, there must be a set procedure for dealing with the follow up and dispatch of wounded deer.

Culls carried out without taking these welfare considerations into account can become counterproductive, adversely affecting both public and neighbour relations; more importantly they can cause unnecessary suffering to the deer.

Benefits

Where deer are in high densities a collaborative cull, be it on a landscape scale or small team cull on a single estate, can provide the mechanism to reduce deer numbers significantly to a sustainable level, allowing traditional stalking methods to continue and maintain the population. The number of animals shot during a single collaborative cull could take a lone stalker in some cases an entire season to achieve. Provided they are conducted for the right reasons and are organised efficiently they can bring a number of benefits, for example:

- They make more efficient use of stalker's time
- Large culls can be achieved over a short time scale
- Culling can be concentrated over a shorter period causing less disturbance and minimising the redeployment of resources later
- They can be operated over a vast area – on a landscape scale
- Culls can be achieved in sensitive areas where traditional methods are not practical or safe
- They have the benefits of a team effort using greater resources than would otherwise be available
- They can provide a level of sustainable management in areas where a stalker's presence is not desired throughout the year
- They provide a forum in which all individuals involved in deer management are able to engage, exchange ideas and discuss future plans and tactics.

Collaborative culls may have negative impacts if they lack adequate risk assessment, welfare considerations and organisation. They will be less effective, exposing participants and the general public to unnecessary risks. They can disrupt the management plans of stalkers on neighbouring property where traditional culling takes place either on a recreational or professional basis. They may also attract unfavourable media attention, resulting in negative public reaction regarding deer welfare. Not all stalkers are attracted to the idea of spending long periods of time in high seats in circumstances where their activity is restricted. On the cynical side, they may be seen adversely by the outside world and due consideration needs to be given to the need for such culls, how they are conducted and why.

Tactics

The success of collaborative culls is dependent on accurate assessment of deer numbers, knowledge of their movements in the area and how well matters are organised and controlled on the day. Where culls are continued year on year, assessment of their effectiveness should be made over the long term. Culls can be effective for a couple of seasons and then subsequently fail for no apparent reason.

One of the reasons for apparent failure is that fallow are quick to adapt to the danger of such operations and learn the patterns of behaviour, even when this may only occur once or twice a year. If they are not moved around during the cull they simply resort to safe havens and couch up until it is safe to move and return to their preferred habitat. This can occur in areas where collaborative culls have been successful previously and have relied on the disturbance of the shooting, rather than by a walker, to move deer to the marksman. So your tactics need to be flexible and judged over a number of seasons.

If deer are to be moved by walkers it is essential all parties involved are fully briefed as to their role and responsibilities to ensure the safety of all concerned. They should wear high visibility clothing and be made aware of the high seat locations and routes for them to take. They should attend the main briefing of the stalkers. The nominated walkers need to have a detailed knowledge and understanding of the ground and should be in radio contact with the cull organiser at all times during the cull.

Managing the Day

The Organiser's Role and Responsibility

Operating a collaborative cull does not necessarily entail the need for a formal Deer Management Group to be formed. They can be organised by neighbouring landowners on an ad hoc basis. The Deer Initiative supports such culls through the provision of infrastructure such as high seats, chiller trailers and radios and also through provision of expertise. If you are faced with organising such a cull you may seek its advice and guidance*[53].

53 www.deerinitiative.com

There are a number of initial considerations to be made. Having ascertained the need to reduce numbers through various population assessments and sought the co-operation of landowners, your objectives should fall within an overall deer management plan. An agreed strategy should be established by meeting those concerned. This will take account of a risk assessment prepared at an early point in the process, see Chapter 12 for advice on preparation. You may find the following checklist useful:

Date and Time

A collaborative cull of fallow will be most effective during the doe season, i.e. between November and March. It should not be conducted too late in the season when the vast majority of does will be heavily pregnant. There is benefit in choosing midwinter days when the woodland cover is low and clear safe areas are afforded around the high seat positions.

A mutually agreed date and time will need to suit the majority of those stalkers to be invited. You should be sensitive to the needs of others within the countryside and check whether there is any forestry of farming work that may affect your plans. Try to avoid weekends and bank holidays when there is a greater chance of the general public being in the area. The duration of shooting should be long enough to take account of deer returning to favoured areas. Equally, it should not be extended to the point whereby stalkers become fatigued, cold and inattentive. They will not shoot well under these circumstances. Three hours should be seen as an optimum period.

There are advantages and disadvantages to commencing a cull at first light. In opting for an early start you will have the advantage of natural deer movement and may not have to deploy walkers to move deer that have settled. On the downside, organising and briefing personnel in the pre-dawn darkness can be difficult. If you have visiting stalkers who do not know the ground it is unreasonable to expect them to find their seats in the darkness without clear guidance. This effectively means arranging for them to be guided to their seats. This is extremely important and essential from a safety point of view. Panic sets in when, in the darkness, stalkers become disorientated and cannot find their seat. There is then a real danger of them walking into another's shooting zone during the poor light when deer may be starting to move.

Providing a map and nothing else is not an adequate control measure to mitigate the risks. I have had experience of both these risky situations, i.e. not being able to find a seat and being in my seat when another stalker has crept into my area seemingly lost.

The latter reaffirms the advice of not using your rifle scope to confirm potential targets. I was initially convinced that what I could see with my bare eyes in the pre-dawn darkness was a black fallow pricket coming straight toward me along the ride. It was not until I checked it out with the binoculars that I realised it was a fellow stalker. He had inadvertently walked past his own seat some 300 yards away! Alarmingly, this is not an isolated case and emphasises the need for good communication and guidance.

Deciding on the Cull

Ascertain the cull requirement, including the ratio of bucks to does. If your objective is to substantially reduce the population to a desirable level and in line with an overall management plan then such a 'reduction cull' must focus on a high proportion of females. If other species of deer are likely to be present you will have to decide if it is desirable for their numbers to be reduced together with the fallow. If carcasses are to be collected by a Game Handling Establishment they may appreciate advance notice of the cull together with an estimate of numbers. Arrangements will need to be made for the correct disposal of waste products.

High Seats

A stocktake of your high seats will be required, together with a physical safety check in line with your risk assessment. You may need to source extra seats from neighbours and these will need to be obtained in sufficient time prior to the date to enable them to be put into position. A safety check of all seats should be conducted and recorded. Careful thought needs to be put into their strategic positions and this demands a good knowledge of the ground and deer movements. See Chapter 9 for further information.

Mapping the Area

Once the boundaries of the area have been determined you should obtain and copy a sufficient number of large scale maps for distribution to all concerned. These should indicate rendezvous points, all public rights of way, buildings within the vicinity and the position of each seat, which should be numbered.

Participating Stalkers

It is important the stalkers have sufficient experience to defend your choice and faith in them robustly should things go wrong. You may view this as covering one's back but I can assure you that this element of your responsibility as an organiser will be scrutinised carefully should there be a subsequent claim against the landowner or individual.

It follows that stalkers should ideally possess the basic deer stalking certificates (DSC) 1 and 2 as a minimum. It is of greater importance that they have sufficient experience to supplement their formal qualifications. If you do not know them personally you will have to rely on those that do to vouch for them as referees. They need to possess adequate insurance to cover third party risks, and a firearm certificate with the appropriate conditions. You should arrange for all these documents to be either produced or forwarded to you prior to the date of the cull.

At the risk of being pedantic, do not take it for granted that each stalker has the qualifications and the correct, up to date documents. If you do you may be disappointed and exposed to considerable risk.

Communication

Communication will be a key factor on the day. The provision of handheld radios will be an advantage; alternatively you may have to rely on mobile phones provided you are in a good signal area. You should circulate a list of all participants and their contact details to enable contact to be made with anyone involved should the need arise. You should notify all other interested parties of the forthcoming event, e.g. adjacent landowners, residents in the area, forestry and farm workers. You should also consider notifying the local police for their information only.

In sensitive areas open to the public, consideration should be given to the preparation of a draft press release or response. This should provide an explanation for the action taken and be used in the event of complaints or concerns being expressed by members of the public or the media.

Briefings

There are benefits to briefing all participants together prior to dispersal to their various tasks. It is advisable to use a written aide-memoire to ensure items are not forgotten. The briefing note is an important document that should be retained as there may be a need to subsequently provide evidence of the instructions given.

An example of what a typical briefing may include is shown overleaf. The list is by no means exhaustive and should be tailored to meet individual needs:

Collaborative team briefing **Date............................** **Time..................**

1. *Please make sure your vehicles are secure and you have taken steps to safeguard against loss or theft of ammunition or firearms.*

2. *Check that you have your mobile phone and have the list provided showing all contact details of everyone involved. If you have a radio check that it is working and you have the appropriate channel information before you depart. Your call sign will be your seat number.*

3. *You have been issued with a map showing your allocated seat number and the transport arrangements into the woodland. Is anyone not aware of their allocated position? Once near the woodland and en route to your allocated seat keep quiet and don't use torches unless you have a problem.*

4. *Once you are in your seat you are 'live' to shoot up to the time given to remain in position, after which there should be no shooting. Shooting is to end at ..... We will meet outside the wood at ..... prior to returning here unless alternative arrangements are agreed.*

5. *Rifles should be carried to your seat in their slips. Please double check that they are unloaded prior to climbing up and down the seat. Seats have been checked previously but you should still check they are safe prior to climbing.*

6. *There is to be no shooting other than from the high seat with the exception of dispatching a wounded beast at close range, which will be dealt with separately as discussed next. Avoid taking long shots. Shooting moving deer is forbidden with the exception of a wounded beast providing it is safe.*

7. *The follow-up of any wounded animal will be conducted separately following the cessation of shooting. If you suspect that a deer is wounded and has not been accounted for this should be notified to me and subject to a follow-up check with tracker dog. On no account should you conduct the searching of a suspected wounded animal prior to this being authorised.*

8. *May I remind you to ensure you identify your target and that a safe backstop exists; remember, dogs may appear without owners.*

9. *Any (insert species) can be shot. No (insert species) are to be shot. No other species including foxes to be shot (include guidance relating to ratio of bucks to does to be shot).*

10. *Deer are to be shot in the chest (heart/lung area).*

11. *If you take a shot you are to remain in your seat until the given time. Do not stray out of your area looking for a shot beast at any time without contact with neighbouring rifles and myself.*

12. *Make a note of the deer you shoot and their location. Use the compass card and pencil provided. A guide to its use is on the card. You will note the arrow on the card indicates the direction that your seat faces.*

Compass card

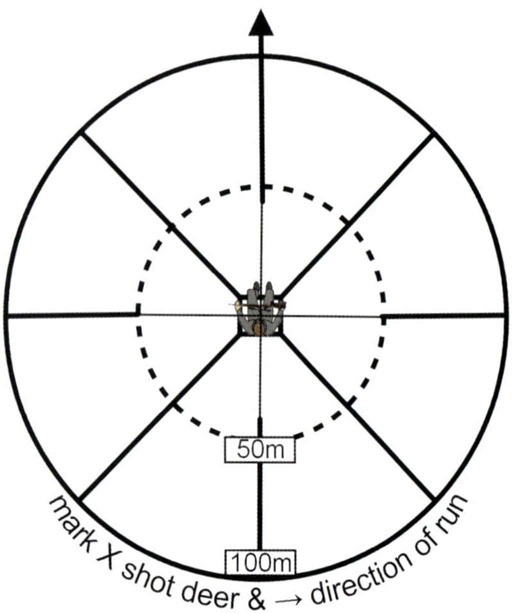

Cull Clock Card							
Fallow	**B**	**D**	**F**	**Other**	**B**	**D**	**F**
Shot							
Seen							
No of shots							

13. *Don't be embarrassed if you have a miss but don't assume you have either. Mark the place where you think the point of shot was with the tape provided.*

14. *Carcasses should be/should not be gralloched and brought together at an appropriate collection point.*

15. *You should be aware that walkers wearing fluorescent clothing will be quietly moving deer throughout the day. You may see them on several occasions or not at all.*

16. *Should you be confronted by anyone you should unload and provide them with an explanation courteously. You should notify me of the incident whether resolved or otherwise. The information will then be circulated.*

17. *A basic first aid kit is available and in my possession should anyone require this at any point.*

18. *Refreshment arrangements.*

19. *Any questions?*

Assistants

You may consider an additional briefing is necessary for individuals who are deployed to move deer. This should include checking they have fluorescent clothing and are fully conversant with their role and knowledge of the ground. On a practical note they should be discouraged from getting into conversation with stalkers in the high seats and should resist the temptation to shout to them on finding a carcass, which they should not move. Those involved in carcass extraction and preparation should have adequate protective equipment and qualifications for all aspects of their task, i.e. ATV use and carcass examination and preparation.

Those deployed to move deer should have a thorough knowledge of the ground and resist moving carcasses they may find.

Safeguarding Public Safety

Signs should be conspicuous and placed at all access points

Signs providing information on what is taking place and warning of the potential danger may be prepared and placed at appropriate access points in the area before stalkers are deployed to their positions. These should be of conspicuous design.

If the cull is within an area normally open to and used by the public then you have a duty of care to ensure they are not endangered in any way. This duty of care also extends to those that may wander off the public right of way. This risk should be well documented in the risk assessment. You may therefore consider additional steps to safeguard their safety. Advising the general public in advance of the day's event through display notices, using physical barriers to close certain access points and having security personnel to guard key entry points are all reasonable steps you would be expected to take.

Extraction of Carcasses

A large cull of fallow deer focuses the mind on the need for adequate transport and larder facilities so consider the capacity of chillers and number of 'back room' staff required for carcass preparation. Be careful not to underestimate this as it can be the most resource intensive aspect to the day. Transport for extraction of carcasses needs to be capable of getting close to the shooting positions. While there may be short

Consideration should be given to the capacity of chillers to ensure they are adequate

drags to nearby accessible woodland rides, an all-terrain vehicle(s) will normally be necessary. Handling fallow on this type of day should be treated as a two-man job. You may consider periodic extraction of carcasses throughout the cull period. This will reduce the time carcasses are left un-gralloched and provide better deployment throughout the day for those responsible for their preparation at the larder. All personnel involved will need to be made aware of these arrangements and individual stalkers contacted for clearance prior to any interim extraction.

Follow-Up Procedures

You should have a clear policy on the follow-up of wounded deer and have a tracking dog available. This is best carried out by a dedicated individual after shooting has finished and in liaison with the individual stalker involved. This issue must be addressed clearly in the shoot briefing, as detailed above.

Maintaining Management Records

The debrief will give you the opportunity to record all the necessary details required for deer management purposes, e.g. numbers of bucks/does culled, approximate ages, condition including abnormalities, weights, location shot, disposal, number and species seen. If you have used the compass cards, as shown earlier, these will be invaluable for your record keeping. They will serve as a cross reference to the larder record and also provide an indication of which seats have been the most successful.

Refreshments

Arrangements should be made for appropriate food and drinks at the end of the cull and this can also serve as an opportunity to debrief and thank all involved.

The Stalker's Role and Responsibilities

Being invited to take part in a collaborative team cull should be treated as an acknowledgement of your marksmanship and stalking skills. It should not be treated lightly as you will be under some pressure to maintain your reputation and the trust bestowed in you. There are a number of measures you can take that will give you confidence in your role and ensure you fulfil your responsibilities.

Stalkers invited to take part in team culls should take their responsibilities seriously. Prior knowledge of the ground will provide confidence

Knowledge of the Ground, Documents and Equipment

Having accepted the invitation to take part, if there is an opportunity to help with the organising of the day in some way this should be offered. If you are unfamiliar with the area to be covered in the cull there may be the opportunity to visit beforehand. Knowledge of the ground will give you confidence and some comfort when you arrive on the cull date.

Make sure you provide all the relevant documents promptly as requested by the organiser, e.g. firearms certificate, insurance and stalking qualifications, and make a note in your diary of the date and time of the event. There will be the potential of using far more ammunition than for a normal stalking outing so ensure you have a good stock. Have at least forty rounds with you on the day. Zero your rifle immediately prior to the date and ensure it is clean and in good order. Clean the lens of both your telescopic sight and binoculars. Take with you a spare, large capacity, magazine if you have one.

Selecting your clothing is a matter of personal preference but you should be mindful of the weather and the extraordinary length of time you will be in a seat, so dress for warmth and the possibility of rain.

On the Day

Allow adequate time to travel to the venue and aim to arrive promptly. On arrival you will no doubt meet some old stalking friends and there will be a temptation to get into discussion instead of getting your boots on, etc. Pay particular attention to the briefing by the organiser, who will be under pressure co-ordinating the day's event. Following the briefing he should ask if there are any questions. If there is anything you are unsure of you should clarify the matter. In doing so the response may well benefit your fellow stalkers. Above all, be confident of knowing your seat location and the means to get there.

Once settled into your seat make sure your radio is switched on to enable you to monitor any information circulated. Make a mental note of all shots taken and the location of carcasses. Even better, make a written note of shots and location of carcasses in the quieter moments in your seat. I recall being issued on a team cull with a compass card as shown earlier for this purpose. Although I thought it to be rather bureaucratic at the time, rather than relying on my memory, I did use it and found it a great help in maintaining an accurate record of events.

If there are assistants deployed to move the deer then you should expect to see them at any time during the shooting period and possibly more than once from different directions. If carcasses are to be extracted periodically you should expect to be contacted in advance to enable this to be done safely. The techniques of using high seats and action to take in public confrontations are covered in detail in Chapter 6 and 9 respectively.

Be honest in any debrief when asked with regard to the number of shots and possible misses you may have had – remember we all make mistakes.

Conclusion

Collaborative culls should not be regarded as a panacea by deer managers. They should never replace traditional, discrete deer management methods practised effectively by both recreational and professional stalkers. They have their place where deer are in such large numbers that urgent action is necessary to prevent serious damage and in sensitive areas where the traditional methods have failed or are not practical, e.g. park and estate situations that are used intensively by the public. In isolation, one-off culls rarely achieve a reduction in the population over time without a concerted effort to maintain a realistic cull each year. Therefore, consideration may have to be given to running them over a number of years to be effective.

With all the knowledge available at home and abroad, stalkers are able to benefit from the experience of others when organising or participating in collaborative team culls. Best practice guides are available covering both Cross Boundary Liaison and Team Culling*[54].

Moving Deer to Strategically Placed Rifles

There are situations where neither traditional stalking techniques nor collaborative team culls are practical. Small areas of woodland close to urban development, parcels of dense cover sandwiched between motorway networks and airport perimeters are all places in which fallow deer can be found and their presence can present a real danger to public safety. These situations often call for deer to be moved in a controlled manner to strategically placed rifles. The idea is certainly not new and has been practised for years by stalkers in an effort to achieve their cull targets. Many of the basic safety measures applicable to collaborative team culls are relevant to these small-scale manoeuvres. These tactics, typically involving perhaps only two or three stalkers, can be quite productive and exciting, too.

Advance Planning and Tactics

With a good knowledge of the ground you should be able to plan a series of manoeuvres in areas known to hold deer. The weather will influence your plans; the wind being a key factor in dictating tactics. The waiting rifles will need to be positioned downwind of the chosen area, ensuring their scent is not carried to the deer. Their positions will need to provide good, safe zones of fire in areas that are clear enough to shoot into safely. Ideally you should seek positions overlooking natural breaks in the woodland cover or wide rides where the deer are likely to hesitate before moving on. If there is to be more than one waiting rifle it is essential that all involved know exactly where everyone is located and their corresponding shooting area. An understanding by all involved of the tactics to be deployed and the timing is vital. A clear safety briefing covering all aspects of the operation prior to commencing the manoeuvre is therefore necessary. The waiting rifle(s) should be concealed, taking advantage of any natural cover available. Once their positions have been determined they should not

54 www.thedeerinitiative.co.uk/uploads/guides/123.pdf

move from their position other than a short distance to facilitate a shot. If you are able to use existing high seats or make use of portable ones on the day, then this will add to the safety and effectiveness of the operation as the rifle(s) will be able to cover a greater area than at ground level.

Waiting rifles must take up their positions quietly, without chat to fellow stalkers, and well in advance of the walker going to his starting position. The use of two-way radios is a great advantage, allowing for the waiting rifles to be given advance notice of any relevant issues and deer movements. With the walker moving to an upwind position, prior to moving downwind towards the waiting rifles, he will often be unaware of deer that have picked up his scent and moved on. The first indications of this will be the sound of a shot from those in wait.

The waiting rifles should therefore expect to see deer moving without any advance notice. They need to be alert to early movement once the walker has left. Even if, as a patient waiting rifle, deer do not come in your direction you will gain a valuable insight into the effects upon other wildlife as the stalker moves through the woodland towards you. These effects are elaborated upon in Chapter 6 on stalking techniques. It is this experience that will enhance your stalking expertise in future years.

The stalker with the task of moving the deer has to be careful not to encroach too closely into the woodland before getting to the starting position as he risks his presence being detected prematurely. The result will be deer will exit by the side door and avoid the ambush. A wide berth should therefore be given to the holding area until the carry of human scent is such that it will influence the deer to move in the desired direction. There is no reason why the walker should not take the opportunity to shoot deer during the operation provided it is safe to do so. These opportunities can arise in the crosswind areas that have not been affected by the carry of scent. As the moving stalker gets closer to those in wait an acknowledgement that he will be entering the shooting area should be communicated in some way, but not relied upon.

As with collaborative team culls, such methods can be overdone and, by using the same tactics too often, you will educate the deer to a point that your efforts will be to no avail.

Chapter 12

Safe Stalking

It was a warm, late summer evening in Shropshire and I settled back into the high seat, content to listen to the chorus of birdsong. I pondered over what I may see. The roe rut was drawing to a close, but it was a fallow pricket I had in mind. I was in a small woodland valley and to my left I had a view over our boundary and into a field of long grass. My son, Lewis, was stalking a long way off; on the opposite side of the wood. I had not been in the seat long when I caught sight of a roe doe over the boundary. I looked hard but I could not see a buck in attendance. The doe nervously grazed among the grasses, constantly looking back to the wood where perhaps her kid lay or maybe a buck. She eventually disappeared. Suddenly a shot rang out from close by to my left. I immediately tensed up in surprise, it was so close, and I was unaware the neighbouring ground was stalked. Was it a poacher or a legitimate stalker over the boundary?

I sat motionless for a while, watching and listening. Then over the boundary I saw a dog working its way through the grass. I watched with interest and, soon after, a man with a rifle followed up. Had he shot the doe? Whatever, I felt the need to announce my presence not only from a safety point of view but to ensure the individual was aware of the boundaries involved. I alighted from the seat and, with a shout, made contact over the boundary fence.

It became clear the stalker was legitimate and had shot a roe buck, which lay in the long grass. We were about to exchange details when a third stalker appeared from the long grass. He appeared somewhat angry. I presumed he was a friend of the stalker I was talking to – but I was wrong. An alarming story unfolded. He had been stalking the same roe buck and had been beaten to the shot! They both seemingly had an arrangement with the same farmer, without knowing of the other's existence. A confrontation ensued but eventually peace was restored and they left. My thoughts dwelled on what I had witnessed. Two stalkers, both unaware of each other's presence in the long grass stalking the same roe buck at the same time! I pondered the risks involved. In my experience, such coincidences often lead to serious consequences.

The Risks

Stalking is a potentially hazardous activity and we owe a duty to others to take reasonable care so as not to cause foreseeable injury. While there are obvious risks to the individual associated with stalking, e.g. being alone, climbing high seats and lifting heavy weights, the greatest risk arises from the use of high powered rifles.

If you take a reckless shot that results in someone being injured or killed you may be liable to legal action both under civil and/or criminal law dependent on the individual circumstances. Should an investigation reveal that gross negligence or recklessness was involved the consequences could be serious and a manslaughter charge may follow. This was the result following an incident near a campsite in New Zealand where a twenty-five-year-old woman was shot in the head. She had been cleaning her teeth outside her tent before going to bed. The rifleman mistook her head torch for the eyes of a deer and shot her dead. The shooter was also in breach of a number of conditions of his permit, including shooting during the hours of darkness.

In Devon some years ago an equally tragic accident occurred when a man shot dead his stepson with a .243 rifle. A colleague and I assisted with the investigation and found the man had failed to identify the target. He thought what he was shooting at was a fox. The man was charged and later convicted of manslaughter.

The latter incident did not involve deer stalking and occurred at night, during a lamping expedition for foxes. Had it been a stalker failing to identify a legitimate quarry target in poor light the liabilities involved would have been the same. The fact that deer are crepuscular by nature results in a high percentage of deer being culled in conditions that negate good identification. This, therefore, becomes a high risk issue. It is essential that stalkers consider and take heed of best practice if they are to guard against mistaken identity or failing to ensure an adequate safe backstop. Extra care is needed in your identification of deer when visibility is poor.

Best Practice

All stalkers, whatever their experience, should take time to read the best practice guidance, which is readily available through The Deer Initiative both via the internet or hard copy*[55]. This gives valuable guidance on handling firearms including, security, maintenance, zeroing and action to take in the event of a misfire. The section on 'Firearms: Safe Handling' covers all the key safety points when handling a rifle and taking a shot. Particularly relevant here are the first four essential guidelines:

1. Be familiar with the surroundings and know where the potential hazards are.

55 www.thedeerinitiative.co.uk/best practice/Assessing the backstop

2. Ensure targets have been identified beyond any doubt.
3. Ensure there are no obstructions in the path of the bullet. Even small twigs can cause deflections or ricochet; the closer to the rifle the obstruction is, the greater the effect on the bullet path. Be aware that the bullet does not precisely follow the line of sight at all distances.
4. Before taking a shot ensure the backstop/background is safe and remains safe if the target or shooter moves. A safe backstop is one that could reasonably be expected to capture a bullet and bullet fragments without causing ricochet, damage or danger.

On the open hill, where long distances can be viewed in areas of relative wilderness, assessing the risk to ensure safe shooting should be achieved easily. However, this a far cry from stalking some of the lowland woodland for fallow, where at certain times of the year the canopy has closed, reducing the view and creating hidden dangers. Consequently, midwinter, with the cover down, tends to provide more opportunity for safe shooting with more caution being required at other times when the canopy has closed.

Assessment of the backstop is essential to ensure public safety. This is a no-shoot situation

Provided the view is unobstructed the key considerations are identification of the target and the nature of the backstop. Can the target be identified clearly as your intended quarry and of what does the backstop consist? Tree trunks, large round bales, rock faces and the like have all been used by stalkers as backstops but should a problem arise from such a shot then the individual will be found wanting and at risk from legal action. You may be surprised at the variance of views between stalkers as to what they consider a safe backstop. I recall one stalker, whom I later assumed had little experience, regarded water as safe! Maybe hc had never played as a child at skimming stones across the surface, an activity on the National Trust's to do list before you are twelve.

How far does one go into assessing the risks associated with thick cover, such as bramble? Not many deer would be taken if we physically had to check this out prior to taking every shot. Provided a safe backstop behind the low cover exists then it would be difficult to criticise a shot taken that results in a hitherto unforeseen problem, unless of course special conditions exist of which the prudent stalker should have been aware. I relate one such situation later.

Safe Handling of your Rifle

Ensuring the safety of others and yourself when handling your rifle is a prerequisite to stalking. Being safety conscious should become the norm, as should demanding the same from fellow stalkers. In addition to the above best practice guidance the Health & Safety Executive (HSE) has published its own advice on the safe use of guns*[56]. The following is relevant to the use of rifles:

- You need good judgement and reactions – that means being calm and not having your senses dulled by fatigue, alcohol or drugs
- To shoot accurately and safely you need to be in a position where you can adopt a firm, steady stance. Make sure you have a clear, unobstructed view of the target
- When aiming a rifle, always check that there is nothing in line with the muzzle that isn't visible through the sight
- Develop 'muzzle awareness' – a sense of always knowing exactly where your gun is pointing. Be constantly alert to the positions of other people in the area – not only other guns and helpers, but also members of the public. Take special care near public rights of way and roads
- Keep your finger off the trigger until you are sure what you are shooting at and only release the safety catch immediately before firing
- Keep the magazine and breech of a rifle empty except when actually stalking.

56 Safe use of Guns, Agricultural Information Sheet no 43

This was the result of a mistake by an experienced stalker who, not realising he had left a live round in the chamber, placed his 30-06 calibre rifle on the rear seat of the vehicle and accidentally caught the trigger! Fortunately no one was injured. He had the door repaired and bought himself a new pair of binoculars

Developing Muzzle Awareness

A sense of always knowing exactly where your gun is pointing and its status is an essential element of the safe handling of any firearm. This should be backed up by the practice of always treating your rifle as if it was loaded. It is not acceptable, having pointed the barrel carelessly at someone, to excuse yourself by the fact that it is unloaded. If military and police personnel, with all the intensive safety training they receive, can shoot colleagues accidently then it behoves us all to take the matter seriously and guard against the risks. You will be very lucky indeed in your stalking career if you escape the experience of suddenly realising there is a round in the chamber, or the safety catch is off, when you thought otherwise! No one is perfect.

You have a personal responsibility when carrying rifles in the company of others to ensure you minimise the risks of an accidental or negligent discharge, which may cause injury or death. Even in the presence of experienced stalkers it is not uncommon to witness a lack of muzzle awareness by rifles being carried in an unsafe manner, often over the shoulder with the barrel pointing precariously at times in the faces of those behind. This problem has been exacerbated by the popular use of sound moderators, which are often heavy, causing an imbalance of the rifle when carried.

While you may feel it an embarrassment you need do something about it and you should not be afraid to speak up and draw attention to what amounts to bad practice. It is now viewed as 'good practice' to point out the failings of others.

Even the most experienced of stalkers occasionally need a wake-up call. What is required is the setting of ground rules of how each of you is to carry your rifles when together in different situations. Remember, you may not get a second chance to alleviate the risk of someone being shot. If you are accompanying another stalker you need to feel safe. If you do not, your concentration will be on your own safety, rather than the stalking, and looking down the muzzle is not an enjoyable experience.

Basically, you should establish a safe system of working together. This is now well practised on the hill in Scotland, where historically a number of professional stalkers have come to grief over the years, having been shot up the kilt by their guests. Not a pleasant experience. This has led to the practice of rifles being kept safe in their slips religiously until almost the last minute, when the rifle is passed to the guest for the shot. The situation of stalking lowland fallow, often in woodland, calls for a different but equally safe approach. The following photographs depict both good and bad practice.

Above: Note where the muzzles are pointing which is not safe for either stalker

Above right: A safer position for the rifles and stalkers!

Security

A safekeeping condition is attached to all firearm certificates. This requires the holder to store their firearms and ammunition securely at all times, so as to prevent, so far as is reasonably practicable, access by unauthorised persons. This is a legal requirement and you should take reasonable precautions to ensure you comply with this condition. You should also be familiar with the Home Office Guidance on firearms security*[57].

In the Home

Security begins at home and your rifle and ammunition should be stored in a secure cabinet when not in use. The overall security of your property is also taken into

57 Home Office – Firearms Security. A Brief Guide

account in ensuring the right level of security exists in individual circumstances. Ideally, ammunition and bolts should be secured separately. The location of your cabinet(s) should be as discreet as possible, not in a garage or annex away from the main living accommodation. If possible it should be located out of the view from an outside window.

Keys to cabinets also have to be safeguarded to prevent access by unauthorised individuals, even if they are members of your family. Modern digital, coded cabinet locks, have the advantage of being keyless, provided you remember the code settings. How you secure cabinets is important; if they can be levered off the wall or base relatively easily then your security is totally breached, as the cabinet can be removed in its entirety. Your local firearms licensing officer will give you advice in this respect.

Taking your rifle out of its secure place prematurely, in readiness for an early morning start, should be resisted. Many burglaries are committed during the night while the occupants are asleep. You may be able to afford the loss of your ancillary stalking equipment, stored either in the vehicle or hallway ready for loading, but the theft of your rifle in this situation would be compromising.

In the Vehicle

Transporting your rifle and ammunition should not present security problems if you are simply travelling from home direct to your stalking ground. However, you should be mindful of unexpected events that may involve others having to search or examine your vehicle at short notice, e.g. road accidents in which you are injured. Consequently, the more secure your rifle is during transport the better. Ideally ammunition, magazine and bolt should be stored separately within the vehicle until you arrive. Remember, while your vehicle is on the road you are effectively in a 'public place', and the rifle should not be in a loaded state. Legally, even if there is no round in the chamber, if there are rounds in the magazine capable of being fed into the chamber, it is classed as 'loaded' for the purposes of firearms legislation.

Security becomes an issue if you have to leave your vehicle unattended with the rifle inside. This is occasionally unavoidable as walking around with the rifle in a slip is not always acceptable and is not risk free. You should ensure the rifle is out of sight and if possible in a locked area of the vehicle or secured by a safety device, e.g. security cable. Ammunition should be secured separately and you should remove and keep the bolt with you. Where you park your vehicle is an equally important consideration in crime prevention. Try to park in a conspicuous position, avoiding the quiet, dark corners, on the perimeters of car parks. Having a cup of coffee and being able to see your vehicle through the café window is a comforting situation to be in.

In the Hotel

If you have an overnight stay with friends or at a hotel you should not leave your rifle in your vehicle. Ideally have it in your possession in your room, perhaps with the bolt secured in your vehicle. The chances of them both being stolen are then remote and you have taken reasonable steps to keep them secure. If you have to leave your room temporarily you may have to secure the rifle in some way out of sight within your locked room, ensuring you have possession of the keys. In this situation it would be advisable to have the bolt with you. I have some concerns over some hotel security that is offered. If you do use this you should do so with assurances that no unauthorised personnel or guests have access to your rifle and ammunition.

If in doubt as to any aspect of firearm security you should seek the advice of your local firearms licensing department or officer.

Signs Warning of Stalking Activities

There is no specific legal requirement on the landowner or stalker to erect signs to warn other users of the countryside of your deer stalking activities, even in areas of open public access or where there are footpaths crossing private land.

There are legal obligations on landowners in certain circumstances under health and safety legislation to conduct risk assessments to ensure no one is put at risk from activities on their land. This may include deer stalking and is elaborated upon later. Typical risk assessments in these situations often include the provision of warning signs as a control measure. Many large landowning bodies do, in fact, use signs to warn members of the public of any activity from which there may be a risk of injury and this includes the use of firearms.

There are also legal obligations (a common duty of care) on landowners under the Owner's Liability Acts that require steps to be taken to ensure persons visiting the land are not put at risk and this can even include trespassers! In some circumstances where the risk is obvious, e.g. an unguarded mineshaft or pit, then the landowner may be liable for damages should an accident occur.

Clearly each individual case will be judged on its merits depending on the level of risk. In many deer stalking situations signing may not be necessary with the risks being minimised through other control measures. However, where collaborative team culls are undertaken in areas in which rights of way are used regularly by the public, it is recommended that appropriate signs are used. See Chapter 11. Warning signs specifically for high seats are discussed in Chapter 9.

Risk Assessment

Keeping up to date with all our rules and regulations these days requires considerable effort and an enquiring mind by everyone involved in deer management. Take, for example, our health and safety legislation, quite a turn-off to most, but despite the fact that the legislation has been around for a long time (Health & Safety at Work Act, 1974) many stalkers are ignorant of its requirements and their legal responsibility, which of course is no defence in law. The problem is that to ignore these may cost someone or yourself their life. If it happens to be the former it may be extremely costly in this increasingly litigious society.

Both employers and employees have responsibilities under the legislation. It is clear that those involved in professional deer management, e.g. forestry rangers, have legal obligations. However, the legislation will also cover many who stalk deer on a more recreational basis, whether for payment or not.

The majority of recreational stalkers who, through their various permissions, take on the responsibility for deer management will be caught by the legislation. If they conduct an 'undertaking' involving the use of firearms they have a legal duty under health and safety law to take all reasonably practical measures so no one is put at risk. The key here is in the meaning of an *undertaking*, which in this sense does not necessarily need to involve employment or commercial gain. So, if you have the stalking rights and undertake to manage the deer for an owner of land, providing cull returns, using equipment and high seats, etc, then this may be classed as an undertaking.

The legislation includes provisions for both the protection of people at work and the prevention of risks to the health and safety of the general public that may arise from work activities; the latter being most relevant to stalking activities. The Management of Health and Safety at Work Regulations, 1992 require employers to identify significant hazards arising from their work activities, assess the risks and to take steps to control those risks.

If a landowner (employer) employs five or more people, including those who may be classed as conducting an undertaking such as a stalker, then a written health and safety policy must be completed together with an appropriate risk assessment. This should cover all activities where there is a risk of injury or ill health. A risk assessment is still a requirement for any work-related activity regardless of the number employed. Only where five or more are employed must it be documented. In reality many employers will conduct written assessments or require stalkers to complete one.

This practice is commonplace for established businesses employing large numbers of people. It is the self-employed and those involved in smaller undertakings that are often ignorant of the legal obligations upon them and it is they that are potentially at greater risk from prosecution and/or litigation.

Many large landowners are now requiring their stalking tenants to abide by a risk assessment and many require the stalker to complete one as part of the arrangement. Hitherto, for the prudent stalker, this exercise would have simply been a mental process; in just the same way as a window cleaner working alone decides to rope his ladder to prevent it slipping. The same analogy can be applied to the stalker. We all hopefully conduct mini risk assessments prior to taking a shot – identifying the target and ensuring a safe backstop, etc. In doing this we are minimising the risks and liabilities involved, particularly with such an increase in public access to our countryside.

If you are tasked by the landowner to complete a risk assessment or assist in its compilation then you need to assess the risks of your deer management activity to yourself and others. So write down the hazards together with the steps to be taken to minimise the risks and include an element of monitoring and review. There are a number of key areas to address including safe use of rifles, high seats, public access, mode of extracting carcasses, use of knives and larder work.

Risk assessments should be kept simple, straightforward and proportionate, and should include relevant examples of best practice. Once written they should stand the test of time with only occasional amendment prompted by a change of circumstances or review. Stalkers with existing agreements or those taking on deer management for the first time should consider conducting a full risk assessment as part of their management plans before embarking on shooting deer.

The example risk assessment is given as a guide and includes additional risks associated with collaborative team culls and culling in areas where public access is high. It lists the potential risks and associated control measures to minimise those risks. It is neither exhaustive nor prescriptive and any location can generate its own individual risk. You should use the HSE guidance on risk assessment to evaluate the level of risk from low, through medium to high. Apply the proposed appropriate control measures and re-assess the level. Clearly, stalking fallow in woodland on an urban fringe generates more potential risk than stalking red deer in a remote Scottish glen and will merit stringent control measures. Conversely, working alone in a remote Scottish glen in the depth of winter carries a greater risk than sitting in a high seat in Suffolk.

The risk areas shown within this standard format, covering the measures taken to reduce the risks, should cover most stalking situations. However, it should not replace a practical and common sense approach to the task to ensure it is relevant and not just a paper exercise. A walkabout without the rifle can be most rewarding from a deer management point of view, enabling you to concentrate on the risks involved and note them accordingly. This should take into account just what high velocity bullets are capable of doing, particularly in terms of penetration, trajectory and distance travelled. It should also encompass the activities of other users of the woodland.

By way of example, I share some woodland stalking ground with a survival course business. You will appreciate that a risk assessment in these circumstances would be a necessity in an effort to prevent accidents and protect the stalker from legal action, particularly since part of their training involves disappearing into the undergrowth and remaining hidden. One season they were practising their tracking skills following fallow bucks around during the rut. Consequently, low ground cover such as bramble, normally accepted as safe, could not be so. To ignore this type of risk, when there is evidence that you have been made aware of it, would be a very dangerous path to take. As you may imagine, special precautions needed to be taken, e.g. liaison with the course manager to ensure no stalking took place during training. The point here is that an effective risk assessment should reflect the individual circumstances of your stalking area; they need to be bespoke.

I would recommend once completed in draft form you let someone who has relevant experience read it. Be prepared to amend the document until you are satisfied all risks are adequately assessed together with the actions to minimise them. And, above all, ensure you make provision to monitor and review it periodically. This should be at least every twelve months or whenever circumstances change the risks involved, e.g. changes in land use, building developments and access.

Most of us drive and appreciate many accidents in life are avoidable. How you react when conditions change can reduce the risks, e.g. we reduce our speed when the road is icy. You should take the same approach to your stalking, ensuring your own safety and that of others. In this way you may avoid the 'deer stalker's funeral' and enjoy your stalking for years to come.

The Deer Stalker's Funeral by Bill Tidy, MBE

Risk Assessment

Hazard	Location	Persons at Risk	Risk Level	Controls	Implementation and Monitoring
Danger through use of high powered rifles **Accidental shooting causing death or injury** **Property damaged**	Estate woodland, adjacent land and property	Estate workers/ volunteers and residents Farming community Members of the public (recreational) Motorists Deer stalker Horse riders Trespassers	High, med or low	All stalkers involved to hold appropriate firearm certificate, DSC qualifications level 1 & 2 (incorporating trained hunter qualification complying with food hygiene regs) and insurance covering minimum of £5 million public liability (BASC now £10m). In addition, appropriate references or knowledge of experience to be documented Use of firearms restricted to the named competent individual as per licence/agreement Identification of estate activities likely to affect stalking activities, e.g. equestrian use, wildlife tours, farming Stalkers to notify relevant estate personnel of stalking intention and ensure contact via telephone wherever possible whilst on the estate Rifles to be made 'safe' when negotiating steep terrain or obstacles Awareness of buildings, public rights of way and highways Safety procedures and advice to be adhered to as per the D.I. Best Practice Guidance and H & S leaflet Guns, in particular identifying of target and backstop/developing muzzle awareness Rifle and scope to be kept clean, regularly serviced and zeroed Collaborative/team culls: • Distribution of maps to each stalker ensuring awareness of public access points, highways and adjacent rights of way, estate and farming activities • Safety briefing of all stalkers prior to commencement of cull • Advance signing of activities at all access points • Safe positioning and use of high seats • Stalkers to be allocated known high seat positions or escorted to seat on day of cull	Safety procedures to be reviewed annually or at any time when conditions change /risk exposed/ or concern raised Qualifications and certification of individual stalkers to be examined and reviewed annually taking into account legal changes and firearm certificate conditions Best practice guidance as published by The Deer Initiative to be followed in respect of all culling activities Rifles to be subject to annual maintenance check Injury or near miss to be reported as per the H & S legislative requirements (RIDDOR)

Hazard	Location	Persons at Risk	Risk Level	Controls	Implementation and Monitoring
Legal liabilities associated with the use of firearms – civil or criminal proceedings	Estate	Deer stalkers and estate management deemed responsible	High, med or low	No shooting into or from land designated as no stalking areas at that particular time Use of firearm and ammunition only within conditions of firearm certificate of each stalker Lawful target species only to be shot Compliance with close seasons unless legal exemption applies, e.g. crop damage, diseased or injured deer No night shooting of deer except injured or diseased animal or where permitted by law No shooting from public highway Security of firearms and ammunition to comply with Home Office guidance, particularly in relation to vehicles Stalking authority to be displayed in vehicles left unattended Liability issues to be covered in safety briefing of stalkers Adherence to best practice guidance issued by The Deer Initiative. All stalkers to be insured adequately	Annual review to be conducted of all licensing requirements Relevant changes in legislation or firearm certificate conditions to be implemented immediately Firearm certificates to be produced annually by individual stalkers and record maintained
Horses – risk of injury to horse or rider through use of firearms	Estate	Horse riders, grooms, members of hunt and followers	High, med or low	Areas identified as higher risk requiring special care, e.g. permitted equestrian access areas Safe and unsafe areas for control identified Communication with stable management to ensure no riding activities at times of cull operation Stalkers to anticipate persons/horses in restricted or prohibited areas at any time Use of sound moderated rifles	Annual review and immediate consideration of any incident reports Injury to be reported as per the H & S legislative requirements (RIDDOR)

Hazard	Location	Persons at Risk	Risk Level	Controls	Implementation and Monitoring
Public con-frontation	Estate	Stalkers and visitors, unauthorised members of public, nearby residents and motorists	High, med or low	Explanatory notices displayed and information to media available though estate management Stalkers to immediately unload rifles identify themselves and provide explanation for the action being taken in line with estate/owner's policy All interactions with members of the public to be reported to the estate owner The gralloch and any by-products of shot deer to be removed in sensitive areas. Carcass preparation to be conducted away from public access areas of the estate Trained tracking dog to be available to aid recovery of any injured beast likely to cause public concern	Annual review and immediate consideration of any incident reports
Injury while stalking/ working alone	Estate	Stalkers	High, med or low	Nominated person to be aware of location and expected time of return of individual stalkers Compliance with safety briefing procedure on arrival Suitable footwear and weatherproof clothing to be worn Immunisation against tetanus Awareness of other infections such as Weil's disease [a form of leptospirosis contracted from rats] and the tick borne Lyme disease (further details below re risk of disease) When it is not safe to carry out particular stalking related tasks alone, e.g. high seats, the work to be planned when assistance is available Radio or mobile phone to be carried First aid kit to be available	Information item: tetanus – the organism causing tetanus is widespread and can enter your body through cuts, abrasions or puncture wounds made by splinters and thorns. It is potentially fatal and immunisation BEFORE infection is the only certain way of dealing with the disease Annual review of working practices and equipment Injury to be reported as per the H & S legislative requirements (RIDDOR)

Hazard	Location	Persons at Risk	Risk Level	Controls	Implementation and Monitoring
Injury from wounded deer **Legal liability by causing unnecessary suffering**	Estate	Stalkers or assistants	High, med or low	Despatch of wounded animals to be carried out humanely and in accordance with the Deer Initiative Best Practice Guidance, thereby avoiding unnecessary suffering of deer and/or injury to stalker Ensure animal is dead prior to handling to reduce risk of injury from hooves or antlers	Annual review
Injury or disease through carcass handling	Estate, location of shot deer, transport to larder/ chiller. Site of carcass prep-aration	Stalkers, assistants and carcass handlers, e.g. game dealers, butchers and the public via the food chain	High, med or low	All carcasses to be visually inspected as per the D.I. Best Practice Guidance with particular attention paid to the lymph nodes. All stalkers should wear disposable gloves for handling and inspection of internal organs If TB is suspected the carcass should be isolated and the district veterinary officer and estate management informed without delay All stalkers to carry a mobile phone and have ready access to a first aid kit Use a sharp knife for carcass preparation with suitable glove protection All stalkers should be aware of the correct methods of lifting and use of appropriate equipment to aid extraction of carcasses where necessary. Use of a winch/tilting cradle for high lift positions Avoid twisting and difficult lifting situations where possible to prevent injury Awareness of the risk of tuberculosis, Lyme disease and their symptoms Stalkers should have a good awareness of TB incidence in the local area and nationally All carcasses to be visually inspected as per D.I. Best Practice Guidance All stalkers should wear disposable gloves for handling and inspection of internal organs Stalkers must be aware of the presence of ticks that can be picked up from vegetation and deer carcasses. Awareness of the risk of Lyme disease and its symptoms. Suitable clothing covering the skin to be worn. Attendance to GP immediately if symptoms occur When gralloching disposable gloves to be worn. Maintain good standard of personal hygiene to avoid infection	Annual review All incidents of suspected disease or abnormality to be reported upon Carcass for game meat establishments to be appropriately tagged by trained hunter in compliance with F. S. A. game meat guide Injury to be reported as per the H & S legislative requirements (RIDDOR)

Hazard	Location	Persons at Risk	Risk Level	Controls	Implementation and Monitoring
Noise and deafness	Estate and adjacent areas	Stalkers and visitors, unauthorised members of public, nearby residents. Horses and riders	High, med or low	Awareness by stalkers of noise pollution and potential hazard of sudden shot report Rifles if capable of being adapted to be fitted with a sound moderator to minimise disturbance Ear protection to be worn when appropriate	Annual review
Injury or damage from use of vehicles	All areas of the estate	Stalkers and persons present on the estate	High, med or low	Awareness of steep gradients in certain areas Only all terrain vehicles to be used in extreme off-road situations Restrict use of vehicles to estate roadways and accepted routes off-road No driving on cultivated land or growing crops Firearms to be unloaded when being transported All persons to adhere to estate safety procedure when operating from vehicles	Annual review
Injury from knives during carcass preparation and liabilities of possession	Site of shooting and larder Estate property while stalking	Stalkers and assistants	High, med or low	Appropriate glove protection to be worn when using knives for carcass preparation Gralloching and use of knives to be in accordance with DSC 2 qualification & training and D.I. Best Practice Guidance Use of a sharp knife of type complying with guidance in food hygiene regs [non-porous] Guards to be placed on saw blades when not in use Knives to be stored in sheaths Awareness of proximity of assistants and other stalkers when using knives Particular care to be taken on the removal of lower foreleg to guard against slipping of blade Knives not worn when not stalking on the estate or at any time in a public place without reasonable excuse	Stalkers to take responsibility for their own safety in addition to the responsibilities of the estate owners Methods to be reviewed annually

Hazard	Location	Persons at Risk	Risk Level	Controls	Implementation and Monitoring
High seats – **Injury from fall or firearm discharge unauthor-ised use or theft of the seat**	Estate woodland and adjacent land	Stalkers, members of the public, especially children	High, med or low	Ensure safe construction and erection of high seats in accordance with the D.I. Best Practice Guidance High seats should incorporate a suitable rifle rest to facilitate safe shooting Location of high seats to provide unobstructed field of shooting and solid backstop Rifles to be unloaded prior to climbing up and down ladders of high seat All high seats to be inspected prior to climbing by the stalker Notices to be placed at the bottom of each high seat forbidding unauthorised use High seats to be located in areas less vulnerable to misuse and where possible away from public rights of way	All seats to be inspected regularly by the stalkers and prior to each use (to be documented) in addition to annual maintenance review
Spread of notifiable contagious disease, e.g. FMD and Bluetongue	Estate	General public, livestock owners	High, med or low	Compliance by stalkers with DEFRA guidance, legislation and restricted zones when outbreaks occur	Maintain awareness of national restrictions or spread of disease via DEFRA website and media coverage

References and Bibliography

Acharjvo, L. N. and Misra, R., 'Effect of amputation of a hind limb on the growth of antlers in deer in captivity', Indian Forester. 98. 507–508. (1972).

Aebischer, N. J., Wheatley, C. J. and Rose, H. R., 'Factors associated with shooting accuracy and wounding rate of four managed wild deer species in the UK, based on anonymous field records from deer stalkers', PLoS ONE 9(10): e109698. doi:10.1371/journal.pone.0109698 (2014).

Aebischer, N., Wheatley, C. and Rose, H., 'Kill, miss or something in between?', Deer, Vol.17, No.4. (2014–15).

Apollonio, M., Andersen, R. and Putman, R. (eds), *European Ungulates and their Management in the 21st Century* (Cambridge University Press, 2010).

Brown, R. D. (ed.), 'Antler development in cervidae', Caesar Kleberg Wildlife Research Institute, Texas (1983).

Cadman, A., *Dawn Dusk and Deer* (Country Life Limited, London, 1966).

Cadman, A., 'The Fallow Deer', Forestry Commission Leaflet No.52. (1966).

Chapman, D. I. and Chapman, N. G., *Fallow Deer* (Coch-Y-Bonddu Books, 1997).

Chapman, N. G. and Chapman, D. I., 'The Fallow Deer', Forestry Commission, Forest Record 124. (1982).

Critchley, C., 'Enough to make your toes curl?', Deer, Vol.17, No.6 (2015).

Davis, T. D., 'Antler asymmetry caused by limb amputation and geophysical forces'. In Brown, R. D. (ed.), Antler Development in Cervidae. Caesar Kleberg Wildlife Research Institute Kingsville Texas. pp 223–229. (1983).

DEFRA and F. C. England, *The Sustainable Management of Wild Deer Populations in England. An action plan* (2004).

De Nahlik, A. J., *Management of Deer and their Habitat* (Wilson Hunt, 1992).

Dixon, D. R., Dixon, P. J. and Jolly, M. T., 'Scraping by', Deer, Vol.17, No.2 (2014).

Ferretti, F., Sforzi, A. and Lovari, S., 'Contact', Deer, Vol.15, No.9 (2011).

Forest, J. (pseudonym), 'The stalker's knife', Deer, Vol.7, No.5 (1988).

Forestry Commission Bulletin 102, 'Forest Fencing'.

Forestry Commission, Forestry Practice Advice note 2, 'Managing Deer in the Countryside'.

Green, P., 'Electric antlers', Deer, Vol.13, No.6 (2005).

Green, P., 'The paradox of deer parks', Deer, Vol.14, No.7 (2008).

Green, P., 'Deer – friend or foe to the UK farmer?', Deer, Vol.16, No.9 (2013).

Griffith, D., *Deer Management in the UK* (Quiller Publishing Ltd, 2011).

H & S publication – 'Safe use of Guns', Agricultural Information Sheet No.43.

Hodge, S. and Pepper, H., 'The Prevention of Mammal Damage to Trees in Woodland', Forestry Authority Practice Note.

Home Office, 'Firearms Security, A Brief Guide'.

HSE leaflet, 'Safe Use of Ladders and Stepladders'.

Johnson, J., 'The BDS Deer Distribution Survey 2000', Deer, Vol.12, No.1. (2001).

Kierdorf, U. and Kierdorf, H., Schultz, M. and Rolf, H. J., 'Histological structure of antlers in castrated male fallow deer (Dama dama)', The Anatomical Record. Part A, 281A (2004).

Langbein, J., 'How do deer cross Britain's busiest motorway?' Deer, Vol.17, No.5 (2015).

Langbein, J. and Putman, R., 'Collision cause', Deer, Vol.13, No.10.

McKelvie, C., 'Anatomy of a stalk', Shooting Times & Country Magazine, (6 May, 1999).

Millais, J.G., *British Deer and their Horns* (Henry Sotheran & Co., London, 1897).

Ohl, F. and Putman, R.J., 'The Effect of Levels of [Hunter] Competence on Deer Welfare – Defining and Measuring Welfare', Report for Scottish Natural Heritage, Inverness (2013), supplemented with additional material from Aebischer and Wheatley (2012).

Ozoga, J., *Whitetail Summer* (Willow Greek Press, 1997).

Pace, B., 'Tackling the incline', Sporting Rifle, No.106 (2014).

Parkes, C. and Thornley, J., *Deer: Law and Liabilities*, 2nd edition (2008).

Pitcher, B. and McElligott, A., 'Call of the big bucks', Deer, Vol.17, No.1 (2014).

Prior, R., *Modern Roe Stalking* (Tideline Books, 1985).

Prior, Dr R., *Deer Management in Small Woodlands*, The Game Conservancy/BDS (1987).

Prior, Dr R., *Trees and Deer,* 2nd edition (Swan Hill Press, 1994).

Putman, R.J., *The Natural History of Deer* (1988).

Putman, Dr R., 'Deer management on national nature reserves. Problems and practices', English Nature Research Report No.173 (1996).

Putman Dr R., *The Deer Manager's Companion: A Guide to Deer Management in the Wild and Parks* (Swan Hill Press, 2004).

Putman, R., and Apollonio, M. (ed.), *Behaviour and Management of European Ungulates* (Whittles Publishing, 2014).

Putman, R., Apollonio, M. and Andersen, R. (eds), *Ungulate Management in Europe: Problems and Practices* (Cambridge University Press, 2011).

Putman, R., Watson, P. and Langbein, J., 'Assessing deer densities and impacts at the appropriate level for management: a review of methodologies for use beyond the site scale', The Mammal Review, Mammal Society (2011).

Putman, R., Langbein, J., Green, P. and Watson, P., 'Identifying threshold densities for wild deer in the U.K. above which negative impacts may occur', The Mammal Review, Mammal Society (2011).

Simpson, Prof. J.W., 'Aladdin's Slippers', Deer, Vol.16, No.9 (2013).

Springthorpe, G. D. and Myhill, N. G., *The Wildlife Ranger's Handbook* (Forestry Commission, 1985).

Sykes, N., '1066 and all that', Deer, Vol.15, No.6 (2010)

Sykes, N., 'Keeping up with the Godwinesons', Deer, Vol.15, No.5 (2010).

Sykes, N., 'The Deer that walked the world', Deer, Vol.17, No.8 (2016).

Tabor, R., 'Assessing deer activity and damage in woodlands', Deer, Vol.13 No.1 (2004).

Tabor, R., 'Plants as indicators for assessing deer activity and damage', Deer, Vol.14, No.5 (2007).

The Deer Initiative, 'A Guide to Writing Management Plans' (2009).

The Deer Initiative, 'Deer Best Practice Guides England and Wales' (2010).

Thornley, J., Good, Better, Best, Deer, Vol.16, No.8 (2013).

Trout, R. C. and Pepper, H. W., *Forest Fencing*, Technical Guide (Forestry Commission, Edinburgh, 2006).

Wallace, G., 'Training dogs for woodland deer stalking', Deer, Vol.13, No.5 (2005).

Whitehead, G.K., *The Whitehead Encyclopedia of Deer* (Swan Hill Press, 1993).

Work at Height Regulations, 2005.

Index